MW01284883

THE STADIUM STEPS

GARY L. JORALEMON

ISBN 978-1-63784-249-2 (paperback)
ISBN 978-1-63784-250-8 (digital)

Copyright © 2024 by Gary L. Joralemon

All rights reserved. No part of this publication may be reproduced, distributed, or transmitted in any form or by any means, including photocopying, recording, or other electronic or mechanical methods without the prior written permission of the publisher. For permission requests, solicit the publisher via the address below.

Hawes & Jenkins Publishing
16427 N Scottsdale Road Suite 410
Scottsdale, AZ 85254
www.hawesjenkins.com

Printed in the United States of America

To Alex, sons Joe and Vince, and my entire family. You're my source of inspiration and unconditional love. For Brad and Erin, we'll take it from here, boys. Finally, to the American Probation Officer. Sometimes working beyond the limelight with honor isn't such a bad thing.

ACKNOWLEDGMENT

Knowing that only a select few have their work published, my wife, Alex, never allowed me to wallow in self-pity, wondering, *Who would ever want to read this crap?* Spending untold hours in a home office trying to tell one's story can be lonely and frustrating. But Alex has always ensured that my tumbler was full, the house quiet, and my writing a priority.

Friends Susan Rotalo, Christine Ertman, Dana Hansen, Chris Smith, my nephew Jesse Sanford, "Grampa" Bob Sanford, and my wife, Alex, read early drafts and provided invaluable input and counsel.

Finally, I'd like to thank an elderly groundskeeper assigned to maintain the field at Edwards Field on the University of California, Berkeley campus. I never learned his name, and he certainly didn't know mine. But as a seventeen-year-old who would run the stadium steps early in the morning on the way to high school, this kind gentleman would give me a friendly wave and thumbs up when observing me climb over a security fence designed to keep townies like me at bay. For whatever reason, he never ran me off, and he remains a part of my youth.

FOREWORD

The Stadium Steps depicts the roller-coaster ride of moral development that is often a part of our human condition. Joralemon is unafraid of diving into the fact that despite the unfairness of life, our choices determine who we become, and this is often messy and complex.

We are engaged in a delightful mystery as we watch O'Shea, Father Iggy, Detective Harold Davis, and others wrestle with issues involving morality, sin, and redemption. Is O'Shea, like the Archangel Michael, a defender against sin and wickedness or simply a beyond control vigilante?

The Stadium Steps explores the paradoxes that can and often do have serious effects and outcomes. While the events of life—violence, rage, and selfishness—have serious consequences for our soul, our choices can redeem us. This story is unafraid of confronting these challenges and, like Michael O'Shea, can lead us to mercy, grace, and ultimately redemption.

—Father Mike Cicinato
San Luis Obispo, California

PROLOGUE

"Sixty-three, fifty-six in foot pursuit," Deputy Probation Officer Michael Ignatius O'Shea spoke into his radio with amazing calm. No huffing and puffing, no screaming, no dramatics.

Guy's got ice in his veins, thought the dispatcher on the other end of his radio.

"Northbound Front Street, four hundred blocks. Suspect, White male, blond-blue, twenty-five, five ten, two hundred. Dark baggy shorts, white tank."

"Copy, 63-56," replied the dispatcher.

"Adam 29, en route, two minutes," came the reassuring voice of a nearby deputy sheriff's unit.

Not too soon. Let 'em run himself out. He'll put up less of a fight, Mike thought. Fortunately, his daily stadium step workouts had kept him in top condition despite his age. Mike would be fifty years old in a few weeks. His tactic wasn't complex. Even though his suspect had the physique and fitness level one would expect from a youngster raised on junk food and YouTube, he *was* half Mike's age with limited judgment. *Dummy with no impulse control. Won't miss mutts like this when I retire.*

Mike was a good twenty yards behind his suspect, a local spousal abuser who had missed a probation violation hearing, thus the active warrant motivating the foot chase.

"Edwin, stop now and this all ends nice and easy!" yelled Mike, now closing to ten yards.

"Fuck you, old man! Hey, why ain't you breathin' harder?"

"C'mon, Edwin, no need to add a resisting charge. Go to the ground!" commanded Mike, looking side to side for the sheriff's unit.

"Fuck you!" gasped Edwin between breaths.

Edwin Andrew Bagley had all the energy required to periodically beat his girlfriend and mother of their three children, but on this given evening, he was quickly losing what little strength he had. As they turned the corner, Edwin slipped on some gravel but was able to right himself and continue his attempted escape.

"My name's not Edwin, old man. It's *E-Bag*!" whined Edwin.

"Right. Sorry, Edwin," proclaimed Mike with an emphasis on the *Edwin.*

This should be just about right. Mike unclasped the retractable baton from his duty belt. Unlike his younger counterparts who preferred the Taser to an "impact weapon," as they were called, Mike still preferred his baton. He drew it from a scabbard tucked snugly behind his 9 mm Glock 26 pistol, and with a smooth flick of the wrist, the six-inch baton became thirty-six inches of mean aircraft grade titanium. A Taser would have been easier, but for some reason, Mike couldn't shake his fear of electrocuting *himself* with the five-thousand-volt device. He knew his phobia drew behind-the-back snickers and comments about his age and inability to adapt to new technology, but Mike had little interest in anyone's opinion about his age. In fact, he had little interest in anyone's opinion about most things.

He continued to close the gap on Edwin, who was by now starting to stumble from exhaustion. With both hands on the tips of the baton, he brought the weapon down against Edwin's throat and hooked his foot around the probationer's shins. Gravity completed the task, and both fell to the ground, Edwin face-first, Mike cushioned by his probationer's girth. He tossed the baton aside, straddled Edwin's back, and grabbed one of two handcuffs kept in pouches placed on the left and right sides of his duty belt.

"Give me your hand, cheese dick," Mike said, almost in a whisper.

In a momentary fit of defiance, Edwin tried to roll over onto his back. Mike grabbed his wrist and twisted it with brutal force, dislodging Edwin's forearm ligaments from the bone.

"My God, he's a maniac! He's gonna kill me!" he screamed.

"Shut up, Edwin," said Mike impassively.

Mike got to his feet, retrieved his baton, and caught his breath. *Not bad for a damn near geriatric.* He looked around for his backup from the Sheriff's Office, grabbed his radio, and depressed the transmit button. Nothing. Mike couldn't speak. *What the hell is this about? Try it again.* He stared at Edwin, whimpering and mumbling something about a lawsuit. *How'd he get cuffed? Is someone else around?* Mike looked over his shoulder and saw that he and his prisoner were alone on the dark street.

"Sixty-three, fifty-six, status?" asked the dispatcher. "Sixty-three, fifty-six, status?"

Seconds passed as Mike looked at his radio in confusion with a vague feeling that he should do *something*. Dispatchers only ask for status checks if they suspect the officer may be in some peril, and Mike understood that few things upset a good dispatcher more than ignoring a request for the officer's status.

"Sixty-three fifty-six, negative contact," stated the dispatcher, urgency creeping into her voice. "All units, 63-56 is in foot pursuit and not responding to status check. Last known, northbound Front Street, Pacific Beach."

Mike stumbled to the curb and sat down. He stared at the street and tried to process the dispatcher's last transmission.

Got to help that guy. Sixty-three, fifty-six. Shit, that's me. What's wrong with me? He looked down and saw wetness in the front of his khaki duty pants. *Why are my pants wet? My God, I pissed my pants.* Mike fell back on the sidewalk, felt a tingling sensation in his head, and marveled at the bright lights and melodic sounds of approaching sirens as everything proceeded to go dark.

CHAPTER 1

Twenty-seven years earlier

Mike wheeled his aging Volkswagen Beatle off the coast highway at a gas station perched above the Pacific Ocean in the tiny town of Gorda and found a pay phone. By the glow of the fluorescent light of the phone booth, he dug the number of his old friend from his wallet. Tommy Sagapalu was the son of an Oakland police officer who had been a close friend and colleague of Mike's father and a pallbearer at Emile O'Shea's funeral. Tommy and Mike had been youth boxers in the Oakland Catholic Youth Organization boxing program. Tommy was able to skip the awkward adolescent growth stage many boys experienced and, by the age of fifteen, had the body of a grown man. Mike had many friends but counted Tommy as his closest.

After several rings, a female voice answered with a loud "Hola?" Mike could hear loud music in the background.

"Is Tommy in?" Mike asked politely.

"Un momento," said the female.

The unmistakable gravelly voice of his friend answered, "This is Tom."

"Tommy, me lad, Michael O'Shea," said Mike.

"Mike!" yelled Tommy into the phone. "Where are you?"

"About seventy miles north of you on the coast," answered Mike.

"What the hell are you doing up there?" Tommy asked.

"Needed some downtime. Oh, by the way, can I crash on your floor for a couple of days?" Mike asked, knowing his old friend would allow no other accommodation.

"Are ya kiddin' me? Mi casa es su casa!" Tommy shouted.

"I'm not interrupting anything?" asked Mike, recalling that a female voice had answered the phone.

"Nah, that's Alma, and you're gonna love her. See you when you get here…and pick up some beers, ya bum."

A little over ninety minutes later, he reached the town of Serra. Mike had visited Serra several times during his college rugby career. He liked the coastal beauty of Santa Barbara to the south but loved Serra, or what the locals called it, "S-Town." The small college community nestled between the Santa Lucia Mountains and the Pacific Ocean was midway between San Francisco and Los Angeles and had the climate and scenery of Santa Barbara without the glitz, glamour, and celebrities. Serra was home to California Coastal State University, and like most college towns, the school and city had grown up together. The town had a sports-minded population and active nightlife that appealed to Mike.

As promised, he stopped at a liquor store a few blocks from Tommy's apartment and picked up a case of Coors. Tommy lived in the Lanai Apartments, a small complex near the campus that was painted bright pink and surrounded by tall palm trees, suggesting to Mike that he had truly arrived in Southern California (although the residents of Serra were quick to deny any association with the greater Los Angeles area and preferred the term Central Coast when describing where they lived). Mike pulled into a stall in the complex parking lot, gathered his duffel bag and beer, walked past a well-tended swimming pool, and found Tommy's apartment.

Just as he was about to knock, the door swung open, and there stood his large friend, dressed in a traditional Samoan lavalava (a skirt worn by natives of the South Pacific Islands), no shoes or shirt, and the most ridiculous sombrero Mike had ever seen perched atop his head. With outstretched hands, Tommy gave his old friend a bear hug. Although it had been years since Tommy had boxed, Mike was impressed with his friend's still chiseled physique.

Mike walked into what may have been the most prototypical bachelor pad he had ever seen. An odd but appealing collection of cheap pieces of Mexican and Samoan art, serapes and blankets, and a large print of Samoan warriors paddling an outrigger canoe adorned the walls. Tommy brought some of the pieces from home in Oakland. The rest had been brought back from a road trip to Rosarito Beach in Northern Mexico. A very used couch, which Mike assumed would be his sleeping accommodation, lined one wall. An old black-and-white TV sat atop a makeshift bookcase made of an old surfboard atop two wooden apple crates. In a small kitchen alcove was a trash can over-flowing with beer cans, tequila bottles, and pizza boxes.

"Mike, you know you are always welcome in my home," announced Tommy in his most earnest tone, which belayed his obvious state of inebriation.

"Appreciate it, my brother," responded Mike with a hug.

Although the Eagle's "Hotel California" was blasting from a stereo, Mike could hear a female voice coming from the rear of the apartment.

"Tomas, has your friend arrived?"

"That's Alma. She's a peach!" explained Tommy, attempting to remain steady on his size seventeen feet.

Alma Sotoro Hernandez-Santana was a stunningly beautiful five-foot, two-inch brunette who had come to Serra from her native Mexico to study nursing at Cal Coastal University. She bounded out of a back bedroom.

"Miguel, I am so pleased to meet you!" Alma announced with kisses to both of Mike's cheeks. "You help me convince Tomas to clean up the apartment, yes?"

"It's a warm night. Let's take some beers out poolside," Tommy suggested, clearly wanting to change the subject.

The three reclined in a semicircle of lounge chairs beneath a cloudless night. Mike immediately noticed that living in Oakland, he couldn't recall the last time he had been outside in the evening without a sweatshirt, but tonight was truly spectacular. Mike and his old friend caught up. Tommy, it turned out, was one of the rare Cal Coastal graduates who had been able to establish a career in Serra and, like his dad, had gone into law enforcement. But, as Mike discovered, not as a traditional cop. Tommy had become a deputy probation officer for the County of Serra.

Tommy explained that probation officers were "like counselor-cops," with the dual role of bringing about (or at least attempting) the rehabilitation of criminals, while being ever prepared to track them down and arrest them if they didn't go along with the program. Mike was intrigued.

Tommy gave Mike a brief introduction into the world of community corrections.

Probation, he explained, was a second chance for the offender with certain conditions. The job of the probation officer was to give the miscreant some guidance in staying out of trouble but always being ready to take them into custody *if* their misdeeds could hurt someone or themself.

"How come I've never heard much about probation work?" Mike asked. "Lots of cop shows on TV, but no shows about probation officers."

Tommy reached for another beer out of a small ice chest between their lounge chairs. "We're pretty low-key. Most people don't know much about us unless they're on probation or someone on probation is hasslin' them. It's a pretty cool gig."

Transfixed by a swan diving coed in the bikini, Mike heard only about a portion of what Tommy had said.

"But it seems like such a nice, safe place to live," said Mike.

"Oh yeah," his friend responded. "Serra is great, but we got some real charmers in this county, I'll tell ya. You should see some of the asswipes I have on my caseload."

Mike gave this comment some thought and asked, "What do you do with them?"

I gotta work in the field tomorrow night. You want to come along? See what it's all about?" asked Tommy.

"You betcha," said Mike.

*****

At a little after five o'clock in the afternoon, Tommy appeared at the door of the apartment. Only it wasn't the Tommy Mike was accustomed to seeing. He sensed immediately that *this* Tommy was all business. Mike reminded himself that he was about to enter Tommy's world, a foreign world he didn't fully comprehend. Tommy was dressed casually in jeans, hiking boots, a T-shirt, and an oversized flannel shirt. He could tell immediately that Tommy was wearing body armor, with the flannel shirt concealing a 9mm Beretta semiautomatic pistol holding thirteen rounds and another twenty-six rounds in magazine pouches on his belt. Tommy led Mike out into the parking lot to an unmarked gold sedan. Through the tinted windows, Mike noticed a cage-like barrier separating the rear from the front of the vehicle. A police radio was affixed to the console between the driver and passenger seats.

"Take your shirt off," commanded Tommy.

"What?" asked Mike.

"Your shirt. Take it off."

Mike did as he was told, still a little intimidated by the dramatic change in his friend's demeanor.

Tommy opened the trunk of his work vehicle, fished around a large black equipment bag, and pulled out an old blue T-shirt with a probation department badge on the left front.

"Here, put this on," he said, handing Mike the shirt.

Again, Mike did as he was told.

From the trunk of the car, Tommy pulled out a Kevlar vest. The vest was held within a white cotton shell covered in sweat stains and looked as though it had seen better days.

"Bulletproof vests don't exist. Just Hollywood bullshit. A direct shot with high-capacity round or even a sharp knife will penetrate it. But it's better than nothin', am I right?" Tommy said, now smiling for the first time since picking Mike up.

Tommy helped Mike with the vest, connected the Velcro side straps snugly, and handed Mike back his own T-shirt to put over the vest.

"A couple of things I need to go over with ya before we take off," said Tommy, reaching for a small radio attached to the left side of his waist. Tommy pointed to a transmit button on the side of the radio. "I go down, grab my radio. Press this button, give them our location best you can, and tell them to roll medical and backup. Got it?"

Mike stared in disbelief. *What have I gotten myself into?* "Got it," he said weakly.

Tommy then reached to his right side, pulled back his shirt, and exposed his pistol.

Mike's eyes widened. *I don't think he's showing off. I think carefree Tommy Sagapalu has turned into an assassin.*

"This is real worst-case scenario shit, O'Shea, so listen up. If I go down and you think you or me are about to *die*, grab the gun, point it at your target, and squeeze the trigger. Got it?"

"Got it" was all Mike could choke out.

"Oh, by the way, if, for some reason, my Berretta misfires or I lose it, here's my backup," said Tommy. He pulled up his left pant leg, exposing a smaller gun tightly fitted into a holster attached to his ankle. "Taurus thirty-eight caliber revolver, so it has fewer rounds and isn't as accurate, but it's a cannon. Just like the other one, point and shoot."

Mike stared into his friend's cold dark eyes. "Ya know, Sagapalu, I'm startin' to get the idea that not all your probationers are too interested in you tryin' to help them stay out of trouble."

"Right!" said Tommy.

"I thought probation officers are like counselors," Mike observed with slight concern in his voice.

"Sometimes we are, just like sometimes cops are. But other times, we're more like cops. Just depends on the probationer and what's goin' on," explained Tommy. "Like you said, sometimes people just don't want to be helped and go along with the program."

Tommy was casually flipping through the pages of a massive blue binder he had pulled from the trunk of the car. He explained that this was his route book, and that each of his sixty or so probationers had a few pages dedicated to their vital information, probation terms, and residential and criminal history. A booking photo taken during their most recent jail stint was stapled to the first page, which included the probationer's background information. On a small writing pad, Tommy started scribbling names and addresses as he developed a rough itinerary for the evening. Tommy explained that he had a general caseload with a variety of offenders from throughout the county, which he preferred over the more specialized caseloads.

"I got 'em all," he explained. "Perverts, gangsters, thieves, dope addicts, wife beaters, you name it." Tommy closed the binder and said, "I got about fifteen people I'd like to see tonight, but we'll be lucky if we find ten or so. Let's get about halfway through and then grab some dinner."

"Sixty cases to keep an eye on seems like a lot," said Mike.

Tommy nodded. "It is, but at any given time, I got a dozen or so in jail. That's still lots of cases, but manageable. But you have to get out in the field and stay on top of 'em. We've got officers who try to work banker's hours, and it usually backfires and makes more work for them. Let's hit it!"

*****

Tommy drove down a narrow dirt road in the town of Pacific Beach in southern Serra County, known as home to several generations of gang members. He made one pass by a dilapidated stucco home on a corner, glanced about, then continued down the block.

"Hear that whistling?" asked Tommy. "Means we've been made."

"Made what?" asked Mike.

"Means the local gangsters have seen us and are sending out a warning to one another."

"That was quick," said Mike.

"Just because they're in a gang doesn't mean they're not really smart," said Tommy.

He pulled into a dirt alley which bisected two roads and parked the caged car. Tommy explained that one of his probationers had just gotten out of jail and was due for a visit.

"Jericho Swaine," Tommy explained, pulling out his jail photo.

Mr. Swaine, Mike observed, looked like a rather rough character with a shaved head and a goatee that hung well below his chin. The words *Born Loser* were clearly tattooed across his forehead.

"Kid's just twenty-two. Dad's an OG, and Mama's out of the picture. Older brother in the joint, along with a couple of cousins and some uncles. Connected family," said Tommy.

"What's an OG, and what's he connected to?" Mike asked.

"Sorry. Original gangster. Kid's third generation gang involved. Dad's done serious time, but now he's getting old and pretty sick from diabetes," said Tommy, taking one more glance at the route sheet page as he reached for the radio mic.

"Control, 63-29," Tommy said into the mic.

"Sixty-three, twenty-nine," the voice of a sheriff's dispatcher squawked.

"Sixty-three, twenty-nine, I'll be 10-6 at 1590 Twenty-Fourth Street, Pacific Beach. Request status."

"Sixty-three, twenty-nine, copy," replied the dispatcher.

Mike stared at his friend. *Shit, he really seems to know what he's doin'.*

As they slowly approached the house, Mike could see Tommy's eyes dart from side to side. The front door was open, and as they got closer, Mike could hear the voice of Los Angeles Dodger announcer Vin Scully calling a game. Tommy reached for a doorbell and gave it a ring.

"What's up, Mr. Swaine? Sagapalu from Probation. Jericho around?" asked Tommy amiably as he peered into the house.

A massive man lumbered to the front door and motioned for them to come in. Ronny Lee Swaine had the same shaved head and scraggly goatee Mike recognized from his son's booking photo. He weighed, by Mike's estimation, a good four hundred pounds, which made him two hundred pounds overweight. Ronny Lee wore a stained white tank top, denim shorts that fell midway down his shins, white socks which came up to meet the shorts, and cheap slip-on sandals. Ronnie Lee reminded Mike of some of the characters who used to show up for his boxing tournaments.

"What's the score?" Tommy asked, motioning to a Dodger game on a small TV in the living room.

"Giants 3–2," responded the older man.

Ronny Lee lowered himself into a worn easy chair facing the TV. He was in obvious pain. *Shitty way to live,* Mike thought.

"You feelin' okay, Mr. Swaine?" asked Tommy with genuine concern.

"Yeah, I'm okay. Got this damn diabetes, and my feet swell."

With that, he peeled off a soiled sock to reveal a disfigured foot, blueish purple in color with all but two toes missing. A milky white substance seeped from some of the narrow cracks around his remaining toes. Mike took a glance and quickly returned his gaze to the TV, trying valiantly to keep his lunch in place.

"Shit, Mr. Swaine, I'm no doc, but that doesn't look real good," observed Tommy.

"I'll be okay," said Mr. Swaine.

Tommy looked around and asked, "Junior home?"

"Yeah, he's out back," Swaine Sr. said.

"How's he doin'?" asked Tommy.

"Workin', helpin' with the bills around here. Can't ask for more than that, I guess."

"Any signs he's back on the shit?" Tommy asked.

"So far so good. You'll be the first to know. I don't want any of that around the house. I got grandkids all over the place," replied Mr. Swaine.

Mike suspected Tommy's term *shit* referred to heroin, which evidently was an issue for the younger Swaine. Tommy had an easy way about him, and Mike admired the way his friend seemed to find a balance between being respectful while maintaining an aura of authority. Plus Tommy's muscular frame and height demanded a level of respect. Mike noticed the incongruity of his friend's shoulder-length mane of frizzy hair tied into a bun and all the law enforcement accoutrements attached to his belt.

"Okay, Mr. Swaine, we'll go round back. You take care of yourself."

Tommy led Mike to the side of the house into a backyard cluttered with beer cans, engine parts, and several disabled vehicles.

Tommy's radio crackled, and the voice of a sheriff's dispatcher said, "Sixty-three-twenty-nine, status?"

Tommy pulled the radio from his belt. "Sixty-three-twenty-nine, I'm code 4."

Music blared from a portable stereo attached to a long extension cord which snaked across the yard and through an open window in the Swaine home. The Purifys were singing the sixties hit "I'm Your Puppet." Under the open hood of an old car emerged a less rotund version of Ronnie Lee Swaine.

"What's happenin', Jericho!" called Tommy jovially.

"Hey, Sagapalu. What are you doin' here?"

Jericho looked as though he had missed very few meals during his recent jail stint. In fact, his jeans could barely contain a rather impressive belly. Mike recognized him immediately from his jail photo by the tattoo across his forehead.

"Here for a sample," said Tommy, pulling a small plastic bottle from his pocket.

"Can I go behind the shed?" asked Jericho, nodding to a small metal shed at the end of the yard.

"How 'bout your bathroom?" Tommy asked.

"Broken. We piss in the yard and shit in the neighbor's."

Tommy motioned toward the shed and tossed his car keys to Mike. "Can you go to the car and bring me the little ice chest, Mike?"

"What's wrong with that dude's ears?" asked Jericho when Mike was out of earshot.

"Boxin'," said Tommy. "Called cauliflower ear."

Mike found the ice chest as directed and returned to the yard. Tommy and Jericho were casually discussing Jericho's automotive project, the plastic bottle on the hood with dark yellow urine filling the bottle to a midway point. Tommy opened the ice chest and pulled out a handful of packages the shape of popsicle sticks. After selecting four sticks, he removed the packaging and dipped the sticks into the urine. The sticks were color coded. If the urine indicated the presence of a controlled substance, the stick turned from clear to a specific color which designated the substance. If the urine was clean, the stick remained clear.

"It'll take a minute," Tommy said. "Hey, Jericho, if I could help you get that tattoo removed from your face, are ya in? To be honest, you look like a bit of a thug. No offense."

The twenty-two-year-old's face immediately brightened as if Tommy had offered him a trip of a lifetime. "No shit, Sagapalu? Hell yeah, I'd get rid of it, homie."

Mike noticed that while Jericho appeared to be White, he had the distinctive dialect of a Latino gang member.

"Here's the deal," explained Tommy. "I help you get that tattoo removed and you stay clean, make all your counseling, keep a job, and help out the old man. Deal?"

An elated Jericho grabbed Tommy's hand and pumped it. "That's a deal, Sagapalu. I'm in!" Tommy went back to the test sticks and pulled them one by one from the bottle of urine. After examining each, he looked up at his probationer.

"You're clean, Jericho. Stay that way and you and me will be good."

Tommy replaced the lid to the urine bottles and tossed it and the test sticks in a trash can. He and Mike said their goodbyes and started back toward the car.

"Hey, Sagapalu," Jericho called out.

"Yeah?"

"Is it gonna hurt, homie? You know, gettin' this taken off?" asked Jericho, pointing to his tattoo.

"Hell yeah, it's gonna hurt like a bitch, but you can take it, tough guy," replied Tommy with a smile.

CHAPTER 2

The next stop on Tommy's "hit list" was the home of Mr. Peter Oakendorf, who resided in the small town of Geneva, which conveniently was the town next to their current location in Pacific Beach.

Tommy opened his route book and turned to Oakendorf's page. The soft face of Tommy's probationer was captured in his booking photo stapled to the upper left-hand corner of the face sheet, along with the probationer's charges, terms and conditions of probation, and various other tidbits of information that assisted Tommy in managing the case.

Mike looked at the picture. "Looks like one creepy dude."

Tommy smiled and replied, "He is just that…a creepy dude. Sex offender. You could say Peter has a problem with his peter." Tommy smiled at this clever display of wordplay. "Oakendorf is a child molester."

"I thought sex offenders went to prison," Mike said.

"Nope. I've got a few, and we have one officer who has a whole caseload of them."

Mike looked at Tommy quizzically. Tommy explained that many sex offenders were spared prison in lieu of time in jail and placement on probation because of plea bargains.

"Why strike a plea with a pervert?" Mike asked.

"Lots of reasons. Maybe testifying would screw the victim up more than they already are, or maybe the DA thinks the victim would make a bad witness. Sometimes the DA will offer up a lesser charge if they think a jury might not buy their case."

Tommy tossed his route book on the floorboard and opened the car door. As with the last visit, Mike noticed that Tommy didn't park in front of the probationer's house. Rather, several houses away and out of sight. Tommy led Mike down the road and up a narrow alleyway between two houses to a rear flag lot. Peter Oakendorf's house was more of a cabin and looked to have been built at least sixty years earlier. After listening for sounds from inside the house, Tommy approached the door and announced his presence with a few loud raps. He stood to the side of the front door and motioned for Mike to do the same.

"In case someone starts shooting through the door," Tommy said casually.

What a job, Mike thought. More rapping on the door and no response. Tommy slowly moved around to the side of the house and tried to see into a window. Nothing. They made their way to the back of the house where the rear door led to a small kitchen. Tommy looked in a window. Mike immediately sensed that he saw something. Tommy reached for the door. The old brass knob turned without obstruction. It was unlocked. Slowly, Tommy pulled a small handheld radio from his rear right hip and depressed the transmit button.

"Sixty-three twenty-nine," he said into the radio in a low voice.

"Sixty-three twenty-nine," responded the dispatcher.

"Sixty-three twenty-nine, 10-6 at 620 Temple Road, Geneva, for a probation check. Believe subject may be in the house and evading contact. Attempting entry," Tommy quietly said into the radio.

Once again, as Mike observed his radio transmission, he was impressed at how quickly his friend morphed from a happy-go-lucky jokester to a professional law enforcement officer. Tommy's eyes were glued to the house. Out of the corner of his mouth, he ordered Mike to stay behind the cover of an ancient oak in the probationer's backyard. Tommy approached the house and unholstered the Beretta from under his shirt. He slowly opened the door and yelled into the house.

"Peter, probation department. Come out slowly and show me your hands!"

Tommy's gun was now pointed down in a forty-five-degree angle. As he stepped into the house and out of Mike's view, Tommy noticed a small utility closet to the side of a stove. On top of the stove sat a tea kettle with steam shooting out of the spout. Instinctively, he reached over and turned off the burner.

"Come out of the closet, Peter," Tommy said in almost a conversational tone that masked his tension.

No response. After a few moments, he raised his gun to the closet door, his index finger slowly moving from the frame of the gun to the trigger. With his free hand, Tommy reached for the latch on the closet door and yanked it open. Immediately, he saw the dumfounded face of his probationer, hands up, trembling, and standing in an apparent pool of his own urine. Tommy quickly lowered and holstered his gun and grabbed Peter Oakendorf by the throat. Without effort, he tossed him to the floor.

"Put your hands behind your back!" Tommy yelled as he placed one knee across his subject's shoulder blade. "You fuckin' piece of shit!" he screamed. "Do you know how close I came to poppin' you?" Tommy quickly reached for a pair of handcuffs from the rear of his belt and secured his now prisoner's wrists behind his back. "Who else is here?" Tommy demanded.

"No one, I promise," replied the terrified probationer.

He grabbed a fistful of Peter's greasy hair and shoved him into a chair next to the kitchen table. Tommy opened the door and called for Mike to come into the house. Mike stood at the doorway, wide-eyed and pumped with adrenaline.

My heart's about to jump outta my chest. Wonder how Tommy feels.

The voice of the sheriff's dispatcher came back over the radio. "Sixty-three twenty-six, what's your status?"

"Code 4, I'm 10-15 with one male," Tommy quickly responded using the police radio code for one subject in custody.

He stood over his probationer, who was now whimpering softly. Mike wasn't accustomed to seeing grown men cry, and the scene unsettled him.

"Why'd you hide from me, Peter?" Tommy asked quietly. The whimpers had turned to sobs. "Peter," he said patiently. "I almost just shot you because you made the bad decision to hide from me. I need to know why."

"'Cause you scare me. You come over here and treat me like shit all the time, and I'm scared of you." Tommy looked at Mike and rolled his eyes.

"Peter, this is Mike. He's going to stay here and keep an eye on you. Mike's slightly off-balance mentally. He's part of a special program to assist crazies with getting back on their feet. He has his own issues, so don't agitate him," he said calmly, as if he was speaking to a child.

Peter looked at Mike with absolute terror in his eyes and tried to push his chair toward the corner of the kitchen away from Mike. Tommy, gun again drawn, slowly searched the remainder of the house for inhabitants. When he was confident that Peter was indeed alone, he holstered his gun and stood in the middle of a small living room adjacent to the kitchen. As he looked around the old house, Tommy smelled something familiar.

Smells nice. Like Alma's hair after she takes a shower. Weird. He looked around and saw nothing out of order. Peter was a competent housekeeper. Books on rock collecting lined the bookcase. Television, chair, coffee table. Nothing out of the ordinary. *What is that smell? Baby powder.* Tommy realized the living room smelled of baby powder. *Oh my God, he's got a baby in here.* Once again, he searched the rest of the house. Nothing. Tommy stared straight ahead, trying to make some sense of the presence of baby power. Talcum powder, to be more precise.

Tommy's eyes lowered. The solid oak floors were original to the house. Age and wear had beveled the wood planks into a wave design. He took a few steps and heard a distinctive squeak common with old floors. Tommy tried it again.

Loose floorboards. Loose floorboards and talcum powder. Old home remedy. Dust talcum powder on the wood floor and sweep it into the cracks between the floorboards to fix the squeaking. Why does a floorboard squeak? He lowered himself to one knee and pushed on the board. Tommy could see the distinctive line of white powder between the boards. From his right pant pocket, he drew a folded tactical knife which he opened with the flick of his thumb. The floorboard lifted away easily, revealing a crawlspace below. From another pocket, Tommy retrieved a small flashlight and illuminated the crawl space. A brown paper bag lay directly below the opening. With the knife, he pried the neighboring boards loose and reached for the bag.

"Mike," Tommy called into the kitchen. "Bring him in here."

Mike grabbed Peter by the arm and led him into the living room. When they saw Tommy, Mike could feel the probationer start to collapse. Mike grabbed him with both arms and led him to a chair.

"I can have those. They're not against my terms," Peter declared with more bravado than he was feeling.

"Sure, Peter," Tommy said with no emotion.

Tommy reached into the bag and pulled out a video cassette in a standard cardboard box. On the cover was the smiling face of Shirley Temple. "Shirley Temple, in *The Littlest Yankee*," read the box. He emptied the bag. There were a dozen videos with young child actresses from throughout the years, from Shirley Temple to the Olsen Twins in a spoof on a spy movie.

"You really are one sick twisted fuck, Peter," said Tommy in a monotone voice.

"What's this all about?" Mike whispered to Tommy.

"He workin' the system. He knows he can't have any porn, legal or otherwise, but he *can* get his rocks off by watching little girls in these flicks. Right, Pete?" asked Tommy, turning to the once again sobbing Peter Oakendorf.

"What are you gonna do?" Mike asked.

Tommy stared at his probationer. Again, no emotion, just a stone-faced stare.

"I'll find something," he declared confidently.

For the next hour, Mike stared at Peter while he wept. Occasionally, Peter would feign gagging as one would just before vomiting. Even with a lack of experience in this field, Mike recognized Peter's attempt to illicit sympathy.

Tommy was in Peter's small bedroom searching for something, anything that he could use to lock Peter up, if even for a short time. Deep in the rear of a closet, he found a small locked chest. With the same knife he had used to pry up the floorboards in Peter's living room, Tommy broke open the cheap lock. The box held various old photos of a young Peter with his parents. By the photos, it looked as though Peter still lived in the house he grew up in. Under the photos was a small manila envelope. Tommy opened it and shook several sheets of paper out onto Peter's bed.

"Big Creek Storage," read one sheet. It was an invoice for a storage unit a mile or so away. He searched for a unit number.

"Bingo," he whispered to himself. At the bottom of the invoice, in faded writing, Tommy read, "Unit 122."

*****

When they had loaded him into the back of Tommy's caged car, Peter assumed he was on his way to jail. Not a good thing, but Peter knew there was no way the judge would uphold a probation violation over some tapes of kids' movies.

"I'll be out by Friday," he declared confidently between sobs.

Peter remained confident, even cocky enough to start whistling, until Tommy missed the turn toward the freeway that would have taken them to the Serra County Jail.

"Hey, where we goin'? Officer Sagapalu, I'd like to know where we're going."

Peter was now in full "I'm a taxpayer, you know," mode, even though he hadn't paid taxes in years.

He doesn't have a clue, Tommy thought, driving toward the storage yard. As he turned into the industrial park which housed Big Creek Storage, Peter's complaints subsided. Tommy parked and retrieved Peter. If his suspicions were correct, he wanted Peter to bear witness to the search of his storage unit. They walked down a wide row of buildings on either side, each with a rolling garage door to keep the renters' possessions secure. Tommy stopped at unit 122 and noticed a large padlock on a hasp midway up the door.

"Mike, do me a favor. Get my bolt cutters from the trunk." Tommy tossed his keys to Mike.

"You can't open that. You don't have a warrant," Peter said meekly without making eye contact with his probation officer. "I'm protected under the Third Amendment!"

"I don't need a warrant. It's the *Fourth* Amendment, Counselor, and you waived that right and opted to accept a probation term instead of going to jail. Probably would have been a good thing to discuss with your public defender."

After Tommy raised the door, he immediately knew he had struck pay dirt. In the middle of the floor of the unit was a single large cooler, something one might use to store their catch after a day of deep-sea fishing. He pulled on a pair of latex gloves from his back pocket. Tommy pulled up on the lid. As the lid opened, he pulled away from the strong odor of fifty-two pounds of dried marijuana, laying on top of what he assumed to be ten to fifteen pounds of cocaine, packaged into plastic-wrapped bundles. Peter was going to prison for a very, very long time. Tommy pulled the radio from his belt and keyed the mic.

"Sixty-three twenty-six."

"Sixty-three twenty-six," returned the voice of the sheriff's dispatcher.

"Sixty-three twenty-six, requesting a crime scene team and detectives at 11228 Bellevue Road, Arroyo Berros, unit 122. Located 11350 material during a probation search," said Tommy, referencing the penal code section for possession of a controlled substance for purposes of sales.

*****

By the time they finished up at the storage unit and had booked Peter into jail, both Tommy and Mike were bone-tired and hungry.

"Let's get a beer, Mike," Tommy said as the two walked out into the cool night.

"I'm buying, my man," Mike replied. "You earned it."

Over pizza at Jerry's, a local pizzeria in downtown Serra, Mike peppered Tommy with questions about his job. What he liked most about it, what he didn't. He asked about his training and was surprised to find that unlike police officers, probation officers were required to have college degrees. He also found that probation officers had a lower salary and benefit package than police officers.

"Why not just be a cop?" Mike asked.

"Great question," Tommy replied with a grin. "Some POs do become cops, but more cops become POs. I've kept in contact with some of my probation buddies who've gone to work for police departments, and they've all regretted it."

"Why?" Mike asked.

Tommy refilled their mugs from a pitcher before he answered, "For me, it's an ego thing, I guess. Take Jericho's case. Chances are he's gonna be okay. He may pick up a low-level misdemeanor now and then, but he'll probably keep himself clean and stay out of trouble, or at least not go back to the joint. At the end of the day, I know I had a part in that. It makes me feel good."

Tommy grabbed the last slice of pizza. "Don't get me wrong, I love the coppers, and I have some good buds who are police officers and deputy sheriffs. But it's a different job, and the old counselor-cop deal works for me. Plus, couldn't keep this mop if I was a cop. Probation dress standards are pretty lax," Tommy said as he pointed to his mane of curly shoulder-length hair tied up into a bun.

*****

Mike awoke early and waited for Tommy to finish his shower before he took over the bathroom. Over bowls of cereal and diet sodas, the two discussed Mike's interest in following Tommy's career path. Mike's most pressing concern was his eyesight. A severely detached retinae suffered during the 1979 Golden Gloves finals rendered him blind in his left eye. If a half blind applicant was going to be immediately disqualified, he might as well know sooner than later. Tommy didn't think it would be an obstacle but thought it best for

Mike to do a little research before he left town. After breakfast Mike packed his duffel bag and gave Tommy a tight bear hug.

"Did ya have fun?" Tommy asked enthusiastically.

"Are you kidding? I had such a good time I'm thinkin' of moving here!"

Tommy followed Mike to his VW. "Say goodbye to Alma. Tell her I still think she's way too good for you, ya mutt."

"Will do, amigo," said Tommy. "She told me to say goodbye and apologize for staring at those freak show cauliflower ears of yours," Tommy said with a wink.

CHAPTER 3

Four years later

After Mike's initial training, which included six weeks at a basic probation academy in Sacramento, he was ready for his first assignment, a caseload of adult felons. Probation officers were, Mike discovered, an entirely different breed. Some were former delinquents who assumed that since they were once criminals, they must possess a supernatural ability to understand the criminal mind. Some wanted to save the world, and some just wanted to discover a probationer misbehaving so they could mete out whatever random punishment suited them for that day. A few of the single male officers assigned to juvenile cases liked telling women they "worked with troubled kids."

A few officers were interested in the criminal mind and ways of changing the socially maladjusted. Some were interested in becoming police officers but were deterred by the discipline and rigid schedules. This oddball combination led to a complete disregard for any type of uniform appearance and contributed to the department being labeled as the "Continental Army" by some of the more professionally attired local law enforcement agencies. In fact, as a group, probation officers prided themselves on their offbeat approach to not just how they looked but also how they went about supervising criminals.

In the four years since Mike had joined the probation department, one of the habits which made him stand out from his peers was his willingness to work odd hours—in fact, any hours—allowing him to monitor his "fellas" (as Mike referred to his probationers). As a bachelor, he had no personal obligations. It wasn't unusual for him to start his day in court at nine o'clock in the morning and end it at two or three o'clock the next morning after a night of trying to locate and apprehend a probationer who wasn't interested in going along with whatever rehabilitative plan Deputy Probation Officer Michael O'Shea had to offer.

On such an evening, Mike was blanketing the town of San Sebastian in northern Serra County. Mike knew the town well and was able to troll the streets with his headlights dimmed and a list of absconders nestled on his lap. He knew his wayward probationers tried their best to evade him. Nonetheless, Mike felt a personal obligation to bring them in. But this evening was not his night, and like the fisherman whose love for fishing never dimmed by a lack of catch, he returned to Serra with an empty back seat but content with his effort.

Mike parked in a space in the front of the probation department and collected his gear from the trunk of his departmental car. A dilapidated pickup truck with what looked like a homemade camper shell perched precariously over the bed was parked in a corner of the parking lot. A collection of peeling bumper stickers covered the sides, declaring the owner as a supporter of everything from socialism to the Second Amendment. Mike peered over the open trunk of his vehicle as he loaded his field equipment into a black nylon duffle bag with "O'Shea, County Probation" embroidered on the side.

The truck obviously didn't belong to anyone within the department. *Probably a homeless guy looking for a quiet place to spend the night*. With a high-powered tactical flashlight in his left hand and his right resting on the butt of his Glock model 26 pistol, he slowly approached the truck.

Mike jumped as he heard a male voice yell from the shadows of the building, "Hey, get away from my truck!"

He looked up to see an older man wearing dark pants and a dark hooded sweatshirt with the name of a local auto shop on the front. He was carrying two plastic water jugs in his hands. He indeed looked homeless and seemed to be using the building's water spigot to replenish his supply.

"No problem. Take all ya need," Mike assured him in as soothing a voice as he could muster.

The man was now within ten feet of Mike, close enough for the stench of alcohol, tobacco, and living on the road without a bath to permeate Mike's nostrils. His curly salt-and-pepper hair was matted and greasy. Something about his general appearance and eyes altered Mike's senses.

"Who the fuck are *you*?" the man roared as he took a step toward Mike.

Mike withdrew his wallet badge from his left hip pocket and identified himself. No response, just more wildness in the eyes.

"That badge don't mean nothing to me. Get away from my truck!"

Mike's holstered gun was placed on his right hip, handcuffs in pouches in the small of his back to allow easy access with both his right and left hands, and a flashlight in his left hand. The rest of his equipment—baton, pepper spray canister, and his radio—were tucked snugly into his duty bag. Close, but not as close as he would have liked.

You got a problem here, son, leavin' your nonlethals and radio in the bag before you talk to this guy was a rookie move. Mike knew the man in front of him was either mentally ill, under the influence of any variety of substances, wanted by the law, or perhaps a dangerous combination of all three. Either way, he couldn't just retreat and let him be on his way. Based on his behavior, Mike knew that there was an expectation from his department and the public in general that he would make at least a token attempt to find out what the man was up to.

"Sir, please turn around and put your hands behind your back. I'm going to put you in handcuffs until we figure out what's goin' on here," ordered Mike in a calm voice.

The cement block came from behind and hit Mike squarely on the back of his head. He staggered but tried vainly to remain upright. The second blow was again aimed at his head, but the fourteen-year-old runaway mounting the attack missed and struck Mike on the right shoulder blade, sending him to the ground. She was petite, just over one hundred pounds and barely five feet tall. Kitty was her street name, and she had joined forces with her male companion after meeting him at a local soup line. As is often the case with the homeless, they had forged a bond common among the disenfranchised. When one was threatened, they tended to respond in aggressive packs. The bright parking lot lights were now blurred, and Mike knew that if he lost consciousness, the beating would continue. Or worse, he'd lose control of his gun. He heard the truck door close and the engine start.

For the driver of the truck, this night wasn't quite over. You don't hit a man with a badge over the head with a block of cement and just walk away.

Mike, now on one knee, struggled to regain his footing. The lights of the truck blinded him with what seemed like two spotlights aimed directly into his eyes. The truck slowly started to roll in his direction, past the main road leading into the parking lot, which the driver *should* have taken if he intended to flee. *Shit, got to get away. He's comin' for me.*

The driver pushed his heavy boot down on the gas pedal, clipping Mike hard on his left hip and sent him reeling to the asphalt. He slammed the ancient truck into reverse and repositioned the vehicle in the direction of Mike's prone body. The searing pain in his head, hip, and shoulder was the only thing keeping him from losing consciousness.

The truck was getting closer, now less than twenty feet away by Mike's estimation and picking up speed. He reached for his pistol, unsnapped the level III retention holster, and drew the weapon.

Never cared for this damn holster. Thank God it released. Mike aimed directly at the driver's side and pulled the trigger, again and again, until all thirteen rounds were fired and the gun was empty. Mike hadn't bothered to count his rounds. He had always thought that was a silly part of his training. Count your rounds during combat so you'll know when to reload. *I'm just not that sharp.* Fortunately, he noticed that the slide of his weapon had locked into place, indicating that there were no bullets left in the gun.

The truck veered away from Mike, missing him by inches, and careened into a retaining wall separating the parking lot from an access road. No movement inside. Mike grabbed an extra magazine from a pouch on his duty belt, depressed the small button on the side of his gun expending the empty magazine, and slammed the fresh rounds into the gun. If by chance the driver survived the hail of bullets, he'd come for him again.

Mike began an excruciating crawl back to his vehicle. With his right hand, he grabbed the lip of the trunk and reached for his duty bag. Unable to maintain his balance, Mike fell to the ground, landing on his injured left hip, the contents of his duty bag spilling onto the asphalt. He groped for his radio and found it just under the right rear tire. Pressing his thumb on the transmit button, Mike began to speak, hesitated, and put the radio down. He had the presence of mind to know that his radio traffic would be recorded and that the recording would be played over and over in the days, weeks, months, and maybe years to come.

Take a breath, dummy. Calm down. After a few seconds, Mike again depressed the transmit button.

"Sixty-three, fifty-six, probation unit is 11-99 at the probation department on Johnson Avenue. Shots fired. Repeat, shots fired. Subject on scene in a late model truck with a camper shell. Need medical. Repeat, subject still in the vehicle."

"Sixty-three, fifty-six, copy 11-99 on Johnson Avenue. All available units, respond code 3" came the reassuring voice of a Serra police dispatcher who had just communicated to anyone listening that an officer was in trouble and needed immediate assistance.

Mike turned onto his side and aimed the gun straight at the cab of the truck. From the ground, he could see that about a half dozen bullet holes pockmarked the camper shell. He took some comfort in knowing that at least a few rounds had hit their target and wondered if the rounds fired into the shell had made their way into the cab.

Wait. Talking to the guy, get hit from behind. Shit…there's more than one! Are they in the truck or out? How many doors did I hear close?

Mike quickly looked around. The second attacker was still some-where in the parking lot or in the cab of the truck with the driver.

Mike could now hear the sirens of the police cars speeding in his direction. He quickly grabbed his radio and screamed, "Sixty-three, fifty-six, be advised. There's a second subject. Location unknown. Approach with caution. Repeat, there's a second subject, unknown location!"

"Sixty-three, fifty-six, advise location of outstanding subject and last known location," replied the dispatcher.

"Unknown location!" Mike screamed into his radio. "They may be in the truck or out...I don't know! Got hit from behind. Your guys may be walking into an ambush!"

Shit, now I'll never get out of here. Mike knew that the respond-ing officers would approach very slowly to avoid walking into exactly what Mike had warned them about. He also realized that identifi-cation would be key in surviving the night. The responding officers would be amped and quite possibly a little quick on the trigger. With his free hand, he grabbed the badge he had clipped to his belt and held it up. Mike could hear sirens and the screeching of tires coming from every direction. He suspected some members of allied agencies would also respond, the Sheriff's, maybe the Highway Patrol. Mike felt a warm sticky sensation in his right eye and realized he was bleed-ing. Looking down at his shirt, he saw that he was bleeding badly. Still foggy about what happened after he had tried to handcuff the man he assumed was now dead, he tried to readjust his now throb-bing hip.

On his way into complete shock and adrenaline pulsing through his veins, Mike's pain level was still tolerable.

"Don't move a fucking muscle!" a voice called out from behind one of the cars parked in the lot.

"Do not, I say do not, reach for that gun," came the second command.

Mike realized that he had placed his gun down on the pavement to the right of his head. "Officer Mike O'Shea, County Probation... just take it easy, guys," Mike urged in the calmest voice he could muster.

Surviving this mess only to get shot by a unit dispatched to assist him would be ironic, to say the least. Mike was blinded by the officer's ten-thousand candle power tactical flashlight which was intentionally pointed directly in his eyes. He had used the same technique on dozens of occasions. Blind the suspect, gain the advantage.

"On your stomach, very slowly," the voice commanded.

They're gonna hook me up until they can sort out this clusterfuck. Mike winced in pain as he tried to maneuver onto his stomach. With a head and shoulder wound and what felt like a shattered hip, his hope for a quick trip to the emergency room at Serra Memorial Hospital was fading. The officer swiftly swooped in and placed his right shin over the back of Mike's neck, just above where the second blow with the brick had landed. He groaned but had the presence of mind to offer up his hands in the perfect handcuffing position. The cuffs were applied, and Mike was searched for an additional weapon.

As the officer's hands made their way down Mike's body, he remembered his backup weapon. Mike had a thirty-eight caliber Taurus revolver strapped to his left ankle, used in the event of a malfunction of his primary duty weapon, or just as likely, if he had his primary weapon taken away.

"Hold on. Just hold on," said Mike, trying to catch his breath. "Backup weapon inside left ankle," he said in what amounted to a whisper.

The officer found his five-shot revolver, unbuttoned the release snap, and removed it from his ankle holster.

A second officer and then a third now emerged from the shadows, AR-15 rifles and a tactical shotgun pointed at Mike's back. He knew better than to try to speed the process along by introducing himself, so he stayed quiet.

"Get him back to the perimeter!" one of the officers yelled to an approaching paramedic. With Mike handcuffed and searched, the police officers turned their attention on the truck. Mike heard more yelling. He knew they would approach the truck very slowly.

Damn, I'm sleepy. Probing his face, Mike realized that he had lost his glasses despite the new Velcro strap and duct tape apparatus he was experimenting with.

A few moments later, the truck was secured. An officer pulled Mike's wallet badge from his rear pocket, checked the photo, and confirmed that the seriously injured man on the ground was indeed who he said he was. The paramedics were allowed to move in and take over. Mike was loaded into an ambulance and marveled at the efficiency of the paramedics. In and out of consciousness, he could feel a prick in his arm as an IV was inserted. He started to shiver violently before passing out for the second time that evening.

Mike awoke in the emergency room at Serra Memorial Hospital. Staring up at amazingly bright lights, he realized he was now lying on his back. A man in his late forties with a white coat and a black turban appeared.

"Mike, you're in the hospital. I'm Dr. Khan. Can you hear me? Can you understand me?"

The doctor had a pronounced British accent. *Must be an Indian…but different kind of Indian than me,* Mike thought with a giggle as the morphine drip attached to his hand started to take effect.

"Did he *shoot* me?" Mike asked, almost sounding hurt that his homeless friend from the parking lot would repay his offer of water with such a lack of graciousness.

"No, *you* have not been shot, but you were struck several times with a blunt object. You have many injuries. A severely bruised hip, large gash on your shoulder. You also have a fractured skull, which is the most serious."

Mike looked around and realized that he was now dressed in a hospital gown. He felt instinctively for his right hip.

"Where's my gun? What did you do with my gun?" Mike demanded, now trying to sit up.

"We have your weapon, Mike." This time, the voice was different, no accent and female.

Mike looked to his left and saw the face of Constance Tinker, the Serra Police Chief. Chief Tinker had come to town a few years earlier from the town of Yuma, Arizona, and had a solid reputation for being pro-officer *and* pro-community, not an easy thing in a college town with almost as many ACLU attorneys as family pets.

"My name is Connie. I think we've met at a meeting or maybe some training we both attended."

Mike tried to focus. *Where are my glasses?* "What happened back at the department?" he asked.

"Mike, I want to fill you in, and of course, my investigators will have lots of questions for you when you're up to it. Before you say anything though, I must tell you that we'll handle this like any other homicides until you're cleared."

"Homicides…the guy from the truck? Was there someone else?" he asked, still trying to focus on the police chief.

"Mike, we have two fatalities from this incident. An adult male driver in the truck and a female juvenile in the passenger seat. Looks like the juvenile was a runaway traveling around with the male. This is going to be a tough time for you, but we'll make it as easy as we possibly can, okay?"

"A juvenile? A kid?" Mike asked.

"Yes, a fourteen-year-old girl."

He stared up at the bright light illuminating the room. "I need to throw up," he warned Dr. Khan, who, with surprising agility, had a large plastic bowl for such occasions in front of Mike's lips.

*****

"It looks like a good shoot, Mike. You'll be on the beach until they wrap things up, but you should sail through the investigation," assured Jerome Rosenblatt, who, at seventy-eight years of age, was the oldest practicing labor attorney in California.

Jerome Rosenblat was a celebrity in law enforcement circles. His practice consisted entirely of representing officers who found themselves under investigation for an infinite number of reasons, from graft and corruption to unlawful use of force, the routine sexual harassment case, and on-duty shootings (as was the case with Mike). Rosenblatt received a call at his home in Monterey, about two hours north of Serra, from Tommy Sagapalu, who had rushed to the hospital as soon as he had heard that Mike had been in a shooting. Despite the late hour, long drive, and his advanced age, Rosenblatt had thrown on an old pair of jeans, deck shoes, and a blue "Hastings School of Law" sweatshirt and rushed down Highway 101 to Serra.

Rosenblatt stood in the corner of Mike's hospital room next to Tommy as detectives briefed him on exactly what had happened. Fifty-nine-year-old Terry Brennan, a parolee who had been released after serving thirty years for trying to run over a police officer in Las Vegas. This was no surprise to Mike, and he even found some irony in the situation. The court in Nevada, however, did not find Terry's behavior at all amusing. The sentencing judge's mood further deteriorated when Terry Brennan's defense attorney attempted to blame his client's "issues" on a case of PTSD from his tours in Vietnam. A quick records check revealed that not only was Terry Brennan never in the military, but he also had an old federal warrant for failing to register for the draft.

Terry was homeless and had no known family. He followed a well-known trail of towns along the western United States that were friendly or at least tolerant of drifters.

Fourteen-year-old Darlene Bixby from Phoenix, otherwise known as Kitty, had left an alcoholic mother and her mother's sex offender boyfriend when the boyfriend's attention turned from Darlene's seventeen-year-old sister to her. She traveled with a small band of teens who followed the same trail as Terry Brennan. After their attack on Mike and his subsequent defense, both had died immediately. The coroner had removed four rounds from Brennan's upper torso and two from Darlene's. Mike had killed them very decisively and very efficiently. For Mike's part, he had received a deep contusion on his left hip, suffered a moderately severe concussion, and had a wide gash on his shoulder which took over thirty stitches to close. A large cut across the back of Mike's skull required an additional twelve stitches.

"Mike, there are two detectives outside. They want a statement, which is to be expected. Before you answer any question, pause and look at me. This will give me sufficient time to object."

"Got it," said Mike.

Once the detectives had brought Mike up-to-date, they asked him if he was ready to talk. He looked over at Tommy, who shook his head violently from side to side, and then Rosenblatt.

Rosenblatt stepped forward and, in a grandfatherly voice, said, "It's late, boys. What say we all get some sleep, including my client, and reconvene back here in a few days? I'm confident Officer O'Shea will cooperate fully and answer all your questions."

The two detectives stared straight ahead, expressionless. Having *never* been in an OIS (officer-involved shooting) themselves, they were more irritated with the request for a delay than empathetic.

"Boys, my client is under the influence of an opiate-based pain reliever, and as a matter of practicality, he can't talk to you until he is no longer under the influence of this substance."

Mike, who now held a small pen-like device which controlled his morphine drip, gave himself several jolts and offered the detectives a boozy grin. The detectives looked at one another, shrugged, and left. Rosenblatt had bought Mike some time. Tommy's now wife, Alma, was on duty at the hospital and came in as the detectives left.

She came over to Mike's bedside and checked his vitals. In a soothing tone, she asked, "How are you feeling, my friend?"

"Super, Alma," Mike slurred. "'Cept I'm becoming a first-class addict with this stuff. Hey, when you gonna leave that bum Tommy Saga-what's-his-name and run off to Cabo with me? Do you possibly have a sister I could meet and fall for? We could be fam-damn-ly. Hey, Alma, are you aware that Tommy is of Samoan decent? Very unpredictable, those people, but great dancers. I'll teach you the haka [Samoan tribal war dance] when I get the hell outta here."

Somewhere in the recesses of his memory, Mike recalled spending weeks learning the dance, which Tommy's groomsmen performed at the Sagapalus' wedding.

Tommy rolled his eyes at his wife. Alma smiled. "There's a man outside to see you, Mike. He says he's the chief of the probation department."

"Yeah, Mike. Brewster's outside. In fact, half the department's in the hall. Do you want to see him?'" asked Tommy.

"Usher old cheese dick right in, Tomas," replied Mike, now maximizing the input of the morphine drip.

Tommy walked out into the corridor and over to a dozing man dressed in ratty brown corduroys and blue chambray shirt.

"He's all yours, Chief," Tommy said to Chief Probation Officer Jonathan Brewster.

Jonathan (he insisted on the formal form of his name, never John, Johnny, and certainly not Jack) Brewster had received his master's degree in social work from Oberlin College in 1969 and somehow landed at the doorstep of the Serra County Probation Department. He entered the field when probation officers were essentially social workers for the criminal courts. Brewster had been a conscientious objector during the Vietnam War and fancied himself a pacifist. To this day, Brewster enjoyed agitating fellow law enforcement executives by wearing a small peace symbol button on his lapel at various official meetings. After marrying a superior court judge's flower child of a daughter, he procured a job at the probation department and, by means which remain unexplainable, had risen to the top spot in the organization.

It was rumored that Chief Brewster smoked copious amounts of marijuana with his friends, an assortment of artists, musicians, activists, and philosophy professors from Cal Coastal. Much to his mortification, Jonathan Brewster had passively witnessed a statewide trend of probation officers turning in their love beads and sandals for penal codes and firearms. Not finding sufficient comfort in marijuana, the chief had begun drinking heavily. He hated his job, hated his life, and wanted nothing more than to retire and write a book about the decline of social work in America. Although professionally disengaged, he continued to work because his wife, who had morphed from flower child to capitalistic real estate broker, liked his paycheck. Earlier in the day, Brewster had been wine tasting with some friends from the Arts Council and was in no shape to drive, let alone pay his respects to an injured employee who had just killed two people.

Brewster weaved into Mike's hospital room, despising the very idea that one of his staff members would have involved himself in such a barbaric act. He contemplated how he would get rid of that "executioner" (as he now thought of Mike). Of equal importance, Chief Brewster wondered how he would explain this to his father-in-law, who was still on the bench and, as a sitting superior court judge, one of his bosses.

"Hey there, old-timer. How are ya?" Brewster slurred.

"Okay, Chief. Thanks for comin' down."

"Listen, guy, you need anything, I mean *anything*, call me! Ya hear, homeslice? Call me, my man!" Brewster grabbed Mike's right hand and attempted a 1970s soul shake but somehow got turned around and ended up grasping Mike's wrist. Realizing his error, Brewster harkened back to his days as a self-proclaimed urban guerilla, waved a closed fist in Mike's direction, and mumbled, "Solid."

Mike stared at his boss who smelled like the inside of a wine cask. *Even in* my *fucked-up state, I can tell that this jackass doesn't know my name.*

Brewster turned and walked toward a closet door. He opened it slowly, and when he realized that it wasn't the way out, he turned to Mike, gave a jaunty salute, and exited through the correct door.

Alma, who had remained in the room under the guise of reading Mike's chart, was mesmerized by the chief's behavior. She looked up from the chart, eyes wide, and said, "Miguel, that man is *drunk.*"

Mike just smiled and gave his morphine pump a couple of squeezes.

CHAPTER 4

Mike slept for the next twelve hours. It was now nine thirty in the morning, and as he awoke, he had two sensations—pain in his hip, head, and shoulder and intense hunger. He also noticed that at some time throughout the night, a killjoy had removed the morphine pump, leaving him to rely on pills he was given by Alma and a cadre of nurses every four hours. Tommy strolled in with Rosenblatt close behind and handed Mike a white bag with the word *Fred's* in red lettering.

"You are my absolute best bud, Tom," Mike said. From the bag, he pulled out a breakfast burrito from Fred's Hot Dogs, a local institution.

With a mouthful of burrito, he turned to Rosenblatt and said, "Morning, Counselor."

"You look good, Mike. They're going to release you day after tomorrow. Feel like a field trip?" the old attorney asked.

"You betcha," responded Mike.

Forty-eight hours later, Mike carefully changed into a clean pair of jeans, a T-shirt, and sneakers that Tommy had picked up from his apartment. As he was dressing, Tommy handed him a 9 mm Smith and Wesson pistol and a holster.

"The detectives have yours, Mike. Take mine until you get yours back."

Mike looked at his friend's gun. "Thanks, Tom" was all he could muster with a significant lump in his throat.

Mike would need a walker until his hip healed, a fact which annoyed him to no end. With Tommy's assistance, he gathered his things and slowly shuffled out of the small hospital room and into the parking lot. Tommy helped Mike slowly and gingerly lower himself into the rear of Rosenblatt's 1972 Mercedes sedan.

"Where we headin', Mr. R?" asked Mike from the back seat.

"Mike, I never let my clients in these cases give a statement before they've had a chance to go back to the scene of the shooting," said Rosenblatt.

Mike considered this and immediately saw the logic. Too many officers had hurt their cases by insisting that they give statements directly following their shootings. Mike's confidence in his attorney's skills were reinforced. Rosenblatt turned left on Johnson Avenue, past the old General Hospital which now housed various county government offices, and up the hill to the probation department. Although it was a typically foggy coastal morning, Mike felt sweat trickle down his neck as he returned to the scene of an incident he would never forget. Rosenblatt parked his car exactly as the truck had been parked the night of the shootings. From the trunk of the Mercedes, he pulled a camera with an attached flashbulb that looked like something from a Kodak Museum. With Tommy looking on, tape measure in hand, Rosenblatt had Mike slowly, step by step, go through the events leading up to the shootings.

After nearly two hours, Rosenblatt was satisfied. As he took copious notes, Mike marveled that a man close to eighty possessed such an incredibly sharp legal mind. After studying his notes, Rosenblatt looked up and said simply, "Okay, boys, I think we're ready."

Rosenblatt dropped Mike off at home and returned to a room at a Holiday Inn. As Mike walked toward the entrance to his upstairs flat, he saw Wong sticking his head out of a side door to the restaurant kitchen below.

"All okay, Mike?" asked Mike's landlord and the proprietor of Wong's Café, a Serra institution.

"You bet, Wong. Just a little banged up," replied Mike. "Hey, if you could have a big bowl of wonton soup brought up, I'd really appreciate it."

Mike retrieved his key from a pocket and unlocked the door. An initial assessment of his apartment indicated all was as he had left it nearly four days before, except for an envelope that had been slipped under his front door. Mike opened the refrigerator and saw nothing he found particularly appetizing, other than bottles of ice-cold Pabst Blue Ribbon staring at him longingly from behind a carton of milk.

Wonder if I should drink with all the dope they've got me on? What the hell! He flopped down on the couch and tossed his walker aside.

Finally, Mike started to allow the gravity of the last few days to settle in. He thought about the eyes of the homeless man. He wondered what events might have taken place to have brought young Darlene Bixby to the point where Mike needed to take her life to save his own. He opened the envelope that was left at his door labeled "County of Serra Probation Department, Human Resources Division."

Mike read the first two sentences and tossed the letter aside.

> You are hereby advised that pending the outcome of an internal investigation, you are placed on paid administrative leave. An investigator from the Professional Standards Unit will be contacting you for an interview. *You are further advised that until further notice, you are directed to NOT discuss this matter with anyone other than your legal representative and investigative personnel of the Serra Police Department and/or the County of Serra District Attorney's Office.* Should you need to leave the area, please contact this office and your request will be considered.

Nice. They could have told me in person. Mike listened to a few messages from well-wishers that were left on his message machine.

He hobbled back to the refrigerator, grabbed a second beer, and collapsed on the couch. *Head hurts. Hell, everything hurts.*

Mike took from his pocket three small vials of pills the hospital had given him when he was released. The first was a strong antibiotic to ward off postoperative infections. The second was a painkiller. Vicodin, to be specific. And the third was something to help Mike sleep. He hopped to his bathroom, unscrewed the caps on the pain and sleeping pills, and tossed them into the toilet. Mike had been a competitive boxer and rugby player for much of his life and had never relied on medication, although the opportunity certainly presented itself enough times. He hobbled back to the couch and, in a fit of frustration, kicked the walker across the room.

Damn if I'm gonna use that thing. He held the cold beer can up against his forehead and tried to numb the pain from the skull fracture.

Despite a valiant effort, Mike's mind continued to wander back to the night in the parking lot. Could he have done something differently? *Should* he have done something differently? He received enough winks, nods, and under-the-breath "good jobs" from the police once they identified Mike as an on-duty probation officer, but who knew? Would he really sail through the shooting investigation as his colleagues had predicted? If he didn't, he'd be out of a job. If he didn't, he'd probably end up in front of a jury, and then anything could happen. This *was* California, after all. Mike allowed his mind to wonder.

Wonder how'd I'd do in prison. *I can still box. Maybe I'll walk into the chow hall and beat the baddest inmate over the head with a food tray like in the prison movies.* As a former law enforcement officer, Mike knew that prison time would be lonely time as he would be kept in protective housing. *Stop it, dummy. No one's goin' to prison. I hope.*

Thankfully, Mike's daydream about the worst-case scenario was interrupted by the ringing of the phone.

"Michael, are you okay?" It was Iggy, and by the tone of his voice, Mike could tell he had heard about the shooting. Father Ignatius Sean De la Rosa was Mike's priest, Godfather, former boxing coach, close friend of his late parents, and if Mike was being honest, the closest thing to a father he had.

Mike apologized for not calling and explained that he had little recollection of the time in the hospital. "How did you hear about it?" he asked.

"I got a call from the priest at Our Lady Church, who, by the way, said he hasn't seen you for a couple of Sundays."

Mike smiled.

"Mike, Father Bob says that you're all over the news."

Father Robert Anthony, known to locals as Father Bob, was the senior priest at Our Lady Church a couple of blocks from Mike's apartment. Mike liked Father Bob and had even met the priest for beers one night after work.

"Mike, I'm coming down. You shouldn't be alone at a time like this," said Iggy.

Mike sighed. "Iggy, I really appreciate it. I'll do you one better. I'll come home for a few days as soon as they're done with my interviews. I'll need to get out of town by then."

Mike hung up the phone and stared at the dark TV perched precariously on an entertainment center, which was actually a few pieces of lumber stacked on top of cement blocks holding a TV and stereo. The blocks and lumber had been spray-painted maroon, a domestic touch Mike thought was the height of sophistication. He felt a moist sensation on his cheek and realized that at some point following his call from Iggy, he began to cry.

I'm no expert in this area, but don't believe I'm handling this thing so well.

Mike heard a loud knock at the door, but he was not in the mood for company, so he ignored the rapping.

"O'Shea, I know you're in there!" yelled Tommy Sagapalu. "We need to discuss your recent 314 charges."

Hilarious, Mike thought. Section 314 of the California Penal Code referenced the crime of indecent exposure. Mike wiped his eyes and blew his nose on a rather ripe T-shirt hanging off the end of his couch.

"Come on in, Tom," Mike called.

The large Samoan had trouble fitting into Mike's doorway. The apartment was built in the 1940s for much smaller people. Tommy held groceries in one hand and a sleeping bag over his shoulder.

"You look like shit, fool," Tommy said with a smile that belayed real concern.

"I'm all right," Mike said. "What are you up to?" Mike inquired, suspiciously noting the sleeping bag.

Tommy laid the groceries down on the kitchen counter and helped himself to a Pabst from the refrigerator.

"Mike, I've never been through a shoot, but I know some guys who have, and it's a pretty shitty deal. Not a good time for you to be alone."

He thought about putting up a good argument, but knowing his friend, it would be wasted breath. Tommy Sagapalu was one of the most loyal people Mike had ever met.

"I hear my thing made the news," Mike said as he grabbed a third beer from the refrigerator. *I don't need the calories, but damn, my head and shoulder hurt like a bitch.*

"Yep, it's in the last couple of paper editions and on TV. Remember what Rosenblatt said. Don't talk to anyone, especially the press," Tommy warned.

"I got it. No talking," said Mike. "Actually, it gets better." He handed Tommy the letter from the probation department.

Tommy read the letter, looked up at Mike, and then read the letter a second time. "You got this in the mail?"

Mike nodded in the negative. "Slid under my door."

"Wait a minute," said Tommy. "I get the IA part [internal investigation]. That's to be expected. But no one from the department has called you? This is how you find out you're on the beach? At the very least, they should have given you a counseling referral by now."

Mike considered Tommy's line of questioning. "The suspension with pay with an OIS is standard, but yeah, I would have expected a more…" Mike struggled for the right word. "I guess a little more compassion. Kinda cold-blooded."

Tommy's brown eyes seemed to turn a shade of black. "This is a bullshit way to treat one of your guys, O'Shea," said Tommy, now trying to maintain his temper. "I just want to break that mother-fucker," he said, making a violent motion with his hands as if break-ing a piece of kindling in two.

"Which motherfucker? We know so many," asked Mike, start-ing to feel the effects of the beer on an empty stomach. "Ya know, you South Pacific Islanders are a very violent people. You should spend more time with my people. Actually, I'm not exactly sure who my people are," Mike said with a laugh. "Take your pick. Smoke peyote with my native ancestors or get hammered on whiskey with the Irish who adopted me!"

"Chief Brewster," said Tommy. "That piece of shit is entirely incapable of handling this. They should turn the whole fuckin' department over to the Sheriff's. The SOs deal with this kind of thing all the time. Fuckin' amateur!"

"Easy, my brother," Mike said dreamily, now feeling the full effects of the beer. "You must join me in my place of peace and tranquility."

"And you're in the land of fucked-up-ville, *my brother*," said Tommy. "Oh, speaking of which, in the bag on the counter is a han-dle of Cazadores Tequila from the Serra cop who tried to spin you into a pretzel."

"Gosh, that's swell," Mike slurred.

Deep down, Mike knew Tommy was right. Chief Probation Officer Brewster could barely handle the stress of a call from down-town reporting that monthly vehicle mileage sheets were submitted late to the County Auditor's Office, let alone one of his officers kill-ing not one but two people. The fact that one of the deceased was a runaway teenage girl made matters more politically sensitive.

Mike was never the chatty type but made up for lost time over beer, a shot of the tequila sent over by the Serra Police Officer, and the frozen pizza Tommy had brought. He talked about their train-ing and how, at some point in the parking lot, his mind shut down and was on automatic pilot, just responding to threats, not thinking. Muscle memory is an amazing thing, they agreed. Both knew that Mike was lucky, very lucky one of the police officers hadn't mistaken him for an unfriendly and taken him out. They talked about the old man with the camper. The toxicology test hadn't been released, but the investigators told Mike they found a useable amount of methamphetamine and a small glass pipe in the truck.

Tommy reminded Mike that this was the second time the old man had tried to run down a law enforcement officer. Mike admitted that he seemed devoid of any strong sense of remorse at having shot the old man. The girl was something else. Tommy could tell this was going to be hard for Mike and just listened. Where was she from? Why had she run away? Had her parents been found and told their daughter was wrapped up neat and tidy and ready for pickup at the Serra County Morgue? Mike wondered if she had any brothers or sisters. What grade was she in? Did she have a pet? Why wasn't she in school? What was she doing with an old man, living out of a camper?

Mike went on talking for the next five hours. Feeling his head spin from the alcohol, he switched to iced tea around midnight.

"Well, I got the interview with the detectives in a few hours. Better hit the sack," Mike finally said close to three o'clock.

He looked over at Tommy, who was splayed out in an easy chair next to the couch, eyes clamped shut, mouth wide open, long hair askew, low snores. Mike wondered how long Tommy had been asleep.

Probably when I started asking about the kid's pet. Mike grabbed a gold blanket with a large blue *Cal* written in script across the center he kept folded over the end of the couch. The Wongs were a great family but cheap as hell and seemed to ignore Mike's subtle comments about his ancient wall heater and the chill in the apartment during winter evenings. He placed the blanket lightly over his friend, turned off the lamp in the living room, and limped to the bedroom.

CHAPTER 5

Surprisingly, Mike got a solid six hours of sleep and woke to the front door closing. He slowly limped from his bed to the living room and read a note from Tommy, who was due in court later in the morning and needed to go home, shower, and change. He promised to check in on Mike later in the day. Mike was under strict orders not to get the sutures in his shoulder and scalp wet, making showering a challenge. He did his best and toweled off. As was his morning routine, Mike had turned on the TV to catch up on the news while he dressed. As soon as he heard his name mentioned, he wished he hadn't been such a creature of habit.

Standing in his living room, still wet from the shower, towel wrapped around his waist, Mike watched the news report. They showed some old footage of him giving an interview after he had tracked down a particularly nasty probationer with a warrant issued for murdering his in-laws. Next, they showed a driver's license photo of the man in the truck and gave a respectable synopsis of his criminal history. Finally, they showed an eighth-grade school photo of the girl Mike had killed.

Oh God. He looked into the eyes of a little girl who could have easily been one of the kids he saw every morning walking to the small parochial school near his apartment. Blue shorts, white shirts, big smiles. *What the hell were you doing there that night with an old man?*

Mike's obligatory interview with investigators with the district attorney's officer-involved shooting team was scheduled for ten o'clock that morning. As agreed upon, he met Jerome Rosenblatt at the Spilled Beans Coffee Shop across the street from the courthouse at eight thirty. Mike was a regular here. He liked the kids working the counter, liked the eclectic clientele, and liked the coffee. As soon as he walked through the door, Mike sensed that something was different.

"Hiya, Patty," he said as he greeted a young barista.

Patty was an English major at Cal Coastal, and when she learned that Mike, despite his gruff exterior, had two English degrees from the University of California, she began to look to him for academic advice.

"How'd you do on your midterm? Did you go for the comparison of the *Iliad* and *On the Road*?" Mike asked. He had suggested the idea to Patty, who was prepping for an important exam in her senior English Literature class.

"Haven't gotten my grade back yet," she said with her eyes down.

Usually, his young friend couldn't wait for his daily appearance and peppered him with questions about literature. Not today.

Guess she knows. Mike got his coffee and a dry bagel and limped to a table outside. As the morning traffic made its way down Cuesta Street, he picked at his bagel and wondered just how many changes he would encounter in his life following "the deal," as Mike now referred to the shootings. Jerome Rosenblatt pulled his ancient Mercedes into a rarely unoccupied parking space reserved for patrons of the coffee shop. He slowly got out of the car and walked over to Mike.

"You look tired, Counselor," observed Mike.

"I am tired. You think I'd listen to my wife and give up saving the skins of you trigger-happy cops," said the attorney.

Mike looked up from his bagel. *Did he call me trigger-happy?* As soon as the words left his lips, Rosenblatt regretted them.

"Mike, I'm sorry. This was a good shoot, as good as I've seen. I'm just tired, and my feet hurt. Bunions are the Lord's curse on the aged."

He smiled and patted the attorney on the back. "No prob, Mr. R."

Rosenblatt explained that after dropping Mike off, he returned to the probation department parking lot for a second look. "I'm good because I'm very thorough, Mike," he said.

Rosenblatt took a yellow legal pad out of his briefcase and went over anticipated questions which would be asked during his meeting with the investigators.

"Mike, what do you know about this county's DA investigators?"

"They seem like okay guys." He paused. "Actually, they seem a little different from the rest of us."

"How so?" asked Rosenblatt.

"Well, they're better dressed, that's for sure. Dress more like attorneys than cops or probation officers." Mike took a bite of bagel and sip of coffee. "To be honest, most of the ones are a little stand-offish, like they're better than the rest of us."

Rosenblatt smiled and sat back. "Yes, Mike, there are some fine and honorable investigators employed by the district attorney's office. However, some joined the DA's office only after a few years of police work, and only then because of political connections with the DA, who, after all, is an elected official."

Mike hadn't decided if the local district attorney's office handling his investigation was good or bad news.

"Some want to see you get an absolutely fair shake." Rosenblatt tapped a bony finger on the table to make this point. "But, and this is a big *but*, some are unscrupulous and would love nothing more than to find a crack in the story of a popular local probation officer and use the carcass of his rotting career as a badge of honor for theirs."

Mike looked out onto Cuesta Street, wondering if a career teaching seventh-graders to appreciate Mark Twain might have been a wiser career move. *He's telling me to get ready to take it right up the ass.*

"What I'm saying is this. Just because these investigators have badges, don't be fooled into thinking they have *your* best interest at heart. Right now, you trust *me* and your family. No one else. Understood?"

Mike nodded. Sobered by his attorney's insight, he listened carefully as Rosenblatt went through every conceivable question that might be asked and the most appropriate answer. He soon realized that his story was what it was, and it was supported by facts. But Mike also realized that there was more than one way to answer a question truthfully, and that this difference might tip the scales in his favor. After close to ninety minutes of prepping, Mike and his attorney walked across the street to the district attorney's office. They were ushered into a windowless room by a receptionist Mike had said hello to dozens of times when he visited the same office in his capacity as a probation officer. She was usually friendly. This morning, she looked at him like he hadn't bathed in some time.

Mike and Rosenblatt entered an interview room and took two chairs. After several minutes, there was a quiet knock on the door, and a friendly face appeared. Investigator Hortensia Ruiz had been with the district attorney's office for ten years and had worked with Mike on some mutual cases. They were friendly enough, but not so close where Investigator Ruiz would need to recuse herself from being involved in the investigation. Hortensia introduced herself to Rosenblatt and greeted Mike with a handshake and wink. The wink, he hoped, was a sign that he had done the right thing and that all would be well. Hortensia explained that she was assisting the primary investigator, who would join them in a moment. Rosenblatt asked for the name of the primary.

"Dwight Dickhard," replied Hortensia.

"Pardon me," said Rosenblatt, looking up over his bifocals.

"Dwight Dickhard," said Mike.

"How do you spell that?" asked Rosenblatt.

"D-I-C-K-H-A-R-D," interjected Mike with a smile.

After a light tap on the door, the impeccably dressed investigator Dwight David Dickhard entered the room. Dark blue suit, starched light blue Oxford shirt, maroon silk tie with matching handkerchief tucked into the jacket pocket, and black patent leather Florsheims buffed to perfection. Dickhard's ridiculously dyed auburn hair sparkled with some type of thick hair care product.

Rosenblatt stood. Mike followed suit.

"Jerome Rosenblatt, Investigator Dickhard," Rosenblatt said reaching out his hand.

"Incorrect. It is pronounced *Dick-Herd*," replied the investigator, voice dripping with pomposity.

Of all the investigators in the Serra County District Attorney's Office, Dwight Dickhard was absolutely the last person Mike would have wanted involved in his investigation. Dickhard had spent all of three years as a member of the Santa Barbara Police Department, where he was the victim of an "accidental discharge" on the shooting range during quarterly qualifications. Dickhard didn't shoot *himself* accidentally. Rather, he was shot in the foot by one of the police department's range masters, specifically the senior range master.

The fact that Dickhard had expressed great dissatisfaction with the training procedures employed by the senior range master, a retired Army master sergeant, and had taken it upon himself to spend lonely Saturday evenings rewriting the senior range master's complete training manual, was later examined in an internal investigation into the matter. So was the fact that the senior range master was an expert marksman and knew his way around a firing range. Additional factors examined were the facts that there were no witnesses to this unfortunate event and that not only had the senior range master attained expert status as a marksman, he had also been a member of *two* United States Olympic shooting teams. The most prominent factor examined, but one which never made its way into the final incident report, was the fact that Dwight Dickhard was universally despised by his colleagues, family, fellow police academy cadets and instructors, and most of the citizens he encountered.

Unlike some who merely *appear* overly confident as a mask to disguise insecurity, Dwight Dickhard thought of himself as intellectually superior to the rest of the Santa Barbara Police Department and community at large. Dwight Dickhard's application to the Serra County District Attorney's Office sailed through with stellar recommendations from his superiors. No better way to get rid of a problem employee than to give him or her a glowing reference.

Dickhard stared at Mike without speaking. Thirty seconds, a minute, minute and a half, two minutes. The same stare that had melted so many college students and mentally ill homeless people into admitting to a variety of low-level crimes back in Santa Barbara.

Mike had enough. "Are you trying to intimidate me, punkass? You think you're a tough guy? I deal with *real* tough guys, clown." *Hmmm, possibly an overreaction*, he immediately thought.

Hortensia looked up at the ceiling and said something under her breath in Spanish, a prayer perhaps for her friend to regain his sanity. Rosenblatt simply stared at his client and cleared his throat.

"Perhaps we could take a brief break so I may confer with my client?" suggested the attorney in a pleasant voice. Dickhard gave a dismissive shrug and casually waved his right hand.

"What exactly does that mean?" asked Rosenblatt, mimicking the wave.

"Go ahead and break," Dickhard said with a sigh.

Rosenblatt and Mike walked out a side door and onto a pedestrian bridge between two county government buildings.

"I'm damn near eighty years old, son. Do you think you could behave yourself for just the duration of the interview?" asked the attorney in a tired voice. "I'd really enjoy going back to Monterey and sleeping in my own bed tonight, *if* at all possible."

Mike looked down at his scuffed boots in a look of self-disgust. "You're right, Mr. R. I'm sorry."

Back in the interview room, Dickhard walked Mike through his activities leading up to the shooting. But he wasn't just interested in the time between Mike's conversation with the owner of the truck and beyond. Step by step, hour by hour, Dickhard took Mike through his activities during the forty-eight hours prior to the shootings. How much alcohol had he consumed? Two beers and a glass of wine. How much caffeine did he consume? One cup of coffee the first day, one cup of coffee and an iced tea the second. How much sleep did he get? Seven hours the first night, eight the next. Prescription drugs? None. Had he had an argument with his spouse or partner?

"Don't have one," Mike replied.

"Hmmm" came Dickhard's reply.

Rosenblatt had enough. "Investigator Dickhard, I've been an attorney representing law enforcement clients for a very long time, and this line of questioning is highly invasive and irregular. Just what is it you're trying to get at here?"

"State of mind," replied the investigator in a bored voice, as if Rosenblatt was a six-year-old asking her grandfather why the sun made the sidewalk hot.

"Could you elaborate, please?" asked Rosenblatt.

Dickhard explained that Mike's state of mind was critical in establishing his motives for shooting.

"My client's state of mind was stable and consistent with all the standards set forth in the State Peace Officer Standards and Training requirements, Mr. Dickhard, and his motives were to remain among the living. If you have information to the contrary, you have an obligation to advise my client and I so we can respond."

"Very well," said Dickhard. "Let's start with your arrival in the probation department parking lot."

For the next five hours with an hour break for lunch, Dwight Dickhard asked Mike questions about the shooting from every conceivable angle. He would have happily given a statement the night in the hospital, but now he was glad Rosenblatt had objected. Mike was even more grateful that the old attorney had given him a chance to return to the parking lot and essentially reenact the shootings. By the end of the day, late afternoon shadows were creeping into the interview room.

Surprisingly, Dickhard abruptly announced, "No further questions."

Mike and Rosenblatt rode the elevator down to the lobby of the government center in silence. As the elevator door opened, Rosenblatt said, "You know, Mike, his questions about your personal life the days before the shooting were not at all uncommon. I just put up a bit of a fight for theatrical purposes." The attorney smiled. "Any time an officer takes a life—in this case, two lives—their actions in the days before the shooting will be scrutinized under a very powerful microscope."

Mike shook his head and squeezed the attorney's arthritic hand. "Can I buy you dinner, Mr. R? It's the least I can do."

"I'm too tired to drive back to Monterey tonight. I think I'll just go back to the hotel and take a bath."

"Do you want to stay at my place?" asked Mike enthusiastically. "I'll take the couch. You get the bed."

Rosenblatt smiled. He just couldn't help liking the young officer with the disfigured ears before him.

"Thank you, son. As entertaining as it might be to spend a night in a bachelor pad, I think Mrs. Rosenblatt might be more comfortable knowing I was tucked safely into a room at the Holiday Inn."

Mike led Rosenblatt to his Mercedes, and they said their goodbyes. As he walked the few blocks back to his apartment, still with a noticeable limp from his injured hip, Mike felt guilty for wishing the ancient attorney stayed alive long enough for him to finish his career. He had a feeling he might need a good lawyer again.

Mike dug his keys out of the pocket of his jeans and let himself into the small apartment. Several cards and notes from well-wishers littered the floor by the door, and more goodwill messages were left on his answering machine. He popped a cold Pabst and fell into his couch. Mike's hip hurt. His head was starting to hurt, but he felt some relief knowing that his post-shooting investigation might be close to concluding. After a dinner of warmed leftovers, he called Iggy.

"Want your prodigal son back for a few days?" Mike asked.

"Get your ass up here" came the reply from the priest.

Mike awoke to a glorious Central California morning. After a quick shower, still modified to keep his sutures dry, he packed a gym bag full of clothes and hobbled his way toward the door. The doctor had ordered him to use a walker for another two weeks, but Mike didn't want to arrive at the rectory looking like an invalid. So he left the walker and slowly walked to Mill Street, where he had parked his Jeep. As Mike lowered himself gingerly into the seat, he noticed a small piece of folded paper stuck under his windshield wiper. He reached around and grabbed it. "Murdering Prick," the note said in scribbled print. Mike crumpled the note and tossed it to the street. Unlike most law enforcement officers, he never favored moving into the outlining rural areas of the county where the likelihood of bumping into someone he had arrested, possibly even sent to prison, was ever present. Mike liked living close to work and downtown and knew that regardless of where he lived, if someone wanted to find him and do him harm, it wouldn't be all that difficult. He thought about the small arsenal he kept in the closet of his apartment. *Let 'em find me.*

Mike wheeled the Jeep onto Highway 101, up over the steep Mission Grade, and past the towns of Santa Lucia and Paso Adobe with its vineyards as far as the traveler could see.

After four hours on the road, he pulled up in front of St. Mary's Church and slowly walked up the steps of the rectory. Iggy had been working on his homily for the following weekend and heard Mike's Jeep. He quickly walked to the front door, opened it up, and gave Mike a warm smile. Iggy grabbed him in a bear hug and gave him a kiss on the cheek,

"So glad you're home, son."

Unlike other welcoming embraces, this hug seemed endless. Mike could tell Iggy didn't want to let go, so the two stood there in the front door to the rectory. Finally, he broke loose and looked at Iggy's wide smile and moisture in his eyes. Although used to Iggy's emotional side, Mike had yet to overcome his aversion to seeing grown men cry.

"Oh, come on, Iggy. No tears, please," Mike pleaded.

"Tears are good, Mike. Our Father's way of watering the soul!" Iggy was almost gleeful now, wiping the moisture with the sleeves of his sweatshirt. "You know, Mike, your patron saint, St. Michael, God's cop in heaven, was with you. He protected you that night, and I hope you've been asking him to pray for you."

"You betcha, Iggy. What's for dinner?" Mike sniffed and smelled something spicy and delicious coming from the kitchen.

"I've got a new cook, and I think she's a keeper," Iggy said with a giggle. He led Mike into the kitchen, where a stout woman was furiously throwing ingredients into a large pot on the stove. "Michael, please meet Evelina. She's from Portugal!"

Mike could see that Iggy was beyond thrilled with his new cook. *Poor guy must have been starving.* Evelina turned and almost startled Mike with the face of a bulldog and several missing teeth. She hugged Mike and welcomed him in Portuguese.

"Evelina's put ten pounds on me already," Iggy said with a smile as he patted his stomach.

Mike stretched out his hand and said, "I'm happy to meet you, Evelina. Iggy, she has no fuckin' clue what I just said, does she?"

Iggy cuffed Mike on the back of the head as he had been doing for almost all his twenty-six years and said, "Hey, watch your mouth, mister."

They left Evelina to her cooking, and Mike followed Iggy upstairs. After dropping his duffel bag off in a guest room, the two sat down in Iggy's study.

"How are you holding up, Michael?" asked Iggy, now in a much more serious tone.

In addition to his duties as the senior priest at St. Mary's, Iggy was a chaplain with the Oakland Police Department and understood the nuances of officer-involved shootings and the toll they take on the officer. He walked Iggy through the interview, Rosenblatt's preparation, even his interaction with the barista Patty. Iggy listened intently, understanding that Mike's experience had been standard. He sat back in his chair and stared at his godson for a few moments. Mike braced himself for some true words of spiritual wisdom.

"His name is really Dickhard?" Iggy asked as he burst into laughter.

Mike found Iggy's response to be hysterically funny and just what he needed. Both were now holding their sides and laughing themselves into tears as Mike mimicked the investigator.

After a lull in the conversation, Iggy asked Mike how long he could stay and what, if anything, he wanted to do while he was home.

"If I'm available by phone, I can stay for a week or so," Mike explained. "No real plans. Just like to get a little downtime and start to do some rehab on the hip."

"I'm running the stadium steps up at Cal tomorrow morning. Are ya with me?" Iggy asked enthusiastically.

"How 'bout you run and I just do a slow climb?" Mike countered with a grin.

*****

After catching up on parish gossip with Iggy, Mike limped down the hall and lay down for a long nap. He awoke several hours later to an amazing aroma coming from the kitchen. Iggy hadn't exaggerated. Evelina's cooking skills were epic. Despite their lack of a common language, Mike followed the cook around the kitchen with a wooden spoon, sampling the ingredients of several pots simmering on the stove. Evelina playfully swatted his hand and admonished him in her foreign tongue with a smile. Iggy appeared at the kitchen door. He spoke a little Portuguese and interpreted. Evelina said Mike reminded her of her mischievous son back in Portugal. Mike smiled and gave her a hug.

"Mike, I hope you don't mind, but I invited a friend from the Oakland PD over for dinner. He was stationed in the Azores when he was in the Marines and loves Evelina's cooking."

"No problem," said Mike with a mouthful of stew brewing in one of the saucepans. "Anyone I know?"

"Yes. Deputy Chief Julius Washington."

Mike knew the name sounded familiar, but he had been raised around so many cops that he wasn't quite sure.

"Mike, Julius's wife, Lorene, was the social worker who placed you with your mom and dad when you were a baby. He was also the officer who took down the man who killed your dad."

Mike thought about this, knowing the coincidence wasn't random. Inviting his father's friend was part of Iggy's plan to rid him of any demons which might have crept into his consciousness after the shooting.

Chief Washington arrived a few minutes later, not at all looking like the second-in-command of one of the state's largest police departments but more like a distinguished law professor in khaki pants and a buttoned-down tartan shirt. Over a traditional Portuguese stew, fresh bread, and wine, the trio chatted with no mention of the shooting. After dinner, the men thanked Evelina, who didn't understand a word they said but appreciated the universality of contented eaters. It was a rare but beautifully warm Oakland evening, so Iggy suggested they refill their wineglasses and retire to a small iron table and chairs in the backyard of the rectory.

As soon as they sat down, Iggy, in an almost comical display of theatrics, jerked his head up toward the window of his office and said, "Gosh, that sounds like the phone in my office. I better take it." Off he went, leaving Mike and Julius Washington alone.

"Mike, the last time I fired a gun other than qualifying on the range was when I killed the man who killed your father. It was the best day and the worst day of my life," said Julius. "Your dad was one of the best cops I ever worked with and a hellava good friend."

Mike wasn't sure what to say, so he remained silent. After a minute or two, a simple "Thank you" was all that he could come up with.

"I have some idea of what you're going through and what you're *going* to go through."

Mike stared into the chief's dark brown eyes and looked away. "Did Iggy ask you to talk to me?" Mike asked quietly.

"He's worried about you, Mike."

Julius explained that even in a state as large as California, the law enforcement community is small and tightly knit. He had done some snooping and, with little or no effort, had contacted his counterpart in the Serra Police Department, who, as a matter of professional courtesy, shared the details of Mike's shooting.

"It was a good shoot. *Both* of them."

The deputy chief had correctly surmised that Mike was losing little or no sleep over the killing of the man who had tried to kill him. But the death of his fourteen-year-old companion was another thing. Mike was losing *a lot* of sleep over that. He talked about his own inquiry into the life of Darlene Bixby. For reasons he couldn't understand, Mike wanted to know as much about her young life as possible.

"I found her mother's address. Do you think I should try to contact her?" Mike asked.

Julius smiled at Mike's youthful innocence. "No, Mike, don't call her," he advised. "There's nothing good that could come out of that conversation, not for you and not for the girl's family."

Julius walked Mike through what was sure to be a civil suit against the County of Serra, possibly Mike personally, and any other entities the surviving family members could shake down. Deep pockets run especially deep in cases like these, he explained.

They talked well into the night until the older cop said, "Well, Mike, it's late, and I'm an old man, so I gotta get out of here."

Almost on cue, Iggy appeared from the rectory. The three shook hands, and Mike and Julius Washington promised to keep in touch. Mike hobbled up to his old room and flopped into bed. He appreciated Iggy arranging the dinner, just another in a long line of small acts of consideration the priest had shown to him. Mike shut his eyes and saw the freshly scrubbed face of Darlene Bixby.

*****

The small town of Colma, a few miles south of San Francisco, was best known for having more deceased inhabitants than living. Iggy stood back and gave Mike some privacy as he approached the graves. Mike knelt, crossed himself, and mouthed a prayer for his parents. Iggy turned and walked over to a wooden bench perched beneath a massive cypress tree which sheltered the graves from the cold San Francisco winds.

After a few minutes, Mike walked over and sat down beside Iggy. They remained silent like that for a better part of half an hour. Mike had long ago passed the point where trips to his parents' graves brought on a wave of sadness. Now he felt a kind of peace that always left him feeling better than when he arrived. On this day though, he wasn't finding peace as easily.

Still staring at his parents' graves, Mike asked, "Hey, Iggy, what do you think the Boss will say about my deal?"

Despite being brought up in as Catholic of an environment as one could, Iggy was always a little perplexed with Mike's obvious discomfort with discussing such topics as divine redemption. In fact,

Mike was entirely uncomfortable discussing theology in any form, hence his reference to God simply as "the Boss," a phrase he had started using when he was a teenager. Iggy would try to engage him in similar discussions. Iggy knew—hoped, at least—that this conversation would take place but had wanted Mike to prompt it on his own. During his life as a priest, he had counseled dozens of police officers and combat veterans who struggled with the concept of "just war," a phrase the church used to refer to taking a life in the line of duty.

Iggy took a breath and, in a voice that was as much teacher as priest, explained the mystery of scriptural inconsistencies.

"In the Beatitudes, Jesus says, 'Blessed are the Peacemakers.' Then in the Sermon on the Mount, he tells us to turn the other cheek. Those two statements seem pretty clear on his position that Christians should be pacifists."

Mike continued to stare straight ahead, wondering if this conversation was going to make him feel any better. *Damn, not lookin' good so far.*

Iggy went on. "But then Jesus tells the apostles, 'Let him who has no sword, sell his mantle and buy one.'"

Mike started to feel better.

"Now things get more interesting," Iggy explained in full theology instructor mode.

Iggy went on to explain that by the third century, Christianity was under attack from various sides but continued to grow in numbers. Augustine realized that at some point, the church would need to make a formal statement on war, which evolved into the just war doctorine.

Mike sat back. *Maybe I'm not in as deep shit as I thought.*

"Son, from what you've told me about the shooting, this is my determination, not just as your priest and Godfather but also my objective position as a theologian. First, the man in the truck was the aggressor. You did all that you could to prevent this from happening and were trying to assist him before he became aggressive. Second, you tried to get away to safety, but your hip was disabling, and you took a pretty good shot to the head."

Now we're talkin'. Preach it, brother!

"Finally," Iggy explained. "Your use of force, even in bringing about the death of two living beings, did not bring about evil or disaster greater than *their* desire to kill you."

Mike thought about this and turned to Iggy, eyes wide and mouth open. For as long as Iggy could remember, whenever a light went off in Mike's brain, the same expression came across his face, giving the inaccurate impression that he was a bit of a dullard.

"So I'm gonna be okay?"

The priest smiled. "Yes, son, you're gonna be okay."

CHAPTER 6

Two weeks later

Bob McDougal was the closest thing to a real celebrity the small community of Serra had. For years, the retired Cal Coastal English professor had hosted an afternoon talk show on the town's oldest radio station, KSRA the Mighty 890, as the station was known. McDougal was slightly left of center politically but did a yeoman's job of trying to remain objective and neutral. After over thirty years on the air, a lifetime by the standards of local radio, McDougal had become a local celebrity. He was supported by a legion of loyal listeners, many of whom called in several times a week with their thoughts and opinions on a variety of topics, from the poor behavior of the local college kids to the safety of the nearby nuclear power plant.

Some of the regulars were well-informed and quite rational. Others were simply kooks looking for a public forum to rant and ramble. Despite his liberal social and political bona fides, McDougal had two nephews and a niece who were all police officers in various locales throughout the country. He knew law enforcement was a difficult job and did his best to give them the benefit of the doubt. It was six weeks since the shooting, and the district attorney's office had finished up their investigation. Although not a long time considering that a law enforcement officer had shot and killed two people, one a juvenile. The decision was announced in a press release from the district attorney's office.

"Deputy Probation Officer Michael O'Shea has been cleared of any wrongdoing in a shooting that took the lives of two assailants on September 2 of this year."

McDougal quickly came to Mike's defense despite the volume of calls he received calling for his badge.

"Couldn't he have just shot out the truck tires?" one frequent caller, Gladys from Chumash Hills, whined.

"Shoot his tires out? C'mon, Gladys, what are ya talkin' about?" McDougal implored. "This isn't Hollywood."

"If we spent more money on a local homeless shelter and less on giving guns to probation officers, this kind old man and that innocent young girl would be with us today," pontificated Chet from Pacific Beach.

"Okay, Chet, we all know that not enough money goes toward the homeless, but what's that got to do with a man whose life was at stake? What about him, huh?"

McDougal enjoyed these calls as it livened up his show, and his day further brightened when he took a call from Mike's boss, Chief Probation Officer Jonathon Brewster. McDougal's ageless producer, Bonnie, waved furiously at him toward the end of a Friday afternoon show, just after the DA's Office had released their statement on the findings of Mike's investigations. McDougal knew that Bonnie only got this animated when the show *itself* was about to become part of the news.

"If you've been on hold, I apologize, but we have a special caller I want to fit in before the end of the show," McDougal explained calmly despite his rising blood pressure.

"Line one, you're on the air with Bob McDougal. Hello, line one, you're on the air."

Nothing. Knowing that dead air was the death knell in the talk radio business, McDougal reached for a button to end the call when a man's voice spoke.

"Am I on the air?"

"Yes, you're on with Bob McDougal." Silence.

"Am I on?"

"Yessir, you are on the air."

Despite the hard work of McDougal and his producers to keep the periodic oddball caller off the air, on occasion, one slipped by, so he was accustomed to handling them with all the aplomb of a bar bouncer safely escorting a drunk out of a tavern.

"Last chance."

"This is Chief Probation Ooosifficer Jonathon Brewster calling."

My God, he's drunk, thought McDougal with glee. The periodic inebriated caller was an irritant. An inebriated public official caller wanting to discuss a controversial topic was almost too good to be true!

"I'd like to discuss the fundings of the District Attorney's Offoos regarding the murder of two individuals at the hands of my ossificer, Muster O'Shee."

Bonnie, McDougal's producer, held her head in her hands as she rocked back and forth in disbelief. McDougal's sense of timing kicked in, and he knew he had to engage the drunk on the other end of the line.

"Chief, you, of course, are referring to the findings of the district attorney's office this morning. Officer O'Shea has been exonerated in any wrongdoing in the deaths of two homeless people who apparently tried to kill *him*. Is that correct?"

Chief Brewster stared at the half-empty quart of Jack Daniels sitting on his desk at the probation department. Since Mike's shooting, he had moved on from his daily marijuana habit and the consumption of wine to the hard stuff, which included drinking in his office, clearly in violation of numerous county government regulations. It didn't matter. The stress from employing the murdering O'Shea was more than this ardent pacifist could bear.

"I was at Woodstock, for God's sake," the chief often mumbled to himself during his evening binges. His wife had exited him from their home, which relegated the bureaucrat to a cot he kept in the corner of his office. His surliness had become more than even she could tolerate.

"Am I on the air?" he asked testily.

McDougal stared at his microphone in disbelief. "Yes, Chief, you have been on the air for several minutes, and you were discussing the DA's findings on the Mike O'Shea matter. Please go ahead." Silence.

"Good, 'cause I got some things to say. Ya know, I marshed with Jane Frinda. Have you ever read *Soul on Ice*? My personal bible, if you will," the chief slurred. "Stokley Carmichael's finest work."

"Chief, *Soul on Ice* was actually written by Eldredge Cleaver while he was in prison," corrected McDougal.

"Whatever," he slurred. "How the hell the DAs could a let that barbarian O'Shure off the hook, I don' know."

McDougal knew he had him. "Chief, are you saying that in your opinion, Officer Mike O'Shea was guilty of *murdering* those people and should be charged? Is that what you're saying, Chief?" Silence.

"Am I on the air?"

"Chief, I have to say this has been a rather unusual conversation. Is it accurate to say, Chief Brewster, that you have been drinking this evening?" Silence.

"Hell yeah, I've been drinking! In fact, I'm drunk off my ass! Wouldn't you if you were in my shoes?"

McDougal was in full attack mode and wanted to get as much on the record as he could before the chief dropped the phone, passed out, or simply hung up.

"Chief, where are you right now?"

"In my office, you dick!"

Bonnie placed her finger over the mute button reserved for only the most profane callers.

"Okay, just confirming, Chief. You are intoxicated while on duty at the probation department. Is that correct?"

"Why don't you just go and fu—" Bonnie hit the mute button with all the agility of an F-16 pilot. McDougal sat back, clasped his hands behind his head, and smiled.

*****

60

Deputy Probation Officer Petra Yablonsky got a call shortly after her chief bid Bob McDougal adieu on the air. As the president of the Probation Officer's Association, she sprang into action.

Most who knew her referred to Petra as a "crusty gal," and she wore the mantle with pride. After returning home from her evening walk with her two vicious Rottweilers, not surprisingly named Smith and Wesson, Petra found that her message machine had reached capacity with calls from her union members and Bob McDougal inviting her to appear on his show to discuss her boss' on-air comments. Her heart was racing just as fast as it had on any warrant raid. Petra quickly got back to McDougal and accepted the offer to appear on his show. Next, she called Rosenblatt, the union's attorney.

Not one to exaggerate, Rosenblatt told her that in all his years representing cops, he had never heard of anything like the chief's call and predicted that he would be out of a job by midweek. The next call was to Mike's apartment, and, not finding him at home, Petra got ahold of Tommy Sagapalu.

"Where's O'Shea?" she barked into Tommy's ear.

"Who is this?" Tommy responded.

"Yablonsky, dumb shit! Where's Mike?"

Feeling a bit mischievous and knowing Petra was approaching a state of complete hysterics, Tommy said with feigned joy in his voice, "You know how long I've waited for you two to get together? Petra, I knew you'd finally fall for the loveable old Indian. Think of your kids…half Native American, half Pollack, a brood of drunken idiots. I can—"

"Sagapalu, quit fucking with me! Have you heard what Brewster said on the McDougal show?" Petra screamed into the phone.

After filling Tommy in, he realized two things: Petra Yablonsky was truly one of the meanest women he had ever met, and she really did need to get in touch with Mike. After rummaging through an old phone book, Tommy gave her the number at the rectory. Petra hung up and quickly called Iggy's number. While it rang, she tried to calm herself with a shot of bourbon.

"St. Mary's rectory" came a cheery but thickly accented voice.

"Michael O'Shea, please."

"Yes, yes, Mr. Mike here," replied Evelina.

Mike was lounging at the kitchen table, reading the sports page of the *San Francisco Chronicle*, sipping port and nibbling on olives and the most amazing cheese he had ever consumed.

"O'Shea," he said into the phone as he tried to rearrange a mouthful of cheese.

"We need to talk," said the gravelly voice of his union president. Her two-pack-a-day habit had acted like sandpaper on her vocal cords.

"Petra, how'd you find me?" Mike asked, concern in his voice. "Everything okay?"

Mike spent the next thirty minutes hearing the story. His first response was to laugh.

"No, O'Shea, this isn't funny. There's a lot of people who think you should hang for killing that kid, and this asshole's comments are just fueling that fire and may have helped make things a little *dangerous* for you when you roll into town."

"Good point," Mike said. "What do you think I should do?"

Petra paused and, after weighing their options, said, "Stay up there for a few more days. Give me a chance to do my thing down here. I'll let you know when it's good to come home."

*****

Mike returned to Serra a week later. After unpacking, he got a good night's sleep and walked downtown to the county medical clinic, where he met with the doctor who would determine if he was fit for duty. Mike had a general idea of what the doctor would want to know, and he was ready.

"Does this hurt?" asked the doctor, twisting Mike's shoulder and hip.

"Nope."

"How about this?"

"Actually, that feels great!" said Mike, trying to muster the strength not to whimper.

"On a scale of one to ten, what's your pain like?" asked the doctor.

"Negative five. I'm rarin' to go, Doc!" said Mike through gritted teeth.

Mike passed with flying colors, and as soon as he was out of sight of the clinic, he sat on a bus stop bench and took a deep breath. It was all he could do not to scream in agony when the doctor twisted his hip and shoulder, and he didn't even consider telling him about the headaches, or that ever since he took the brick to the head, he was having some memory issues and blurred vision in his one *good* eye. No, sir, he was heading back to the field and would absorb the pain.

Mike picked up early in his career that when an officer is injured on duty and sent to a physician hired by the county to see if he or she could physically do their job, the ball was firmly in the officer's court. If the officer wanted to go back to work badly enough, they simply said they were pain-free. If they wanted to take a few more weeks off to remodel their kitchen or take a short vacation, they said the pain was intolerable. It was a dirty little secret Mike didn't care for but accepted.

Still in pain and suffering signs of his concussion, Mike returned to work. He accepted the accolades and attaboys from his colleagues and caught up with Petra, who was on her way to court, and thanked her for her help.

Petra simply grunted and mumbled something about being pleased that "that ass Brewster's finally gone."

Mike knew that the union president wasn't one for appreciation, but he felt better after thanking her. After a morning of catching up on messages and paperwork, he treated himself to lunch at Fred's Hot Dogs by the university campus. On his way back to the office, he stopped by a small auto body shop on South Cuesta Street. A large and elaborately hand-painted sign hung over the entrance—"Caspar's Auto Body, Home of the Wrinkle-Free Dent Repair."

Casper was the gang moniker of Diego Salgado, a real OG (original gangster). At fifty years of age, Diego was an institution on the streets of Serra County. A charter member of the Southside Thirteen criminal street gang, Diego had done three stints in prison for a variety of crimes, one attempted murder reduced to aggravated assault, and a slew of narcotics offenses. His most recent sentence came about when Mike discovered a methamphetamine lab hidden under Diego's mobile home. One of the rare success stories in a relatively dismal correctional system, Diego had learned the art of auto body repair in prison. He also had his knee shattered by a correctional officer's baton after the officer mistook Diego for another inmate and made the unfortunate statement in the subsequent investigation, "Hell, they all look alike to me." As a result, the State Department of Corrections simply opened their checkbooks and gave Diego a sizeable settlement.

With this gift from the state, Diego purchased an old body shop and renamed it Casper's in honor of his previous lifestyle. Mike had always liked the gang member and appreciated how Diego would handle his numerous arrests. As Mike would apply his handcuffs, Diego always complied and, with some pride, would say in his gravelly voice, "No hard feelins,' my homie. I'm a professional, ya know?"

When Mike found out about Diego's financial windfall, he visited him at his new place of business and got a commitment that Diego would consider employing some of Mike's probationers. He got out of his Jeep and walked into the shop's cluttered office.

"Casper around?" he asked the young girl behind the counter.

"Out back," she said with a nod.

Mike made his way to the rear of the shop.

"Give me a hand here, homes," Diego commanded as he held out an engine part.

Mike took off his tattered Cal letterman jacket and stuck his head under the hood of the 1955 Chevy Impala Diego was repairing.

"What's new in the zoo, Casper?" Mike asked jovially.

"Casper's my gang name, homie. You know I'm rehabilitated," Diego scolded.

"Then why the name on the sign?" Mike asked.

As though this was the single stupidest question he had ever heard, Diego simply replied, "Because it's good for business, homes. That's my brand."

Mike and Diego chatted as they worked on the engine.

"Got any work for my fellas, Diego?" Mike asked casually.

"Might at the end of the month," Diego replied. "Just don't send me no dope fiends or punks. Got no use for that kind, ya hear, homes?"

"You betcha, Diego."

CHAPTER 7

Twenty-two years later

As he walked out of the door connecting the stairs to his apartment and sidewalk below, Mike heard a familiar voice.

"Hey, young man!"

Oh no. Oh dear Lord, no. What's he wearing? Standing on the curb straddling a used twenty-one speed bicycle was Iggy. Dressed in a rainbow of colorful spandex, a pair of high-tech racing sunglasses over his eyes, and a bike helmet jauntily perched on his head, Iggy could have fit in with the thousands of young cyclists who flocked to Serra County for its climate, open roads, and cycling culture.

"Mike, it's me, Iggy!"

Mike stood, mouth agape, trying to take in the scene. "Iggy, what are you doing?" he asked slowly, as if talking a jumper down from the Golden Gate Bridge.

"Mike, it's fantastic! My doctor told me the knees are shot, so I got to ease up on the step work for a while. Not givin' 'em up completely, but he suggested I try cycling, and I am absolutely hooked!"

My God. Has he been drinking? Can the police pop ya for ridin' drunk?

"What do you think?" asked Iggy as he struck a pose and pointed to his outfit.

"Snazzy," Mike said, still in shock.

"Mike, this has opened up a whole new world for me. You know the seventies are the new sixties!"

"Then how come I'm damn near fifty and feel eighty?" Mike asked with a laugh.

"You know, Mike, those stadium steps are just no good for the legs. Think about cycling. We could do it together!"

"I never learned to ride a bike. I was a deprived child, remember?"

"Bullshit!" hollered Iggy as he mounted his bike. "Taught you myself out on the playground at St. Mary's."

"I just remember falling down and crying a lot," said Mike. "Quite traumatizing, actually."

Iggy smiled at the memory. "You were a clumsy kid. That's why I got you into boxing."

Mike clearly recalled his riding lessons on the playground. In fact, one of his most treasured possessions hanging on the wall of his apartment was an old black-and-white photo of himself on a small bike riding across the playground completely out of control, Iggy running beside him, yelling commands of encouragement, trying to seek the age-old balance between allowing a child to grow while not letting them maim themselves.

"If my knees and hips get much worse, I just may take you up on that. But don't count on me wearin' an outfit like that," Mike said, pointing to Iggy's riding togs. Iggy mounted his bike and turned toward Cuesta Street. "By the by, just remember who taught me about the joys of a stadium step workout."

Over his shoulder, he called out, "Gotta go! I'm meeting some members of the senior cycling club down at Spilled Beans!"

It had been three months since Iggy officially retired as the priest at St. Mary's Church in Oakland. As a nod to his years of leadership and service, his only request to the bishop was granted. He was allowed to ease into semiretirement at the Our Lady Church in Serra, walking distance to Mike's apartment. Despite Mike's irreverence, he enjoyed having the closest person he had to family close by.

Mike slid behind the wheel of his old Jeep and drove five minutes to his office. He turned into his traditional parking spot at the end of the lot, got out of the Jeep, and sauntered up the same brick steps to the probation department he had taken for the past twenty-five years. Across the front door was a banner proclaiming, "Welcome, Chief Jackson!"

What a bunch of suck-ups. She's not even here yet and those fools already have their lips affixed to her ass.

Half the fun of getting a new chief, Mike thought, was to watch the sycophants jockey for the new boss's attention. Mike entered the front door and punched the code on the electronic lock of a secondary secure door. He opened the heavy metal door lined with Kevlar.

As he walked through the entrance, Mike glanced into a small waiting room, already filling up with probationers and their families. As with most probation officers, he kept a mental checklist of his most memorable probationers compiled after a long and colorful career. The list was split evenly between most and least favorite, but there was a third list. This list was thankfully shorter than the others and made up of those probationers Mike truly despised. At the top of *this* list was an individual into whose sadistic eyes he was now staring. *Troop. What a way to start my Monday.*

Mike poured a cup of green tea, greeted a few colleagues, and walked down the long hallway to his small office.

"O'Shea to the front desk. Mike O'Shea to the front desk please," announced the voice of the receptionist from the PA system.

Mike walked down the hallway to the waiting room. He opened the security door and said wearily, "Come on back, Mr. Troop."

Richard Troop was forty years old and a small-time celebrity among the tight and oddly loyal members of Serra's bodybuilding and powerlifting community. At six foot three, he weighed in at an impressive 275 pounds of muscle, upon muscle, upon more muscle. Troop held several bodybuilding titles, including the former Mr. Central Coast, and was the recipient of a few local powerlifting records. But what defined Troop wasn't his physique, as much as how he acquired his stature. Richard Troop could just as easily add the title "Roid King" to his list of accomplishments, as for the past fifteen years, he had immersed himself in the shadowy world of illegal steroid use and sales.

As a fifteen-year-old freshman at Serra High School, Troop had tried out for the football team and impressed the coaches with a magnificent combination of speed, agility, coordination, and strength. Unfortunately, he also possessed an anti-social personality completely devoid of any ability to experience guilt, compassion, or empathy for his fellow human beings. As a strapping freshman, Troop walked onto the campus of his new high school in late August and quickly made a name for himself as a total and multidimensional asshole.

An aged school custodian, who, along with his infirmed wife were skimping by on one income, politely asked Richard to stop casually tossing trash anywhere but in a trash can. Troop responded by pouring sugar in the gas tank of the custodian's relic Ford pickup. Troop and his pals snickered and heckled when they saw the old man sitting at the bus stop alongside the students because he couldn't afford to repair the truck when the engine seized up permanently from the sugar treatment.

At sixteen, Troop and several of his compatriots led a fifteen-year-old girl behind the school gymnasium during the Christmas formal. The group forced the girl to drink grain alcohol until she threw up all over her new dress and passed out. The boys then proceeded to gang-rape her. Although the terrified young lady first impressed police detectives with her certain identification of the boys and stalwart dedication to testify, she later recanted when her family's dog, cat, and her Future Farmers of America project lamb all turned up with their throats slashed.

Richard's reign of terror on the school's campus abruptly came to an end during an expulsion hearing with a vice principal. When it became clear to him that he wasn't going to avoid a final and permanent expulsion, Richard snapped, not because he would miss school, which he wouldn't, but simply because he hated the vice principal. At the end of the hearing, Richard calmly stood and threw a single powerful punch directly into the chin of the 110-pound school administrator, simultaneously shattering most of the bones in the lower part of her jaw. He was later found by the Serra Police hiding in Shell Creek in downtown Serra. While the three responding police officers struggled to put the man-child in handcuffs, Troop bit one of the officer's down to the bones of his hand. Because of his handiwork, he was ultimately sentenced to the California Youth Authority facility in the town of Paso Adobe, in Northern Serra County.

While at the Youth Authority, Richard showed little to no interest in any form of rehabilitative program and quickly aligned himself with a small but extremely violent group of White supremacists. Alongside his "brothers," Richard spent countless hours in the weight lifting pens adjacent to his living cottage. Eight years later, after the vice principal had long since taken a medical retirement because of chronic pain and posttraumatic stress disorder from the attack, Richard emerged from his time as a guest of the state, a hulking twenty-five-year-old sociopath on the precipice of becoming a certified psychopath.

With no investment in any form of mainstream employment or normal life for that matter, Richard turned to low-level crime just to make his monthly living expenses. After all, people who earned honest livings were "suckers," Troop often told his workout partners. However, he soon came to realize that this was no way of life for such an obvious intellect. Troop knew he was destined for much bigger things, none of them legal. He made the acquaintance of a local exotic dancer by the name of Mary Kay Kirkpatrick, otherwise known by the stage name Sapphire.

Mary Kay had three children—ages two, three, and six—by three men who were all inmates in the Central California Center for Rehabilitation, a state prison on the outskirts of town.

Mary Kay's children despised Troop and, somewhere in their innocent little minds, sensed his evil. The oldest was a precocious little girl named Chyna. When Mike first read Troop's file and glanced at his list of family members, he couldn't resist asking himself, *How 'bout sticking with a something a little more benign like Heidi? You'd think a stripper would shy away from giving her daughter an obvious stripper name. Where do these winners come from?*

Chyna's favorite stunt and possibly most endearing—certainly the one Mike enjoyed most—was to *borrow* "Mr. Richard's" toothbrush (Troop insisted that the children show him his due respect by using a more formal title) and swirl it around the toilet bowl.

What a pistol! Mike thought as he read Troop's thick file. After several trips to the emergency room for a variety of stomach ailments, doctors were perplexed as to the cause of his discomfort.

"It's almost as though he's drinking out of the toilet," one ER physician commented to another after confirming the presence of *E. coli* bacteria in Troop's intestines.

Troop had his own suspicions and ultimately coerced little Chyna to confess. He rewarded the child's honesty by throwing her across the small living room of the duplex Mary Kay shared with Troop and the kids (an apartment *she* paid for entirely on her own). Mary Kay briefly considered contacting the Serra County Sheriff's Office but opted to take Chyna for her first pedicure in exchange for responding to any inquiries about her limp with a simple, "I fell off my pony."

Richard knew talent when he saw it and quickly became Mary Kay's "manager." Next, in a spark of inspired genius, he made a trip to the local hardware store and purchased the lumber and supplies necessary to build a stage in the garage of the duplex. Folding chairs, theatrical lighting, and an old bar he bought for a song from the local Eagles Lodge at their annual parking lot sale were added for a more professional touch, a quality to which Richard constantly strove. A few ads in local periodicals and voila, a "Private Gentlemen's Club for Discriminating Men Only."

Richard stocked the bar with watered-down spirits purchased at Costco and assumed the role of bouncer when some of the patrons got a little too frisky with Mary Kay. Mary Kay's contribution (actually Jasmine Rose, as she was now called) was to shimmy across the small stage while earning an impressive sum in tips. Mary Kay's three young children were sequestered in her bedroom with a solid dose of "electric Thorazine" in the form of Cocomelon cartoons, to which their eyes remained cemented for the duration of their mother's performances.

To Richard Troop, his new business venture was almost perfect, until the offensive line of a visiting Southern California college football team in town to play Cal Coastal stumbled in looking for some discriminating, but unfortunately for Troop and Mary Kay, ungentlemanly entertainment. Soon upon their arrival, a 335-pound offensive lineman, a dairy science major from the San Joaquin Valley town of Tulare, jumped on the stage, not as much to fondle Mary Kay but to show off his own spectacularly repulsive dance moves for the crowd. With the urging of his teammates, old number 56, the pride of the San Joaquin, a young man responsible for America's future cheese supply, grabbed the dance pole Troop had installed and attempted to spin around like a Peking acrobat.

Unfortunately, Troop's self-professed creativity and entrepreneurial spirit far exceeded his skills as a handyman, and the pole (a heavy-duty curtain rod with impressive wads of duct tape securing it to the stage and garage ceiling) came loose, and the dairyman-football player flew into the small crowd with impressive trajectory. Chaos ensued, several punches were thrown, and Mary Kay ran off the stage and into the house in tears, bemoaning a general lack of appreciation and respect for her "art."

Neighbors called the County Sheriff's Office, and the dispatcher who recognized Troop's address sent additional deputies. A few arrests were made for disorderly conduct. Troop was arrested and charged with a variety of business code violations and a felony assault stemming from a rather stern beating he gave one of the guests with a hammer he had grabbed from a nearby workbench.

As Mike read the sheriff's report within Troop's file, this last detail reduced him to cackling laughter that could be heard throughout the building. *Guess that's the beauty of having a strip club in your garage. You're never at a loss for weapons.*

Because of this incident, Troop served a year in the county jail and was placed on a five-year term of probation, whereupon he was assigned to Mike's caseload.

For the most part, Troop's first year on probation was uneventful. He had found a local psychologist to deem him disabled because of anxiety, and the Social Security and disability checks were just "rolling in," Troop had bragged to Mike during their first meeting. He was back to his two, three-hour weight-lifting sessions per day, and thanks to an annual membership at a local tanning salon, he looked like a bronzed blowfish. Mary Kay (now with hair dyed jet-black and the new stage name Cheyenne) was happily working in a local and licensed strip club, and business was booming.

Things were "A-OK" in Richard's life. Best of all, by Richard's standards, Mike was of low intellect and had not caught on to his *newest* business venture.

One Sunday a month, Troop had Mary Kay dress the children up in the most adorable clothes they could find at the local Walmart. Mary Kay then dressed herself *down* to look like a typical Central California soccer mom. Keeping in the spirit, Troop had his "Mr. Republican" outfit, as he called it—plaid shorts, a pink polo shirt with the collar ridiculously turned up, and brown deck shoes…no socks. With the costumes on and the car packed, Troop and his brood headed south on Highway 101, past the usual tourist attractions of Disneyland and Marine World, across the Mexican border, and into the family fun Mecca of Tijuana, Mexico.

Troop drove to one of the area's less well-known but elaborately stocked pharmacies, where he loaded up on Dianabol and a variety of other steroids, legally obtained in Mexico but a violation of several federal and state laws north of the border. Of course, this respectable-looking family could then sail back across the border with the "juice," as Troop called it, safely tucked into a special corset Mary Kay wore under her sundress. Once safely back in Serra, Troop would replace the Spanish labels on the vials with labels written and printed in German and sell them to the underground community of body builders and other athletes who wanted to get bigger and stronger without the effort.

The switching of the labels was the brainchild of Troop's lifting partner, Cracker, a White supremacist, parolee, and founding member of the local Nazi party. It was Cracker's belief that only the best steroids came from East Germany, as so often pointed out by Jim McKay on the old *Wide World of Sports* show. Later, Cracker became virtually suicidal when he learned that East and West Germany had unified several years prior, leaving him with a useless supply of "Produced in East Germany" labels.

Mike heard from his own contacts that a local bodybuilder was smuggling steroids across the border and into Serra County. He immediately suspected Troop. Mike's suspicion was confirmed when a probationer he had arrested was looking for a break in his jail time and told him somebody was running steroids up from Mexico, and that this certain somebody might be a neckless meathead known to Mike and most of the local law enforcement community. Mike did indeed make a deal with his chatty probationer and arranged for a reduction in jail time for a tip-off as to when the next Troop family trip was scheduled.

A few calls to Federal Immigration and the International Border Station at San Diego, and reality quickly changed for the little travel-weary family. Social workers were alerted and on hand to take custody of the children. Backup officers, their stun guns charged and ready, were summoned to deal with Troop in the event he became agitated, and several female officers were deployed to search Mary Kay.

*****

Nine months later, Mary Kay was teaching dance classes as a resident artist at the Lompoc Federal Prison. The kids were all in the same foster home and thriving, and surprisingly, Richard was a free man, back in Serra to see his probation officer.

"You skated, Richard. Really dodged the bullet," commented Mike, referring to a suspended prison sentence Troop received for the steroid scam.

"You just have to know the right peeps, O'Shea," Troop said with a cockiness that grated on Mike's nerves.

Troop was no doubt referring to a deal he struck with a federal prosecutor to give up some information on a fifteen-year-old and quite cold murder case involving his old cellmate at the California Youth Authority. As he contemplated this, Mike leaned back and observed his large probationer. Troop was dressed in a ridiculous costume including a strategically torn tie-dyed tank top three sizes too small and the same plaid shorts he used to wear on his junkets to Tijuana. He wore heavy work boots (although he did little actual work) untied with the laces dangling for reasons Mike couldn't even begin to contemplate and a baseball hat worn backward with the logo of a vitamin supplement company. Tilted strategically on his forehead was a pair of sun visors with the words *Main Man* emblazoned across the front.

Troop's hair was a bright shade of platinum, cut into the classic mullet, with a crew cut on the top and a long ponytail in the rear. For the collective oddness of his clothing and hairstyle, what was most impressive about Troop's appearance was his physique and a very angry-looking mass of acne across his back, chest, and neck. Mike couldn't help but stare at dozens of small white-tipped pimples, all of which were standing at attention and appeared ready to burst. Mike averted his eyes as he heard the voice of his mother admonish a six-year-old Mikey for staring at the deformities of others.

Mike glanced through his file and noticed that Troop's weight upon release from jail was an impressive 223 pounds. His career as an amateur boxer gave Mike an uncanny ability to guess people's weight with almost complete accuracy, and he gauged his probationer's weight to now be closer to 275 pounds. Considering his weight and muscle gain and the swath of acne on Troop's neck and back (another sign of steroid use), Troop had quite obviously been using steroids again, a fact placing him in violation of his probation terms to refrain from illegal drug use. Unfortunately, urine tests for steroids are expensive, complex, and take a few weeks for the lab to complete, so an immediate arrest based solely on his suspicion was out of the question.

No problem, Mike thought. Like any good law enforcement officer, he could always come up with some reason, no matter how creative or far-fetched, to make an arrest. Once at the county jail, Mike would collect a urine sample, send it off to the lab, and have the results ready for Troop's violation hearing.

Mike continued perusing Troop's file, which was thicker than most with assorted reports, documents, and Mike's handwritten notes. Toward the top of the file, he found a month-old report from Troop's court-appointed counselor.

Bingo. All probationers are ordered into counseling of one form or another, the type and duration dependent on their offense or recommendations made in a psychological evaluation ordered by the court. Troop had been directed to participate in a program of general weekly group counseling. The report from Troop's therapist indicated that his "attendance was sporadic, his progress marginal, and his conduct disruptive." In the notes section at the bottom of the report, the counselor said:

> Mr. Troop uses his size and vocabulary to intimidate and demean other members of the group. He has been warned that his continued harangues of the other members will result in his termination in the group.

It wasn't much, but it would be enough.

"Stand up, Mr. Troop, and put your hands behind your back," said Mike in a surprisingly calm voice.

Troop remained seated and stared at Mike with the most menacing look he could muster. "I'm not going to jail, you fucking retard," he responded casually.

He picked up a paper clip from a small dish on Mike's desk, straightened it, and began exploring the recesses of his left ear. Troop slowly pulled out the clip and admired an impressive looking wad of wax. After smelling the wad with all the gusto of a sommelier sniffing the cork of a '72 Chateau Montelena, Troop held the clip in front of his face and, with the middle finger of his right hand, flicked his little treasure in Mike's general direction.

Mike remained motionless while contemplating his next move. Troop was now repeating his wax removal technique in his right ear.

I got a master's degree from the University of California, and here I am watching a douchebag core out his earwax. Wonder if the county attorneys could get me off the hook if I jammed that clip right into his eardrum.

"Mr. Troop," said Mike in almost a whisper. "Here's the plan. You're going to go to jail the easy way, and I'll ask the judge to go light on you. If not, I'm going to bust you up bad. You'll still go to jail. You'll just go to the hospital first." Mike wasn't quite through with his threat. "By the way, you should probably know not all is well upstairs, and I've been salivating at the chance to give you one first class and *legal* ass whoopin'," said Mike, tapping a finger on his forehead.

After a moment of contemplation, Troop slowly stood up, put his "Main Man" shades over his bloodshot eyes, and said, "You're a joke, O'Shea. I'm outta here."

As Troop turned toward the door, Mike stepped in front of him and said again in a low tone, "Here's how it's gonna go down, Richard. I'm going to maim you and make sure you never touch another dumbbell again. I mean really fuck you up inside and out. When they start asking questions, I'll just point out your size and age and mine. Who they gonna believe, you or me? After all, I'm just a broken-down old man," said Mike, his tone like that of a used car salesman. It was calm with a tinge of good ole boy neighborliness.

Mike was an experienced officer who knew that he couldn't simply attack Troop based on his snide comments. If rudeness and the hurling of insults to one's probation officer was a crime, probation supervision would look very different. Mike needed to make at least a symbolic attempt to take Troop into custody and give him a chance to resist. He gently grabbed Troop's massive right wrist with his left hand. Troop jerked his hand away violently and assumed a fighting stance. The battle was effectively on.

Mike had learned that closed-fist punches without boxing gloves usually break the small bones in the hand, thus he responded with an open-palmed strike which caught Troop squarely on the point of his chin, jerking his head back and knocking him off-balance. With Troop stunned, Mike grabbed Troop's left wrist and, in one smooth movement, lifted and twisted it with such quickness and force that Troop bent over with a childish scream. As Troop fell toward the ground, Mike stepped in and slammed his knee into Troop's nose. The room filled with the sound of cracking bone and cartilage as Troop's face became a mass of crimson.

Unfortunately, the fight was not yet beaten out of Mr. Richard Troop. He got to his feet, balled up his fist, and swung it up into Mike's crotch with surprising accuracy and speed given his ballooned size. Mike took a step back and attempted to recover as Troop got to his feet and lunged toward him with outstretched arms. His hand shot up and cinched around Mike's throat like a noose.

Hearing the commotion, Tommy Sagapalu sprinted toward Mike's office in time to see Mike's olive skin turning a dark purple as Troop cut off his flow of oxygen. Knowing that this was "getting pretty fucked up," as he later recalled, Tommy quickly repositioned himself behind Troop and brought his arms around the giant's neck so that they snuggly clamped down along his carotid arteries. Troop responded by jamming his thumbs into Tommy's eyes. Mike, now free of Troop's grasp, stumbled toward his desk drawer and grabbed his retractable baton. The baton, also known as an impact weapon, was about eight inches long and made of titanium. Mike expertly flicked the baton open to its full thirty-six-inch length.

In a perfectly choreographed downward arc, Mike caught Troop squarely on his temple. Later, when Mike sat down to compose his Use of Force Report, he would state:

> I swung my baton in a downward combat strike with the intent of striking the suspect on the left shoulder. As I did so, the subject quickly jerked to the left causing my baton to strike his left temple.

Head contact with blunt instruments are frowned upon. However, creative writing in law enforcement is an acceptable and indeed noble art. To those who had been around cops and knew Mike, there was no doubt that his only intent was to do exactly what he did—crack Troop in the ole melon. This blow, combined with a lack of blood flow to his brain caused by Tommy's carotid hold, sufficiently dislodged Troop from consciousness and sent him flailing through the office door and into the hallway. In an instant, Mike was on top of his motionless frame and snapped handcuffs over Troop's baseball bat–sized wrist before he had a chance to shake the cobwebs from his head.

Mike rolled over onto his back and tried to catch his breath. *Too old for this. Should be teaching kids how to write prepositional phrases.*

It's funny what people think about during a crisis. For Mike, as he lay on his back staring up at the government-issued florescent lights illuminating the hallway, he amused himself with the image of Iggy taking off on his bike and looking like a neon beer sign. His daydream was interrupted by the face of a woman.

"Good morning. I'm Cheryl Jackson, your new chief." Cheryl Antoinette Jackson reached down to shake Mike's hand.

Mike thought she was just being polite and offering to assist him to his feet. He grabbed her hand and pulled himself up, almost toppling her off her four-inch heels.

"Nice to meet ya, Chief. Mike O'Shea. Welcome to the Serra County Probation Department."

*****

"We better beat the ambulance to the hospital, brah," said Tommy. "No tellin' what that fool will do to the ER."

Mike turned into the Serra Community Hospital parking lot with tires screeching and parked in a spot reserved for "Physicians Only."

Mike watched the ambulance loaded with Richard Troop speed erratically into the parking lot. *Shit, somethin's up.* The ambulance had barely come to a full stop when the paramedic behind the wheel jumped out.

"Hey! We need help here! Guy's outta control!"

Mike was still feeling a little foggy and tried to focus. *I handcuffed him, right? Yes, handcuffed him, facedown, wrist behind. Should be okay then, right?*

Mike caught Tommy's eye and motioned toward the ambulance door as he grabbed the door handle with one hand and listened. *Somethin' bad's goin' on in there. Let's take this slow.*

Suddenly, the ambulance started to rock back and forth as the door was kicked from inside. Mike took a step back.

Okay, there were two paramedics. One's in front of me scared shit-less. Where's the other? Damn. What's Troop done now? Mike withdrew his weapon and kept it at his side. Tommy did the same. He grabbed the door handle and mouthed "On three" to Tommy as he raised three fingers.

On the count of three, Mike quickly snapped the handle down, yanked the door open, stepped back, and aimed his 9 mm Glock into the interior of the ambulance. In the corner, he saw the prone figure of the second paramedic lying on the floor. It was as if someone had taken a baseball bat to the side of the paramedic's head. His already swollen face was turning a light shade of purple, and his gray uniform shirt was covered in blood. As Mike stared at the paramedic, events started to speed up and revert into slow motion simultaneously. Like a missile, Richard Troop's massive frame shot out of the ambulance. Mike took a step back, but it was too late.

For all his girth, Troop remained athletic. His forehead caught Mike squarely on the chin, knocking him to the ground and sending his pistol sliding across the asphalt. Still handcuffed, Troop strad-dled Mike's body and began an impressive series of headbutts to his face. Ordinarily, Mike would have pinned Troop's arm to his side and gained the advantage by rolling him over, but with his hands still handcuffed from behind, Troop had become a human spear, with no natural places to grab. Troop's fourth headbutt rendered Mike unconscious.

"Go to your stomach, dick slap, or I put a nice hole in the back of your head," Tommy Sagapalu hissed as he drilled the muzzle of his forty-caliber Smith and Wesson pistol into Troop's right ear.

Troop was a psychopath, devoid of *any* ability to feel empathy or compassion for others, but to his credit, he had a definite sense of self-preservation and did as commanded. Tommy holstered his weapon and took a glance around the parking lot. Feeling confident that there were no witnesses, he lifted his left boot and slammed it into Troop's ribs.

"That's for my guy," the large Samoan said under his breath.

*****

After regaining consciousness, Mike looked around and realized he had been taken to an examination room. It was early evening, with the vacant exam rooms filling up quickly, mostly local college kids celebrating the end of mid-quarter exams. A nurse quickly took his vitals, asked some questions, all of which were answered with lies, and cleared him for release. In reality, Mike had received a moderate concussion courtesy of Richard Troop's massive forehead and should have been admitted for a brain scan and observation. Over the years, Mike had developed an impressive ability to convince medical professionals that he was in far better shape than he was. As an English major at Cal, he had taken the requisite drama courses and was a surprisingly competent actor.

After giving a statement to the police, Mike walked slowly to the hospital parking lot where Tommy Sagapalu waited in a marked department vehicle. Tommy made the short drive to the probation department where Mike's car was parked.

"You gonna be okay tonight?" asked Tommy. "You don't look so hot."

Mike was ready with a snappy comeback, but as he opened his mouth to deliver it, the words seemed to stay frozen on his lips. *What's going on?*

"Hey, Mike, you okay?"

After several moments, Mike shook loose whatever was keeping him from answering. "Yeah, I'm good. I'm good."

Tommy stared at Mike, not sure what to do or say. He knew that his friend had suffered more head injuries in fifty years than any dozen people in their lifetimes. He looked down at Mike's hands, resting on his lap. In the glow of the parking lot lights, Tommy could see Mike's left ring finger trembling uncontrollably.

"Mike, what's goin' on?"

Mike looked up. "What?" he said innocently.

"Hey! Your hand's shakin' like a milkshake machine. I'm takin' you back to the ER."

Mike grabbed the door handle and heaved his tired body out of the car. "I'm tip-top. Breakfast tomorrow?"

Tommy knew better than to argue with his friend. "Okay, but call, you stupid Mick half-breed, if you need me."

"You know, Tomas, I wish you'd make up your mind as to which derogatory racist term by which you wish to refer to me," said Mike with a grin.

CHAPTER 8

One year later

Mike had an appointment with Chief Cheryl Jackson, his relatively new boss. He knew little to nothing about interior design, but upon being ushered into Cheryl's office by her assistant, even Mike could appreciate the professionalism the room exuded.

Shit, Brewster kept a sleeping bag in the corner so he could sleep off his benders. We're really moving on up around here.

In the corner facing the door was a large walnut desk built before the Civil War and shipped at great expense from the home of Reverend and Mrs. Jackson, Cheryl's parents, of Atlanta to Serra. The traditional "feel-good" wall adorned with plaques and awards flanked the desk. At the center of the wall was a framed cover of *Ebony* magazine, circa 1984. A younger Cheryl Jackson graced the cover with the heading "Meet Today's Modern Black Woman." Another photo was of Cheryl held aloft by her teammates as she cut down a basketball net at the 1983 Women's National Invitational Tournament, where she captained the team from her alma mater, Howard University.

"So good of you to meet with me, Officer O'Shea," Cheryl said in an airy voice Mike found irritating.

"Just to clarify, Chief," said Mike. "I work for you. If meetings with the boss have become voluntary, let me know, and hell, you'll never see me again," said Mike with a grin.

"Right," said Cheryl, now slightly uncomfortable. "Let me get to the point. I need to transfer you."

"Where?" asked Mike.

"Gang Task Force."

"Why me?"

"Great question!" replied Cheryl, grateful for the opportunity to compliment Mike and hopefully ease some of the tension in the room. "Officer O'Shea, I soon found upon my arrival that despite your, how shall I say, unorthodox ways, you are my best officer and universally respected within the local law enforcement community. Your assignment to the GTF has been specifically requested by Sheriff Teagarten and Serra Police Chief Tinker. Honoring that request is in the best interest of public safety and, to be candid, a politically wise move on our part."

"Can I bring Sagapalu?" asked Mike.

"Sorry, no. No packaged deals. They want you and you alone."

"Wait a minute," said Mike with as much indignation as he could muster. "The GTF is made up of a bunch of White guys. Sagapalu would add, you know, a little diversity to the team."

Cheryl tried to stifle a smile. "Officer O'Shea, I have thoroughly reviewed your personal file, and I am of the belief that, while adopted by a fine Irish couple, you are one hundred percent Native American."

"A gross invasion of my privacy," said Mike, knowing that his boss had a very valid point. "Ah, hell, when do I start?"

*****

Mike quickly adapted to the dynamics of the task force. In the minds of many of the police officers and sheriff's deputies he was working alongside, probation officers were still thought of as do-gooders with more interest in coddling criminals than holding them accountable. But Serra was a relatively small community, and Mike was well-known and respected in law enforcement circles, in part because unlike most of the officers on the task force, he had proven himself in combat and could be relied upon to do so again if things got dicey. His English degrees from Cal also made him the team's most literate writer, a skill which came in handy when writing warrants and crime reports.

A month after being reassigned, Mike got a call from the commander of the task force toward the end of the day, telling him to be at a special meeting early the next morning.

"Don't go to the office. You'll get a text message at 0230 telling you where to meet," said the commander.

Mike arrived home a little after five o'clock in the afternoon. He walked up to his apartment, hung his old letterman jacket on a hook behind the door, turned on Sports Center, and thought about dinner. *Shit. Kind of wound up. Maybe a run up to the stadium.*

Mike looked outside. The product of the heat from the San Joaquin Valley and coolness of the Pacific had created a blanket of fog that settled in over Serra and enveloped Granite Peak. Mike liked the fog. It reminded him of the gray cloak that would drape Oakland from the San Francisco Bay. He laced up his running shoes and threw on an old sweatshirt with *Give Blood, Play Rugby* printed on the front. Mike preferred to begin his workout with a sprint and end it with a casual jog. After a short warm-up, he ran full throttle from downtown Serra to the Cal Coastal Stadium in less than ten minutes.

Mike found the gate to the stadium open as usual. *Enjoy it now. Probably won't always be unlocked.* He made his way onto the field for a lazy jog around the perimeter. *Shit, I feel old.* Up the two hundred steps of one aisle to the top of the stadium, twenty push-ups, and back down to the field. Twenty sit-ups, a quick lap around the field, and another back up the next aisle. Mike would continue this routine until he had run up all thirty-nine aisles of the stadium. A brief rest, some stretching, and then a leisurely jog home. Mike's stadium step routine began as a high school kid in Oakland when he would get up early and drive to the Edwards Stadium on the University of California campus before school. Back then, running the "steps"—as Iggy had phrased it—was a part of his boxing training. Although no longer an amateur boxer, Mike was a creature of habit, so the stadium workout remained as much a part of his life as an adult as it had as a youngster.

"Hey. I thought I was the only one crazy enough to use this stadium as a personal gym."

Mike was laying on his back at the fifty-yard line of the field, eyes closed, thoughts focused on the next day's operation. He slowly opened his eyes and saw a tall figure blocking out the glare of a setting sun reflecting off the fog.

"Hey, you okay?" asked the figure. *What kind of weird accent is that?* Mike thought. *Spanish?*

Mike opened his eyes as he propped himself up on his elbows. He blinked until the figure came into focus. Mike's periodic blurred vision had not improved. *Tall woman. Interesting accent. Silver streak down the middle of wild dark hair.*

The woman was indeed tall, slightly over six feet. She was dressed in running shorts and a gray T-shirt with the words *Cal Coastal Volleyball* across her chest. *My God, what is Pam Grier doing here?* Mike had never outgrown his adolescent crush on the actress who made a name for herself in Blackspoitation films during the 1970s.

"Great minds think alike" was all Mike could muster.

The woman, her golden-brown skin glistening in sweat, lowered herself to the ground in a push-up position, knocked out a dozen push-ups, and turned over on her back. Mike got the distinct impression she wasn't just trying to show off.

"I'm Sylvia Almeida," she said, reaching out a hand.

"Mike. Mike O'Shea," Mike said as he reached out with a firm handshake.

"What a glorious time of day, no?" asked Sylvia.

"This and daybreak. Can't decide which I like more," said Mike.

"Daybreak? I'm from Brazil, and daybreak is just when we're getting to bed," Sylvia Almeida said with a giggle Mike found at once endearing and unsettling.

Sylvia was now going through a series of elaborate stretches, all of which accentuated an athletic physique that camouflaged her age.

Uh-oh, I'm in big trouble. My age but the body of a very fit college kid.

"I've not seen you here, Mike," said Sylvia.

"Must be my impressive speed," he said with a grin. *Too old to be a student. Maybe a faculty member?*

"Well, Mike, I must be off. Early recruiting trip tomorrow," said Sylvia as she stood.

"What are you recruiting for?" asked Mike, self-conscious that he was unable to get to his feet quite as smoothly as his new acquaintance.

"Women's volleyball," said Sylvia with a thumbs up sign. "I'm the head coach here at the university, and I hope to see you again."

*****

Mike has set his alarm for 2:15 a.m. so he'd be awake when the text message from the task force commander came. Like clockwork, he received the message at exactly 2:30 a.m., which simply read, "Odd Fellows Hall, Paso, 0430, park back, rear entrance," which meant the meeting would be held a few hours later in an ancient fraternal hall on the west side of the town of Paso Adobe, north of Serra. To maintain security and secrecy, the officers were told to park in the back and enter through a rear door away from the street. Mike reset his alarm and fell back asleep for an hour.

He arrived early and sat at a table in the rear of the cavernous Oddfellows Hall, along with a variety of cops, firefighters, prosecutors, and for some reason, a few park rangers. Several paramedics stood in a rear corner, not a particularly positive sign, Mike thought. Two large pots of coffee and pink boxes of pastries sat atop a table. A man about Mike's age dressed in a dark suit strolled to the front of the room. *Four thirty a.m., and this guy's spit and polished. Fed or state, I bet.*

"I'm Dana Hansen with State BNE," the man said with a slight Southern drawl.

Mike recognized the acronym. The Bureau of Narcotic Enforcement ran drug interdiction operations throughout California.

"Sorry about all the secret squirrel stuff, but we needed to maintain tight security."

Hansen nodded to a state agent sitting at a table with a laptop opened. On a large screen at the front of the room, a PowerPoint slide appeared with an aerial photo of what looked like a single wide mobile home.

"For the past year, we've had an agent deep inside an OMG [outlaw motorcycle gang] from Northern California called the Savages," said the state agent. "We believe they've set up a remote meth cook in a trailer about ten miles east of here."

"We're going to send in an entry team made up of the local GTF, and if they find anything, the hazmat guys will be staged a mile or so away," said Hansen. "Once we're secure, we'll send the detectives in."

The production of methamphetamine was not only illegal but was also highly toxic. Once the meth was cooked, a nasty byproduct of several deadly chemicals was left and would need to be cleaned up. More aerial photos appeared on the screen.

"This is the trailer. Basic single wide, windows on the one, two, and three sides. [Each side was numbered counterclockwise for easy identification.] A front door here and back door here," Hansen said, outlining the structure with a laser pointer. "Your task force commander will assign you to your positions on the entry team. Any questions?"

Mike looked around the room and saw a hand shoot up from the back.

"Yeah. How do you know for sure there's a cook in there?" asked a sheriff's deputy.

"We've had the place under surveillance for a couple of months now," answered Hansen. He looked toward the agent working the PowerPoint and said, "Slide seven, I think."

Another aerial shot of the trailer appeared, this time from a different angle.

"See how the trailer is surrounded by green foliage?" asked Hansen. "Look at the rear exit. Notice anything?"

Mike began to nod slowly and knew immediately what he was looking at. Among the lush green around the trailer was a definite dark swath of dead brown underbrush leading from the back door down to a nearby creek. The meth chefs had simply opened the back door and poured the chemicals out onto the ground and into the creek, killing anything living in its path.

"We believe the main cook is this subject," said Hansen. "Gregory Allen Rodzinski."

The face of a heavily bearded blond man flashed on the screen.

"He's done time for murder, tried to run over a police officer in San Bernadino with his motorcycle, and has vowed to not be taken in alive."

"Swell," Mike muttered under his breath.

After Hansen's briefing, Mike looked up and saw Tommy Sagapalu standing by the rear entrance.

"What's up, fool?" asked Tommy.

"What are you doin' here?" asked Mike.

"One of your entry guys got sick, so they called me in to pinch-hit," said Tommy. Mike had the upmost respect for the members of his team, but the sight of his large and trusted friend gave him a sense of comfort.

Mike followed Tommy and the six other members of the Gang Task Force into the dark parking lot behind the hall. Car trunks opened, and the gang officers slowly and methodically put on their tactical vests and equipment belts. Mike pulled the Glock from his bag, pulled the slide back to ensure that it was unloaded, and released the slide. He slammed in a magazine with thirteen rounds of hollow-point bullets and pulled back and released the slide once more, loading a round into the chamber. He had three more magazines on his belt and his Smith and Wesson backup revolver strapped to his left ankle. Across his chest, Mike slung a Remington Express 870 tactical shotgun, which he preferred to the Heckler and Koch MP-5 most of his teammates carried.

Across his shoulder was a standard building entry tool called the hooligan. A cross between a pick on one end and an axe on the other, the hooligan would be used in forcing barricaded doors and windows opened. Mike found the tool cumbersome, but his strength and speed made him the obvious member of the team to carry it. The tool was also useful with mobile homes, which, based on their manufacture date, had exterior doors that opened *outward*, making forced entry difficult. Topping it off, Mike carried a small water pack on his back with a rubber tube attached to the top of the mesh carrier which held his body armor and three energy bars in the pouch on the front. In the event the operation lasted into the afternoon, each team member would need a small supply of water and food.

A dark green seven-passenger van with no license plates or government insignias drove up, and the team piled in for the ten-mile drive to a second staging point. This location overlooked a shallow valley with the mobile home directly in the center. Mike and his team members climbed out of the van and rechecked their equipment. A few last-minute instructions from the team leader and a check to ensure their radios were operating, and the group split into two smaller teams for the mile hike to the trailer.

Mike looked up in the northern sky and let out a small sigh of relief for the half-moon. It was bright enough to make flashlights unnecessary, but not so bright as to disclose their location to anyone in or around the trailer who may be awake.

After the ten-minute hike, Mike and his teammates approached the trailer. He marveled at how different the small structure looked from the aerial photos in the PowerPoint briefing and wondered if they were indeed in the same place. The photos made the property appear much larger than it was. The designated team leader held the group up about two hundred yards from the trailer. Mike repositioned his glasses. His latest pair looked more like protective goggles a welder might wear.

"Okay, check your lights, weapons, and let's have one more radio check," the team leader whispered. With this formality out of the way, the team leader said, "Let's go, boys. Get this fucker and go get some breakfast."

As they quickly approached the front of the trailer, Mike held his hand up to the aluminum siding in hopes that he might feel the vibration of activity coming from inside. He looked closely at the front door and, with some relief, saw that it swung inward.

"Police with a warrant, open the door *now!*" the team leader screamed.

No response. The team leader nodded to Mike to unleash the hooligan. Mike reared back in a baseball batting stance and let loose the sharp tool, power bursting from the swift rotation of his hips. The flimsy door gave way, and Mike stepped back, threw the hooligan aside, and grabbed his shotgun. Tommy activated an M84 stun grenade and tossed it through the door. The grenade detonated, creating a deafening roar which always left Mike amazed that such a loud noise could create so little damage. More noise. This time, glass breaking and the figure of a large male jumping out of the window to the right of the front door. As the man hit the dirt, he scrambled to his feet with surprising dexterity, spun around, and sprinted away from the trailer. Mike pivoted, tossed the shotgun to Tommy, who simply stared at him as though he were insane, and took off in pursuit.

No need to get into a wrestling match with this mutt over the shotgun. Pistol will be fine, he thought quickly.

Gregory Rodzinski, the meth-cooking biker who Mike had recognized from the briefing, had no intention of going back to prison for the third and probably final time. He sprinted down a trail, ducked behind some sagebrush, and picked up a large rock. As Mike ran by, the biker brought the rock down directly on the back of his head. He staggered to the ground and briefly lost consciousness, only to come to with the realization that the biker was now straddling him and trying to force the pistol out of his retention holster designed for just such occasions. The retention holster used by most law enforcement officers required a snap and rocking motion which, with practice, releases the weapon. The holster was holding, but Mike could feel something starting to give way on his duty belt.

Mike stunned the biker with a quick blow to the point of his jaw. He tried to angle his body onto his side, which brought him face-to-face with the side of the biker's head. Mike stared directly at his opponent's ear and recalled a pleasant evening spent in his living room with friends, drinking beer and eating pizza, watching in disbelief as former heavyweight champion Mike Tyson bit off a part of rival Evander Holyfield's ear. Instinctively, Mike opened his mouth and clamped down on the ear of the biker, who screamed in disbelief and ever so lightly started to release his grip on the butt of Mike's gun.

Sensing he only had a few seconds before he lost the fight, Mike grabbed the gun, unsnapped, rocked once, twice, and on the third time twisted it as far from the holster as the tight grip of the biker would allow. Mike attempted to aim the gun away from his legs, and in what seemed like an hour but was more like five seconds, he pulled the trigger, repeatedly emptying the rounds into the ground.

Can't let this asshole have any more of my firepower than necessary. Once he was convinced the gun was empty, Mike kicked out to his side and landed his boot in the center of the biker's chest, sending him reeling backward. This gave Mike just enough space and time to draw the five-shot backup revolver from his left ankle holster. He unsnapped the holster, drew the gun, and aimed directly at the biker's chest.

He fired twice, the revolver making a deafening roar. Both rounds strayed to the left of the biker, who was now backing up. Mike blinked his eyes, shook his head from side to side, and fired once more, hitting the biker in the left shoulder.

The biker fell to his knees, left hand limp to his side. "I ain't goin' back...just kill me now...go on!"

Mike got to his feet and slowly walked toward the biker. His revolver pointed at his now prisoner's head. Mike slowly pressed the muzzle of the gun lightly against the biker's forehead and took a deep breath. The biker closed his eyes and mumbled something.

I can pop this motherfucker right now and save the taxpayers a boatload of dough. I'll sail through the IA. After all, his prints will be all over my holster. I'll just say I believed my life was in danger. Easy-peasy. Mike shook this thought loose and lowered his gun. Like a jackhammer, he brought his left fist down, shattering the biker's cheek bone and sending him to the ground.

Mike looked around, took inventory of his condition, and realized several things. First, he and the biker were alive. Mike had won the fight and felt an odd wave of euphoria wash over him. Second, during the chase through the brush, he had lost his radio and had no way to communicate his position to his team members. Third, his thick glasses had broken into small pieces, leaving him blind in one eye. Finally, chasing the biker on his own with no backup was a rookie move he would hear about later.

Mike sat and waited for what he thought would be a relatively short time. Surely sixteen gunshots would create some commotion back at the trailer. A few moments turned into close to thirty-five minutes.

I'm gonna have to carry this prick out of here. The biker was still unconscious from Mike's punch, but the bleeding from his shoulder wound had slowed when Mike wrapped a thick gauze dressing around his shoulder. Small medical kits designed to treat gunshot wounds were standard issues for most tactical teams.

The officers on the warrant detail heard the shots but weren't about to go rushing toward the brush into a possible ambush. In the meantime, Mike's body took over as he slowly slipped into shock. When his teammates found him, he was shivering violently as he lay near the still unconscious biker.

CHAPTER 9

Mike stared at the bright light hanging from the ceiling of the small examination room in Serra Memorial Hospital. A med-evac helicopter had transported him and the biker from the back country of Northern Serra County to the hospital. Tommy attempted to jump into the chopper, not wanting to leave his friend, but he was denied entry when the copilot said he was simply too large to make the flight safe. Mike was leery of being transported with a man he had just shot and made sure the biker was secured with handcuffs and a pair of leg restraints.

"Officer O'Shea? I'm Dr. Vonner. I'm a neurologist. I ordered some tests and can see that you've suffered some previous head trauma. Can you tell me about that?"

"Yeah," Mike said slowly, rubbing his hands across tired eyes and wondering just where the conversation might go. "I boxed up until I was eighteen, played rugby in college. This is the second time I've been clocked since I've been with the department."

"I'm going to refer you for a series of additional tests," said Dr. Vonner.

"What for?" asked Mike suspiciously.

"Just a precaution. You've experienced an inordinate number of skull injuries, and I want to make sure all's well up there," said the doctor, pointing to her own forehead.

If all is well up here, I'd have chosen another profession twenty-five years ago.

"We've done quite a bit of research in this area. Each traumatic brain injury builds upon past trauma, and with your history, I want to rule out permanent damage," said the doctor, her demeanor softening a bit. "You've probably heard about head trauma with professional football players and with our guys coming back from the Middle East. Have you had any symptoms? Headaches, tremors in your hands, or blurred vision maybe?" asked Dr. Vonner. "Also, mental health issues…suicide, moodiness, anger?"

"Nope. Haven't had anything like that," said Mike, looking perplexed. *Liar, liar, pants on fire.*

After being held over for observation, he changed into a fresh set of clothes, courtesy of his fellow members of the task force, and slowly walked into the hospital waiting room. A large group of well-wishers from law enforcement agencies stood to greet him. After the obligatory "Good job" from his colleagues, Mike accepted Tommy Sagapalu's offer of a ride home.

Thinking back on the shooting, Mike felt confident that he would be cleared of any wrongdoing. The biker's DNA was all over his pistol, and his retention holster was now in several pieces from the struggle. Mike also had yet another concussion. *Let's see what Dwayne Dickhard has to say about this one.*

At the urging of the commander of the warrant team, Mike made a call to his union attorney, who was unfortunately out of town representing a police officer from the town of Oildale, 120 miles southeast of Serra. The attorney had advised him to refrain from making any statements and promised to meet with him the next day. He assured Mike that based upon what he knew, it was a "righteous shoot" and that he should be fully exonerated. His attorney on his last shoot, Jerome Rosenblatt, had long since passed away, and Mike cringed at the thought of new and unfamiliar counsel. He also knew that as a union member, he would get whatever attorney the union had on retainer. Getting an attorney with Rosenblatt's experience and skills had been pure luck. On a probation officer's salary, the thought of hiring an attorney of his choice was laughable.

For the next eight weeks, Mike again found himself "on the beach," as they say in law enforcement. It was a paid vacation that really didn't feel like a vacation.

Never in a million years did I think I'd pick up another deal. The fact that the incident took place in a remote location drew out the investigation longer than it would have been if it had taken place in town. To fill his days, Mike ran the steps of the Cal Coastal stadium, read, took naps, became shockingly intrigued with daytime TV, spent time with Iggy, and tried to figure out how to avoid an increasing number of calls from Dr. Vonner's office asking why he failed to appear for the series of tests she had ordered. *I know how this works. They find out my brain is scrambled, tell the county, and bam, I'm in a nursing home askin' Iggy to sneak me in pizza and beer. Not for me.*

CHAPTER 10

"You know, Michael, most cops go through their careers not ever discharging their firearms, let alone being involved in two separate incidents, with two fatalities," said Iggy as they enjoyed their omelets at a sidewalk table in front of Lucy's Cafe in downtown Serra.

"Well, we all gotta be good at something," said Mike. Iggy looked at his godson with the same disappointed expression he used in response to Mike's sarcasm for the past five decades.

"Have you talked to anyone?" He wasn't sure what concerned him more, the fact that this was the second time Mike had fired his weapon in self-defense or that he seemed completely unaffected and devoid of emotional affect.

"You know damn well I had to talk to someone about the last deal, and as always, I found the county-hired psychologist to be nutsier than I am on my worse day. I'm okay," Mike said with a hint of irritation creeping into his voice. He knew that Iggy had been around police work long enough to know exactly what steps were taken after an officer discharged his firearm in a combat situation, a referral to a psychologist for a debriefing among them.

"Yes, I spent three hours with Dr. Seymour yesterday morning, and quite frankly, Father De la Rosa, I have serious concerns about *his* grasp on reality," said Mike in mock earnest. Mike leaned toward Iggy. "In fact, guess what Doc Seymour told me?"

Iggy put his fork down and hastened the chewing of a mouthful of home fried potatoes. "Tell me. Tell me," he said, anticipating that finally, someone had cracked his Godson's emotional veneer.

"Well," said Mike, checking as if someone may have been recording the conversation. "He said he's a Catholic and was an altar boy."

Iggy gave Mike a nod of encouragement. "Go on," he coaxed, waving his fork.

"He said that the priest at the parish where he grew up used to make him wear a little sailor suit under the altar boy's robe he wore for mass." Relying on every ounce of theatrical talent he had, Mike continued, "Didn't want him to feel bad, so I told him that *you* used to make me put on a little Boy Scout uniform before mass. I think we made a real breakthrough in his recovery."

Mike and Iggy engaged in a stare-off, Iggy waiting for Mike to say something reasonable like "just kidding," and Mike waiting for Iggy to challenge the validity of his tale.

After a few moments, Mike could no longer contain himself and started to stifle a laugh. "You're a real piece of work, you know that?" said Iggy in disgust. "Cut the crap, Michael. You've stuffed more into a twenty-five-year career than most, and it *has* had an effect on you," said Iggy. "Hey, did you get the results of the brain evaluation?"

"Yep. All is well upstairs," said Mike, feeling a definite pang of guilt at lying to a priest.

Iggy wondered if Mike was being honest but also knew that at his age, he was no longer one of his young Catholic Youth Organization fighters. Knowing he wouldn't allow the conversation to go any further, Iggy changed the subject.

"Still tackling the steps every morning?" he asked, referring to Mike's stadium step regime.

Mike's face brightened. "As a matter of fact, I ran 'em the night before the deal. Given your prurient fascination with my love life, you might be interested in knowing that while I was at the stadium, I met a very nice lady," said Mike.

Iggy was in heaven. Throughout their relationship, Mike had always withdrawn and remained mum regarding his romantic interests. Iggy knew that he had a wide array of female companions but never felt comfortable discussing them in any detail. Perhaps, Iggy assumed, Mike was simply ashamed that he enjoyed such a robust bachelor's life. Thus, Iggy was determined to savor the lowering of Mike's defense screen by mentioning that he had met someone special.

"Tell me about her," Iggy said as casually as he could.

Mike detailed his encounter with the tall woman with the wild hair and a streak of silver during his early evening workout. "She was really something," Mike said with a mouthful of hash browns.

"Did you get her name?" Iggy asked.

Mike winced. "That's the darndest thing. I can't remember. Having a tough time remembering a lot of things lately." He stared off across the café. "I think she's a coach up at the university though."

The two finished their meals, and Mike paid the bill.

"I got breakfast. You're an old priest on a fixed income, for God's sake. It's bad enough you can't have sex, but they could at least up your salary," said Mike.

Iggy let the comments slide and offered a simple "Thanks, Mike, but next time, we flip for it. No arguments."

After a meandering stroll down Cuesta Street, Mike walked Iggy back to the rectory at the Our Lady Church and then returned to his apartment. *What the hell was her name?*

*****

As was his custom on most weekend afternoons, Mike grabbed a cold Pabst and the morning edition of the *Serra Tribune* and enjoyed the sunshine on the steps leading up to his apartment. Dressed in gym shorts, a T-shirt, and beach sandals, he fit right in with the students emerging from their lairs after a night of overindulgence. Much to his dismay, though not surprisingly, the front-page story was of a local probation officer who had shot a suspected drug manufacturer a few days earlier.

"Second Shooting for Local Probation Officer" read the headline. Mike's thoughts vacillated between reading the article and trying to remember the name of the woman at the stadium.

"Hey, O'Shea, how are you, my love?"

Mike looked up to see the familiar figure of his most recent romantic interest, Greta Beckett. Clad in her traditional peasant blouse, no bra, and a flowing tie-dye skirt, Greta had abandoned her vintage Karman Ghia for an equally ancient bicycle. As she dismounted, Mike marveled at how fit and youthful the forty-five-year-old art teacher looked. Even though she was, by his own estimation, rather unhinged emotionally, Mike enjoyed her company.

"Hiya, Greta," Mike said with a tip of his can of Pabst.

"I read about your shooting, and I've been really worried about you. Are you okay?" she asked.

Mike put down his paper and took a sip of beer. "Tip-top, never been better."

"Bullshit," said Greta. "I've never known a more anally retentive man in my life."

Mike just smiled, knowing that at times like this, his passivity annoyed Greta to no end.

"You're drinking. You know, I'm a recovering alcoholic," said Greta with a sanctimonious tone Mike could never understand. *Why take pride in being a bad drunk?*

Mike took another sip and said calmly, "Maybe *you* are, but I'm not."

Greta simply stared with an expression that somehow attained a balance between amusement and contempt. As she stood in front of Mike, the sun shined through her skirt, giving him the impression that, remaining true to form, she had failed to wear panties.

Greta gently took Mike by the hand and whispered in his ear, "Take me to bed and let me ride you."

For all her craziness, Greta never failed to demonstrate an amazing array of talents and techniques when she and Mike made love, if indeed you could call it that. In fact, after a session with Greta Beckett, Mike always felt a little melancholy. *Why do I like sex with crazy women?*

This day was no different. Mike's bedroom window was open, allowing the warm breeze in, and Greta's unholy screams poured out onto the sidewalk below, commanding him to complete several sex acts, some of which were simultaneously anatomically improbable *and* simply confusing to Mike.

I gotta get her to tone it down, or the Wongs are gonna evict me. While still focusing on the task at hand, he positioned himself just so, which allowed him to curl a toe around the sliding window and slam it shut.

As she lay beside him, stroking his chest, Greta announced, "We need to get married, or I don't want to see you anymore. By the way, I think you need to become more in touch with your indigenous persona. You've become too White."

Mike winced as though in pain. "Get married and give up all this?" he asked, waving his hand toward a pile of dirty laundry in the corner of the room that mysteriously never seemed to decrease or increase in size. "And as for the Indian deal, aren't I a little old to start wearing a feather in my hair and carrying a tomahawk?"

"That's a racist comment, and don't mess with me, O'Shea," said Greta. "I have an education, good job, and my own money. I still have my looks, and I like to fuck. Don't think there aren't *plenty* of men in this town who would jump at the chance to be with me." She was sure to accentuate both syllables of *plenty* so it came out PLENTY-TY.

"I don't know, Greta. Most guys would find your lack of self-esteem to be a real record scratch," Mike said with a giggle.

Greta let out a sigh of disappointment, quickly gathered up her clothes, and was out the door. Mike stood at the window and watched her pedal down the street, never looking back. After a hot shower, he opened another can of Pabst, flopped down on his couch, turned on a ballgame, and shut his eyes.

What the hell was the name of the woman at the stadium?

CHAPTER 11

Predictably, Mike sailed through the district attorney's shooting investigation and received news that he had been cleared of any possible wrongdoing and could return to full duty.

As he showered and shaved for his first day back at work, Mike looked at his reflection in the mirror.

What's wrong with you? You act as though these things are no big deal.

Still dripping from his shower, Mike went to his closet to select his attire for the day: tactical boots, his usual Levi's 501 jeans (selected from a stack of a half dozen or so of the exact same pants), and, as a nod to a marine layer that had blanketed Serra, a thermal pullover. He threw on his old Cal letterman jacket, grabbed his equipment bag, and trotted out to his Jeep parked in front of Wong's.

"Hey, Mike!" yelled Wong from inside the restaurant. "How are you?"

"Can't complain, Wong," said Mike. "How's the fam-dam-ly?"

"Great!" said Wong with a broad smile. "Second daughter, Carolyn, just got into law school, and guess where?"

Mike took a step back. "No kiddin'. She got into *Berkeley*?"

"She sure did!" said Wong. "I'll have my wife bring you dinner tonight to celebrate. Orange chicken, your favorite. Making it with fresh orange juice and some nice local honey we found."

"Hey, that'd be nice, Wong," said Mike. "Tell her she can put it in the fridge. She knows where the key is. And congratulate Carolyn for me. I'll give her a list of spots to steer clear of."

Mike wheeled his Jeep into a parking stall in front of the probation department and grinned to himself. *I've been comin' here damn near every day for the past twenty-five years, longer than most marriages, and I've probably had more fun.* While tempted to attend the seminars held every few months for county employees who were of retirement age, Mike avoided what he viewed as an activity tantamount to meeting with a mortician to discuss one's final wishes.

He walked up the brick steps to the double security door and entered the code on a small pad affixed to the wall. Nothing. Another attempt and still no familiar click signaling the door was unlocked. A third try. No click. Mike stared straight ahead and tried to appear as casual as he could.

No problem. Been off for eight weeks. Forgetting the entry code is perfectly understandable. Let's just not make a scene of it.

"Sixty-three, fifty-six, O'Shea," said Petra Yablonsky quietly. She stood directly behind Mike.

"Pardon?" said Mike innocently.

"Sixty-three, fifty-six. Your radio call sign," said Petra. "We used your call sign last year to program the thing, remember? Kind of as a surprise gift on your last birthday."

"Got it," mumbled Mike as he entered the correct code. "Been off for six weeks for my deal and kind of lost track."

Petra smiled. "Welcome back, O'Shea. Good to see ya."

"Duchess wants to see you, big guy," whispered Tommy, standing at their door of the office. "The Duchess" was Tommy's nom de guerre for Chief Cheryl Jackson. "What's up? She was just down here and said to let you know as soon as you got in."

"Tell her I'm busy, Tomas," said Mike, putting down a mug of tea and his equipment bag in a battered government gray locker in the corner of the office.

"You tell her yourself, cheese dick," hissed Tommy. "The Duchess seems like she's in a no bueno mood."

"What does she want with me?" asked Mike, adjusting his thick glasses.

"Oh, I don't know," said Tommy sarcastically. "Her all-star probation officer chalks up his second line-of-duty shooting," said Tommy, throwing his hands in the air. "Are you kidding?"

Mike gave Tommy his most menacing stare and tapped his fingers on his desk.

After a few moments, Tommy burst out laughing. "O'Shea, I love it when you try to give me a hard look through those Coke bottles you call glasses. You're priceless! One amusing Indian."

Grinning, Mike pushed himself up and strolled down the long hallway toward Cheryl's office. After a deep breath, he knocked.

"Please do come in," said Cheryl in a pleasant but officious voice. "Good morning, Officer O'Shea. I am so happy to have you back."

"Do you know how many bullshit emails I have to wade through after being on the beach for eight weeks, Chief? Can you do anything about that?" asked Mike.

"Understand your frustration," said Cheryl in her best conciliatory tone. "Just keep in mind, electronic communication is a blessing, a blessing indeed!"

She's got bad news for me. Tryin' to be a little too cheerful. Mike assumed his usual seat in front of Cheryl's desk.

"What can I do you for, boss?" asked Mike.

"Well, first, let me officially welcome you back. I've reviewed the district attorney's report, and as you know, you have been cleared in your most recent shooting," said Cheryl.

"Got it," said Mike casually, especially given the gravity of the subject. He didn't particularly appreciate the phrase "most recent shooting" but allowed it to pass without comment. *Wonder if she really believes there's gonna be more.*

"Unfortunately, the shooting, while completely within the law and department policy, was not without, um, issues," said Cheryl.

Mike removed his glasses, took a handkerchief from his pocket, and slowly wiped the thick lenses. The handkerchief was a kitchen towel he had cut into squares for this very purpose. "What kind of issues?" he asked.

Cheryl pulled a manila file from a drawer and placed it on her desk. "You need to see these, Michael."

Mike opened the file. *Transcripts. What the hell?* He recognized the format used when a transcriber typed a conversation picked up from a listening device, either known or unknown to the speaker. The file contained thirty or so sheets of neatly typed pages. Each sheet contained separate conversations delineated by thick solid lines and the dates and times they were recorded. Mike read the first two entries. *Somebody has phones at the jail wired. They're comin' for me. This is a real piss-a-roo.*

After giving Mike a few minutes to read the transcripts of calls from county jail inmates secretly recorded by sheriff's investigators, Cheryl spoke.

"The man you shot, Michael, was, as they say, connected," said Cheryl. "He was the primary meth manufacturer for the Savages."

Uh-oh. "Big cook man means big money man for the club," said Mike calmly.

"Yes," said Cheryl. "You disabled the primary manufacturer of methamphetamine for this organization, and having done so apparently interrupted a significant part of their drug trade throughout the Western United States."

"And?"

"Are you familiar with the phrase *green light*, Michael?" asked Cheryl.

Mike tried to stifle a giggle. After composing himself, he took his glasses and dabbed his eyes with a tissue pulled from a box on Cheryl's desk.

"Is something amusing, Officer O'Shea?" asked Cheryl with slight irritation.

"I'm sorry, Chief. I really don't mean to offend, but hearing you talk street is just, well, you know," said Mike.

"No, Officer O'Shea. I don't know," said Cheryl, her tone hardening.

Quit screwing around. You're starting to piss her off. "Uncalled for, Chief. I appreciate your concern, but lots of things are said in jail. Most are bravado bullshit," said Mike with a shrug of his shoulders.

"Obviously, you are familiar with the gang term *green light*, meaning an authorization from the gang's hierarchy to commit a murder. While you may not take these threats seriously, the district attorney, county sheriff, and *I* do, Michael," said Cheryl.

Mike looked down at his hands. "So what's this mean to me, Chief?" he asked.

Cheryl looked into Mike's eyes. He sensed she was no longer angry with his silliness.

Somethin' else goin' on here. She feels sorry for me.

"Why don't we go back to the reason you asked me to come down to your office?" said Mike.

"To tell you you're being taken out of the field," said Cheryl quietly.

"And why is that, Chief?" *I feel like I'm talking a kid through a math problem.*

"Because of the threats from the Savages," said Cheryl quickly.

"Wrong answer," said Mike. "Be straight with me, Toni." During private conversations, Cheryl begrudgingly allowed Mike to refer to her by the diminutive of her middle name, Antionette.

Cheryl looked down at her desk, wondering if the university might consider her return and a reinstatement of her professor's status. "All right, I'm concerned about your health."

"Wasn't aware you held a medical degree, Dr. Jackson." *At least we're getting closer.* "Any other reasons, Toni?" asked Mike patiently.

"No other reason," said Cheryl, several pitches above her usual vocal tone.

Amazing how bold-faced lying changes the voice, Mike thought.

"You're disappointing me, boss. Be straight with me," said Mike.

Cheryl gave a sign of resignation. "I suspect you know the real reason, Michael."

Mike smiled, eager to get to the truth after fifteen minutes of wasted time.

"You have been involved in two on-duty shootings with two fatalities and a near fatality most recently," said Cheryl in almost a whisper.

"Go on," Mike said.

"All right, Michael. You're so quick to judge me. Let's see if you can handle the reality of the situation," said Cheryl. "We put you back out there, you kill or injure another subject, and the county just opens up the public checkbook."

Mike sat back. After a few moments, he said, "Appreciate the bind I put you in, but my shoots were cleared because had I not done what I did, I'd be dead. Sorry, but that's the unfortunate truth, even if it is too unpleasant for you suits."

"So where does that leave us, Michael?" asked Cheryl.

"Management has reassignment authority, so my feelings on the matter are moot, Chief. Where are you sending me?"

"You're going to be our new training coordinator," said Cheryl brightly.

"Well, that's just damn ducky," said Mike as he stood and turned to leave Cheryl's office.

As was his custom, Mike left Cheryl's office in the same manner he always left a meeting with his boss. He stopped by the office of Cheryl's administrative assistant, Gen Di Tullio, and helped himself to a peppermint from a small glass bowl she kept behind her computer.

"Gen, what say we ditch these losers and drive up the coast to Big Sur? I know a Catholic retreat place, very discreet. No one will talk, I promise. They're not allowed to speak," whispered Mike with a grin.

Genevieve ignored Mike's comment. "How'd the meeting go, O'Shea?" she asked gently. She was aware of the nature of the meeting and knew instinctively that Mike would not be pleased with his pending reassignment.

"Okay, Gen," Mike responded, looking down. "Guess my field days are sunsetting. I tried to bluff her, but the boss knows she can transfer me at will. Nobody around here owns their job."

"You know, Michael," replied the oldest and no doubt the wisest member of the department. "Most men in this business retire much younger and much less healthy than you. Those crazy calisthenics you do keep you young. This change will be a good thing. Trust me."

CHAPTER 12

Two months later

Following a brief transition period, Mike was removed from the Gang Task Force and reassigned to the probation department's training unit. Here, he would spend the final days of his career training other officers on a variety of topics including self-defense, ethics, and report writing.

Whoo boy! One fuckin' thrill after another, Mike thought after reading his formal transfer orders. Despite all that had been said during his meeting with Cheryl, the one thing she had been upfront about was the threat against Mike's life. He knew that if the criminal organization Mike helped put temporarily out of business really wanted him dead, he would be, and possibly anyone Mike was working alongside. Not a good situation for a member of a close team. Mike also knew that while the task force members would welcome him back as a conquering hero, deep down, some would think that the threats made him just "too hot."

Cheryl attempted to temper the move by promising him that on occasion, Mike would be assigned to special details, primarily taking advantage of his specialty of tracking down wanted criminals and bringing them into custody.

Mike spent the morning sitting at his desk and becoming familiar with the state training requirements that would dictate much of what he would do as a departmental training coordinator. Once that task was complete, he started to work on an outline for a course entitled Basic Probation Supervision, a significant portion of which would be dedicated to how to understand and use the court-ordered psychological evaluation.

Mike always found these evaluations helpful in getting a clear picture of the probationer he would be dealing with. If the evaluation gave a diagnosis of sociopathy or in extreme cases psychopathology, Mike's role would be one of an undercover police officer. He would simply monitor and surveil in hopes that he caught the probationer before he or she found their next victim. The problem with socio-paths and psychopaths was that they never developed a conscience and the ability to feel any remorse or empathy. Mike had once super-vised a car thief who justified his actions as a form of just punishment to the "dumb shit" who left his keys in the ignition of his car.

"Maybe the dummy will learn his lesson, and this won't happen again," the probationer had said, smiling. "I'm kind of providing a service to the community, O'Shea," he rationalized.

Sometimes the psychological evaluation would label the pro-bationer as both an offender and victim. Over his career, Mike had known dozens of criminals in this category. It wasn't that they were bad people. Just unlucky. Mike worked with a thirty-year-old strip-per who dealt methamphetamine on the side to support her heroin habit. Literally every male in her life from birth forward had taken advantage of her, from her father who pimped her out to his buddies to the pimp who got her hooked on heroin as a method of control. The woman never had a chance. Mike considered the last category and thought about his own biological mother. He knew little, other than she had been a runaway from a Northern California tribe, who ended up in Oakland with the same fate as the stripper and that both she and her infant son were heroin addicted at the time of his birth.

Not the greatest family tree. Thank God for my mom and Iggy.

The third group Mike deemed to be "just batshit nutsy." Early in his career, he discovered that it was the mentally ill offender who was the most unpredictable and the most dangerous. Limited by the minimal training in working with the mentally ill that probation officers receive, he had no real background in dealing with people who, fifty years earlier, would have been institutionalized.

Mike squinted his eyes, blinked a few times, and took off his glasses. He shook his head as if to shake loose the blurring of his vision that had started slowly a few years earlier but now came on more often. He leaned back in his chair and clamped his eyes shut. *Must be the cheap-ass office lights the county put in here.*

"Hey, O'Shea. Alma's on the nest, and once again, you're the godfather. Congratulations."

"Tom, I know about all the fruitful and multiply BS from Iggy's catechism, but could you two at least try to keep your mitts off-a each other?"

"Can't help it, my brother," said Tommy. "Alma is a hot Latina and I a beautiful son of Samoa."

Mike smiled at fond memories of the baptisms of the Sagapalus' other four children. With Mike standing in as Godfather and Iggy officiating, they always felt like family reunions.

"Nobody wants to work with you, brah," said Tommy. "Other than me, of course."

"What?" Mike was incredulous. He was the best field officer in the department. Young officers used to wait in line to spend time with him and learn from "the master."

Tommy looked a little sad. "Michael, you've shot three subjects and killed two of them."

"So?" said Mike, beginning to understand where the conversation was going. *Why is Tommy calling me Michael all of a sudden?*

"People think you're a shit magnet. Bad luck," said Tommy.

Mike put his glasses back on and stared at his computer. "Fuck 'em then," he murmured.

A week later, Mike wheeled his Jeep around the rear of the probation department. As he rounded a corner to park in his unofficial spot, Mike slammed on the brakes to avoid hitting an expensive Yamaha FZ-09 motorcycle parked directly in the middle of his spot.

I got about one nerve left, and that kid's on it. That "kid" was Whitney Abrams, the department's newest hire. "Whit," as he asked to be called, was a recent graduate in psychology from Cal Coastal

University. Unlike most of his classmates, he had been able to find a *real* job in the area. Whit wasn't big on rules and sneered when it was politely pointed out to him that he was parking in a space reserved for the department's most distinguished officer.

"I don't give a shit," Whit had simply stated. "Old man needs to get to work a little earlier, I guess."

Mike filled his cup with steaming hot green tea and walked down to his office. Tommy was cleaning his gun at a small table in the corner of their shared office. While Mike never mentioned it, his partner's gun cleaning routine was more than unnerving. Tommy had experienced several ADs, or accidental discharges on the firing range, and was notorious for being slightly lackadaisical when it came to firearms. Mike usually found an excuse to leave the office during Tommy's gun cleaning sessions, but this particular morning, his head hurt, he was tired, and his mind was preoccupied with thoughts of Coach Sylvia Almeida.

A day earlier, the Cal Coastal volleyball coach had invited Mike to her office in the campus athletic complex to meet with one of her players who was interested in becoming a probation officer. Mike had tracked her down through the university website, called, and invited her to Sunday brunch. The two had gotten together several times since. Sylvia met Mike in the lobby of the athletic department and greeted him with a light kiss to both cheeks.

"Thank you so much for doing this, Michael. Savannah is graduating next quarter and is really interested in your profession."

"Happy to help, Coach," said Mike.

"You know, Michael, when Savannah was doing some research, she googled 'Serra County Probation Department,' and guess whose name popped up? Quite impressive."

"Lies and fabrications. Tell your girl you can't believe everything you read on the interweb," said Mike.

Sylvia stifled a giggle. "I think you mean the *internet,* Michael."

"Right," said Mike, eager to change the topic. "This is a great office."

On the far wall were three large framed posters. The first was of a much younger Sylvia in midair as she slammed a volleyball toward her opponents. A caption above Sylvia's image read, "Welcome to the Games of the XXIII Olympiad, Los Angeles, United States." The second photo was of Sylvia standing alongside her teammates on the Olympic medal stand, gold medals draped around their necks. Her wild mane of brown curls was secured by a headband adorned with the flag of Brazil. A *C* was sewn onto her jersey, denoting that Sylvia was the captain of the most decorated women's volleyball team in the history of the sport. The final photo was of a woman lighting the caldron at the opening ceremony of the 2016 Summer Olympics in Rio de Janeiro, Brazil, thousands of cell phone cameras lighting up the stadium like tiny fireflies in the stifling Rio heat.

"That you?" asked Mike.

"It is. That was quite an evening."

"Very nice, Sylvia," said Mike.

"A little much, I think, but the university athletic director asked me to hang them in my office," said Sylvia. "He thinks it helps with recruiting."

Mike stared into Sylvia's large brown eyes and smiled. *I'm offi-cially in big trouble.*

"Well, it's workin' for me. When do I get my uniform?" he said with a smile and a wink.

"Saturday night after I prepare you an authentic Brazilian meal, Michael. Sound acceptable?"

"You betcha."

*****

"Oh, Michael, one last thing," said Cheryl as he stood from his customary seat in his chief's office. "I have a message from Petra Yablonsky regarding the progress of one of our newer deputies. She's requesting he spend some field time with you." Cheryl and Mike had just concluded their biweekly briefing on departmental training.

"Gee, Chief, I'd love to," said Mike with as much sincerity as he could muster. "But as you may have heard, I've been taken out of the field and assigned to a training position."

Cheryl gave Mike her thousand-watt smile. "Chief's prerogative," she said in a singing tone Mike found irritating. "Consider it your final performance, and then you can focus solely on your training assignment. After all, this is a training issue, no?"

Mike shook his head. "Who's the mutt, Toni?"

Cheryl sifted through printed copies of emails on her desk. "Ah, here it is. He's a new hire by the name of Whitney Abrahms. You two are going to get on famously."

Mike took a deep breath and turned back to the door. *Gotta call downtown and look at my retirement numbers.*

The following Saturday afternoon, Mike sat back in his chair staring at Deputy Probation Officer Whitney Abrams. Whitney was dressed in regulation black tactical boots, khaki battle dress uniform pants, a black dry wick T-shirt with the department's insignia on the left chest, Kevlar vest held within a black mesh tactical carrier, and a black ball cap with the department's badge on the front and his last name embroidered on the rear. The fact that his attire was brand-new with no signs of previous use added a comical touch to the young officer's appearance. In addition to the standard safety equipment on his duty belt, Whitney had a Smith and Wesson 9 mm pistol on his right hip which Mike determined immediately was too large a weapon for the owner's relatively petite hands.

"I don't have a caseload anymore, Whitney, so tonight's your show. Pick fifteen names of the probationers who live in south county that are your highest priority. Have another five to ten on deck in case we start runnin' dry and can't find everyone in your first tier," said Mike.

"Got it, big guy," said Whitney.

Mike attempted to disguise a cringe. "Let's get something straight, *Whitney*. I don't like nicknames or derivations of names of those I don't know." Mike was trying to blink away a searing headache. "You may refer to me as Mike, O'Shea, or if we get into a shitstorm, 'Hey, fuck wad. But big guy isn't happenin'."

Mike shook his head as he left his office. *I could be home with a cold Pabst watchin' the Lakers game. What did I do to deserve an evening with this fool?*

Mike took the wheel as he and his trainee drove south on Highway 101 toward the small town of River Beach.

"Who's first on your list, Whitney?"

"Edwin Bagley is his name, Officer O'Shea."

Mike smiled at himself. "Well, that's probably a good thing because I supervised Edwin a few years ago, so he knows me, and we have a rapport. What's he think about you?"

"To be honest, we've never met," admitted Whitney sheepishly.

"You've *never* met," Mike said, trying to hide his shock. "What did they teach you in the academy about first contacts?"

"Hmm, I think they said something about having the first meeting with the probationer in a controlled environment, like our office."

"Then why is your first contact with Edwin in the field?" asked Mike.

Whitney looked like he would have preferred to have been anywhere other than locked into a caged vehicle with Michael O'Shea. "Sheriff called and said he's in violation, and he won't answer my calls to come in to meet."

Mike had a decision to make. Under ordinary circumstances, he would skip contacting Edwin Bagley and insist Whitney conduct his first meeting in the department office. But the fact that the sheriffs were requesting some action changed things. Mike always took pride in his reputation as a reliable partner with the sheriff's office and sensed a teaching moment for his trainee.

"Okay, Whitney," said Mike. "Not how we like to do our business. Office contact is always best out of the gate. But I also don't like to give the SOs any reason to say we're not holdin' our mud. So let's go find Edwin."

"Hold our mud?" asked Whitney.

"Yeah, hold our mud. Not crappin' our pants. Holdin' up our end of things," said Mike with surprising patience.

Mike remembered that there was an alley behind Edwin's house that the probationer often used to escape contact. He wheeled the county vehicle around the house and stopped.

"Hear that, Whitney?" asked Mike.

"Whistling," said Whitney. "Why are the neighbors whistling?"

"This is an old gang neighborhood from way back," said Mike. "Whistling is a traditional gang method of tellin' the world probation officers are here."

"Gangsters. Love 'em. Let's roll a few up and show them what's what, am I right?" said Whitney, offering his fist for Mike to bump.

Mike stared at Whitney's fist, glanced away, and said, "I'm just not sure where to begin with your stupidity." Mike had barely finished his sentence when, as if on cue, the pudgy form of Edwin Bagley hurled himself over the six-foot fence separating his backyard from the alley, almost running into Mike's vehicle. Mike slammed on the brakes and unclipped his safety belt.

"I'm gonna go after him on foot, Whitney!" said Mike. "Go to gray channel so we can communicate. Follow me but give me some distance. I talk to dispatch only. Got it?"

Whitney gurgled something unintelligible as Mike threw open the car door and sprinted toward the fleeing probationer.

CHAPTER 13

Chief Probation Officer Cheryl Jackson wasn't accustomed to late-night calls. After all, she had people to handle the after-hour activities of the Serra County Probation Department.

"Hello," she said softly.

"Chief, it's Tom Sagapalu."

"Yes, Tommy, what is it?" Cheryl sat up in bed. She pulled off the satin-covered eye mask she wore, thus avoiding being disturbed by the early morning California sun.

"O'Shea. He's had what looks like a stroke. He's in Serra Memorial."

"I'm on my way."

Cheryl drove into the parking lot of the Serra Memorial Hospital and noticed a large presence of law enforcement vehicles. As she entered through the automatic doors to the emergency room waiting area, Cheryl saw a group of her officers circled around Iggy. He had been up reading, thus avoiding the unkempt look of someone roused from a sound sleep to rush to the hospital. Iggy was dressed casually in jeans and a green Cal Coastal sweatshirt. Although now close to seventy years of age, he remained trim with a sprinkling of gray in his thick dark hair. Only the deep lines around his eyes gave away his age. Sylvia sat on the perimeter of the group, white sweatshirt with "Cal Coastal Women's Volleyball" on the front. Cheryl had met Sylvia at several departmental functions and had been updated on their relationship by her assistant, Gen Di Tullio, who viewed Mike as her younger mischievous brother.

Iggy greeted Cheryl and suggested they step outside for privacy. Tommy and Sylvia joined them.

"How is he?" Cheryl asked.

"Mike was in a foot pursuit and had some kind of a seizure," said Tommy. "The paramedics said he was conscious when they found him lying by his prisoner. They say he had a stroke."

A seizure and a stroke? For a moment, Cheryl wondered if the man the paramedics brought to the hospital was *her* Michael O'Shea.

"Are you Father De la Rosa?" asked a woman in a white coat.

"Yes, I am. Please call me Iggy."

"Iggy?" she said hesitantly. "I'm sorry, Father, but I'm just not accustomed to calling priests by their first name. May I call you Father De la Rosa, please?"

"Of course, of course. I didn't catch your name," said Iggy.

"I'm Maria Rivera. I'm the on-duty physician here this evening. Are you Officer O'Shea's family member?"

Iggy smiled. "Well, not exactly. I'm his Godfather, and I've known him all his life. I was very close to his folks. Mike never married, so his friends here and I are pretty much it."

"I see. May I speak with you in my office?"

"Yes, yes. Wherever you like. May I bring in Michael's friends?" asked Iggy, gesturing to Tommy, Sylvia, and Cheryl.

"That would be a good idea, I think."

The group followed the physician to a small office down the hall from the emergency room. Dr. Rivera was reading a file with some loose documents. Iggy noticed that Sylvia held rosary beads and was mouthing a silent prayer to herself.

"Officer O'Shea suffered a moderate seizure. Just before he arrived, we believe he suffered an equally moderate stroke. That's the bad news," said Dr. Rivera. "The good news is that he's breathing and swallowing on his own. Also, he appears to be in amazing physical condition for a man his age, which will be helpful."

The room became strangely silent.

"Is he going to be okay?" asked Tommy, sounding slightly irritated.

"I can't give you a prognosis. A seizure and then a stroke are simply not consistent with your friend's lifestyle and physical condition. So we're going to need a wide battery of tests to determine the cause," said Dr. Rivera. "I can tell you again he's breathing and swallowing on his own, appears responsive to our questions, and has *some* mobility in all extremities. But for now, he seems to have lost his ability to speak…but that is often temporary. I would like to ask you one question, however," said Dr. Rivera. "Has Officer O'Shea ever experienced any head trauma?"

"Oh my God," said Tommy quietly as he glanced toward Iggy.

Dr. Rivera looked a bit perplexed. "Any head injuries at all over the last few years? His symptoms may be consistent with cumulative head trauma or CTE, as you may have heard it referred to."

"Doctor, Michael O'Shea has been getting banged in the head for the past forty years. I'm sure he's lost count of how many concussions he's had," said Iggy.

*****

Mike was formally admitted to the hospital and given a private room, a common courtesy for law enforcement officers injured in the line of duty. The next morning, he began to shift his body around, trying to find some comfort in the hospital bed. By noon, his eyes were open, and by three o'clock, he was trying to get out of bed, much to the disapproval of the nursing staff, who finally attached soft Velcro restraints to his feet to keep him from moving. The stroke appeared to have affected the left side of Mike's body, all his speech, but none of his will nor his ability to become agitated when people—in this case, doctors and nurses—tried to control his attempts to find his clothes and check himself out of the hospital. As the day went on, Mike's mind started to clear. His speech remained nonexistent. When he tried to talk, Mike had an odd burning sensation in his throat. To deal with his agitation, the doctors applied a heavy sedative.

On day 3 of his hospital stay, Mike awoke from a short afternoon nap to see a sight that could be only bad news. Cheryl Jackson stood in the corner of his hospital room looking more serious than usual and dressed in a pair of sensible shoes, navy blue business suit, white silk blouse, and her mother's pearls. *Must be bad. She's got her news conference outfit on.*

Next to her stood Iggy, who looked presentable as a semiretired priest in khaki chinos, a pressed plaid oxford shirt, and brown loafers. Sylvia sat next to Iggy, eyes puffy and red. Tommy leaned against the wall in the corner of the room, staring at the floor. Standing to the side were two doctors.

"Officer O'Shea, I'm Dr. Cusack." A dour-looking physician stepped forward and grabbed Mike's hand. "If you can understand me, squeeze once. If you cannot, squeeze twice."

I've had a damn stroke and even I know that makes no sense. Who are these clowns? Mike looked at Tommy with a mystified expression.

"I'm sorry, Officer O'Shea. That may have been confusing, wasn't it?" Dr. Cusack took a deep breath. "Let's try this again. One squeeze for yes, two for no. Okay, Sport?"

Sport? Talk to me like a grown-up, you idiot. Mike took his hand and started to squeeze. *Harder...really give it to this condescending dullard.* Dr. Cusack yanked his hand out of Mike's grip and looked toward his colleague with a mixture of shock and disgust. He then turned to Tommy.

"Is he always like this?"

"Actually, this is pretty good for O'Shea. Just don't get your hands too close to his mouth." Tommy tried to control a giggle. Sylvia and Cheryl looked unamused.

Iggy took a step forward. Speaking slowly and quite loudly, Iggy asked, "Michael, can you hear me?"

Mike gave Iggy a vexing stare.

"Mike, it's me, Iggy. You know me, right? You're Michael O'Shea, and I'm your Godfather, Iggy De la Rosa." In a voice cracked with emotion, Iggy was yelling at Mike as though he was hearing-impaired.

Yes, Iggy, I know who you are. For God's sake! Are you crying? Aren't you supposed to be in control at a time like this? And use your inside voice. People are probably tryin' to get some rest around here.

An attractive young doctor stepped forward and took Mike's hand. "Mike, I'm Dr. Vouchilas." He stared into her eyes and suddenly felt a sense of calm.

"My dad was a cop back in Chicago and spent a ton of dough on my education, so no rough stuff with my hands, got it?" she said with a very distinctive Chicago accent. "Mike, here's the deal, okay? You appear to have a serious condition called CTE, chronic traumatic encephalopathy. It comes with the territory when you've had as many hits to the noggin as you have. Father De la Rosa briefed me on your exploits," she said with a smile.

"Boxing as a kid, college rugby, at least three whacks in the line of duty. The man upstairs didn't make our cranial protection with people like you in mind, ya know what I'm sayin'?" Dr. Vouchilas said, tapping her forehead. "This condition resulted in a pretty good seizure. Once they loaded you in the ambulance, you had a stroke… and here we are. On a scale of one to ten, both the seizure and stroke were at about a six. Got all that?"

Mike looked around the room. Iggy was still crying. Dr. Cusack had slipped out of the room. Tommy gave a thumbs-up and winked. Cheryl just looked pissed. Sylvia stared at Mike intently.

She's probably wonderin' if I can still get a stiffy, he thought.

"If you got all that, one squeeze."

Mike gave Dr. Vouchilas a gentle single squeeze.

"Now we're gettin' somewhere," she said. "Prognosis is what we call guarded."

Uh-oh. Bad news coming.

"Mr. O'Shea, we're just learning about CTE," said Dr. Vouchilas. "You've probably heard about brain trauma in the NFL."

Mike nodded slowly. *I should have followed Mom's advice and taken up tennis.* He looked over at Iggy in the corner, holding his face in his hand, weeping quietly. *Don't you fall apart, old man. I'll make an anonymous call to the diocese and tell 'em you've lost your marbles.*

Mike knew instinctively what Iggy was thinking. Somehow, he contributed to Mike's condition by getting him involved in boxing.

Mike opened his mouth to speak and tried to mouth the word *yes*. Out came a guttural murmur that only he understood. *Shit, I really can't talk.* He grasped a handful of bedsheets with his right hand and squeezed in frustration.

"We'll talk about speech in a minute. For now, let's just go with squeezing my hand and the writing board. Do you remember any additional head trauma other than through athletics and while you were on duty?" asked Dr. Vouchilas.

Mike took the pen and grabbed the writing board that had been placed on his lap. "That's it," he wrote.

"Okay, good. That's a start. Here's what we're looking at. Right now, you've obviously lost your ability to speak. Also, you seem to have some impairment on part of your left side. As you've probably noticed, we have you hooked up to a catheter to drain your urine, and we have you in an adult diaper. We're still evaluating your ability to control your bowels and bladder," said Dr. Vouchilas quietly.

Mike pulled up his sheet with his right hand and peeked down at the catheter. He stared up at the ceiling above his hospital bed. *Ya gotta be shittin' me.* Mike felt his eyes start to mist. Dr. Vouchilas looked around the room. Iggy had stopped crying but looked like he might start again at any moment. Cheryl had her arm around Sylvia. Tommy was now at the window, looking out on downtown Serra, wishing the entire scene was a bad dream.

"Is it okay if I call you Mike?"

Mike wiped his nose and then made a rather theatrical display of removing a nonexistent object from his eye. *Don't think she's buyin' it.* He looked up and nodded slowly.

"You're a tough guy. I can tell because I was raised in a houseful of tough guys just like you. Frankly, you all can be kind of a pain in the ass, am I right?"

Mike grinned. *Finally, someone who talks like a real person.*

"This is a load of bad news, I know. Let's brighten things up. First, you're in amazing physical condition. Father Ignatius told me about this stadium step workout of yours. Well, it's paid off in aces," said Dr. Vouchilas with a warm smile. "Second, although you have some tremors in your fingers, no signs of Parkinson's disease. I'm a little surprised after what your skull has been through. I think we can make some serious progress with you. Your speech will respond to therapy, and you may regain complete vocal functioning. With some very intensive physical therapy, I think your left-side functioning may return. We'll just have to see. You must have a ton of questions." She tapped a finger on the dry-erase board. "Write them down here and I'll do my best to answer them."

There's somethin' they're not telling me. Mike looked at Tommy, who quickly looked away.

"When can I get back to work?" he wrote.

Dr. Vouchilas looked up at Iggy and the others. *Guy's lucky. People really love him. He'll need that,* she thought. Dr. Vouchilas reached over and took Mike's hand. "Look, this is no time for bullshit. Given the severity of your brain injuries and the cumulative effects of blunt trauma to your skull, it would be very unlikely that you'll ever be able to return to duty." She stopped and let the news settle in. Mike stared into her eyes with a look she found a little unsettling.

"That doesn't mean you won't be able to work again, just not in law enforcement," Dr. Vouchilas said with all the hope her voice could muster.

Suddenly, and with impressive speed for a man who had just had a major medical event, Mike threw the writing board across the room, sending it crashing into a wall. Dr. Vouchilas stood up from the bed and took a few steps back, startled, not quite sure what Mike would do next. Iggy stepped forward, placing his hand on the side of Mike's head.

"I love you, son. We all love you. We'll be here with you every step of the way." Mike gently pushed the priest's hand away.

"Maybe this would be a good time to take a break and let you rest," said Dr. Vouchilas.

"There's a cafeteria where we can talk. Follow me," said Dr. Vouchilas as she led the group down a long hallway.

Iggy took coffee orders and walked over to the service counter. Cheryl stared at Tommy and Sylvia and shook her head.

"Not good. Not good at all."

"Can he take some kind of a medical retirement?" asked Tommy.

"Of course. Some of the origins of his injury came from employment-related incidents, so he's on solid ground there. We'll just downplay the boxing and rugby injuries." Cheryl gave Tommy a reassuring smile.

Iggy returned with cups of coffee. "Anyone want something to eat?" he asked with much more cheer than he felt. When he was met with blank looks, he continued, "I guess we've all lost our appetites."

"Since you five seem to be the closest Officer O'Shea has of next of kin, here's the deal," began Dr. Vouchilas. "He'll be here for a week or so for more testing. We'll start with some light physical therapy, which, given the little I know about him, should go really poorly. Hopefully, he won't try to choke out the physical therapist," she said with a smile.

"From here, he'll be transferred to a rehab hospital down the coast, Pacific Dunes Center for Medical Rehabilitation. There he'll get some increasingly intense PT. I hear they do good work there," she said.

"When can he go home?" asked Tommy.

"That depends. This could go one of two ways. Either his fitness level and self-discipline will make for a remarkably quick recovery, or, just based on how he responded a few minutes ago, he may become depressed and shut down. We just don't know."

"I've got five kids, so the house is a little cramped as is, but I have a detached garage I could turn into a nice little pad for Mike. What do ya think, Iggy?"

"You're a good man, Tommy" was all Iggy could think of saying.

"How can we help? What's our role?" asked Cheryl, already making plans for Mike's care and recovery.

"A couple of things," said Dr. Vouchilas. "Obviously, a lot of love and support. That will be critical. Does he own a home?"

"No. Michael travels light. Just a small apartment in downtown Serra," said Sylvia.

"Probably for the best. If you can, keep his apartment for him and let him know he still has a home and a normal life to return to.

He's lucky he's a public employee with good medical benefits and low expenses. Trust me, all of this could be much worse."

"It's getting late. Guess there's not much more we can do tonight. If I know Michael, going back to his room to keep him company probably wouldn't go over well. Like a fart in mass, he enjoys saying," said Iggy with a chuckle.

CHAPTER 14

Later that evening

I've had enough. Getting the hell outta here. Gonna sleep in my own bed like a big boy. It was a little past three thirty in the morning. After the doctor and Mike's small entourage left, he dozed for a few minutes at a time but found the outcome the same. He would wake up, feel disoriented, and then realize where he was and what he had become. *I'm a patient. Just another helpless patient. Not for me.* Mike looked around the room. The other two beds were empty. *That won't last long. Where are my clothes? Where's my gun? That ass Tommy is supposed to take care of me at a time like this.*

Mike saw a tall narrow door directly in front of his bed with the name O'Shea written on a removable tag. *Must be a closet. Grab my clothes and just walk on outta here.*

He looked up and saw a bag of clear liquid hanging from a steel IV stand, a long plastic tube running down to the top of his right hand. *They're putting fluids into me.* Mike tried to move his left hand. No movement, just an odd tingling sensation. *Gotta get this damn tube out. Wish they had stuck it in my left hand.* He slowly moved his right foot then bent his knee and tried bringing it up toward his head. *Not bad.* Nothing on the left side, just more tingling. Mike looked back at his hand and the needle covered by a white bandage. *Shit.* He realized that he had yet to use the bathroom since he regained consciousness. He sat back in bed and stared at the celling light. *I can't believe this.* He looked down toward his waist and, with his right hand, grabbed the sheet and slowly lifted it away. Mike groaned as he looked down at another plastic tube. Only this tube was inserted into his urethra. *Right, the doc told me about the catheter. Thank God I was unconscious when they stuck that in me. Couldn't have been fun. Not goin' anywhere soon with that thing in. Wonder if they'll sedate me when they yank it out?*

Mike laid his head back on the pillow. *Think. At some point, that thing has gotta come out. Maybe not. Maybe I'll have a tube up my pecker the rest of my life.* He looked around the room. *Not gonna live like this. Only one option. Just do this thing. Yank the tube out of my hand, loop it around my neck, tie the other end to the rail, and throw myself off the bed. Jail inmates do it all the time. All that Catholic mumbo jumbo about goin' to hell for killin' yourself is just a smoke screen. Take care of your own business. Want to be a burden the rest of your life? Take control like a man, ya pussy! They already know who you are, so no one will have to ID your body. Cleanest suicide ever. Just do it. It's late. They won't hear a thing. Tight around the neck, ease over to the side of the bed, and then boom! Easy peasy. Probably happens around here all the time.*

Mike grabbed the IV tube leading into the back of his hand, took a deep breath, and yanked it out. Ouch. *Shit, wonder what the tube in Little Mikey would have felt like when it came out. Won't have to deal with that now.* He tightly wrapped the tube around his neck once and then twice. *One more time to be safe. Better finish up before I pass out from lack of air.* With the tube tightly secured around his throat, Mike used his right arm to push himself over to the edge of the bed. *Do it, ya fuckin' coward. Just do it. One…two…*

*****

"You've had a tough go of it, lad. I'll grant you that," Iggy said quietly from the dark corner of the room. Instinctively after returning to the rectory, he grabbed his coat and drove back to the hospital.

Mike looked over toward Iggy, shut his eyes, and slowly shook his head from side to side. *I just can't catch a break. The old man will tell the hospital he has concerns about my mental health, and tomorrow I wake up in a rubber room. Just fuckin' swell.*

"You've also had a quite wondrous life, starting with how you came into the world and found yourself in the arms of no better parents than Bridgette and Emile." Mike glared at Iggy as he pulled a sheet over his throat.

"Pretty tough deal you're facing here, Michael. But you know, God is tricky fellow, or being, however you want to think of him. He presents us with insurmountable challenges and then stands right beside us, lifting us up and giving us all the tools we need to overcome them. We just have to listen."

Mike shook his head as he looked up at the ceiling. *Leave it to Iggy to screw up my suicide.* Awkwardly, he loosened the tube and removed it from around his throat. Iggy took a step out of the shadow of the corner of the room. Mike looked up and met Iggy's eyes.

"I'm so sorry," Mike mouthed. Iggy leaned down and slid an arm around his neck as he pulled him into his chest, patting his head gently.

"I love you, Michael, and I'm not going anywhere."

"Go ahead. Let it go. Let it go, son."

*****

The ambulance attendant propped up the gurney so Mike could look out the window as they drove to the small town of Mussel Shores, just south of Serra. He saw the tall palms of the upscale enclave of Shelter Cove pass by.

"Man, your friends are driving like crazy tryin' to keep up," the attendant said with a chuckle.

Mike turned as best he could to look out of the ambulance just in time to see Iggy's aging sedan come up alongside. Iggy, at the wheel, waved frantically, Tommy Sagapalu in the passenger seat, appearing amused by the whole scene. As Iggy aged, his driving had not improved, and Tommy was trying to recall why he had agreed to his driving. Their destination was the Pacific Dunes Rehabilitation Hospital, a facility specializing in stroke and head trauma victims, which rested on a bluff above the water.

"You're really lucky, Mike. This is one of the best facilities for your condition between Los Angeles and San Francisco. I've heard they have done some remarkable things with stroke victims," said Dr. Vouchilas when she broke the news to Mike that he wouldn't be heading home.

Mike had just glared at her, a look she had grown accustomed to after a few weeks as Mike's physician. He grabbed the dry-erase board that seemed to have become a permanent fixture on his bed and tore the cap off the pen with his teeth.

"Want to go home," he wrote.

"You may do just that, but not today, not next week, or even next month," said Dr. Vouchilas with a noticeable chill in her voice.

She's getting sick of me. Can't really blame her. Mike grabbed the board and wrote, "What if I refuse?"

"Let me tell you something, *Jack*," hissed Dr. Vouchilas. "I've about had it with you and that pity pool you've immersed yourself in."

Not exactly digging the hostility, Doc.

"You're alive, Officer O'Shea. Alive and have people who care about you. And if you can manage squeezing a positive thought through that thick-ass skull of yours, think about this. You have health insurance. Fine health insurance in fact. Better than most. And if you ever hope to get home and live independently so you're not *someone else's* problem, you're going to have to work, not just a little but harder than you've ever worked at anything in your life, and that facility where you're heading is your best chance of getting back on your feet. I mean it. I don't give a shit about your stadium calisthenics or whatever you call them. You think you're a tough guy… let's just see."

Dr. Vouchilas stared at Mike with ice in her eyes. "Now if you want to check yourself out, no skin off my prick. You can go home and rot for all I care, you ungrateful ass."

Mike held her gaze, neither wanting to blink first nor look away. He grabbed his board and scribbled out a few words. "No need to get your panties twisted up, Doc. Does everyone from Chicago have a toilet tongue?"

That was the last time Mike had seen his doctor. The next day, he was on his way to the Pacific Dunes Hospital. As the ambulance pulled into the hospital parking lot, Mike cranked his neck to look around. Glancing to the right was fine, but the same movement to the left was a little tougher. The paralysis in his left side had slightly improved, but Mike still had no use of his vocal cords. He did have significant movement in his left index finger and big toe, an achievement Iggy touted as the biggest ecclesiastic event since the resurrection. The doors to the ambulance opened, and Mike looked directly at the smiling faces of Tommy and Iggy.

What are they smiling about? Wonder if I have an anger problem.

Mike's gurney was gently pulled from the ambulance and raised to waist level. Two orderlies in clean white uniforms lifted him from the ambulance and wheeled the gurney toward the hospital entrance.

They must spend a fortune on landscaping. Probably tryin' to hide somethin'. Gotta get out of this pissy mood.

"Gosh, Michael, this place is beautiful," said Iggy as Mike was wheeled into a private room with a nice view of the hills above Mussel Shores. Mike looked around the room. Someone had done their best to make the surroundings look less like a hospital room and more like a home. *Just not mine.* A flat-screen TV was placed directly in front of his bed, which Tommy turned to a sports channel.

"Mr. O'Shea, my name is Jean DeFord. I'm from the dietary department, and I'd like to speak with you about your meals," said a petite young woman dressed in colorful medical scrubs.

Tall and fit, she had braided her hair into cornrows that Jean had long ago given up trying to manage. She reviewed an impressive menu with Mike and asked him to check his meal choices.

"Mr. O'Shea, if you're not feeling well or would like to do this some other time, I can come back."

Sweet kid and someone's daughter, you jerk. Don't take your problems out on her. Mike slowly took the menu in his right hand and, after a few moments, put a check by what sounded appetizing. He had lost almost twenty pounds in the hospital and knew that he would need to bulk back up if he was going to make any progress at all. Mike grabbed the board and wrote, "Thank you, Jean. It's nice to meet you." He looked over at Iggy, who had a pleased look on his face. After Jean left, Mike wrote, "Guess I'm not such an asshole after all!"

"Ah, my newest partner!" bellowed Dr. Jason Shapiro from the door to Mike's room.

The man in the doorway was of average height, thick in the waist, with a wild gray beard and wilder mane of salt-and-pepper hair pulled back into a ponytail. A purple yarmulke sat atop his head. He spoke with a thick East Coast accent and, as Mike would soon learn, was rarely seen wearing anything other than khaki slacks, hiking boots, and a plaid shirt with a wad of pens, papers, and other odds and ends stuffed into his chest pocket.

"Mr. O'Shea, I'm Jason Shapiro, the clinical psychiatrist here on staff. How are you doing?"

Mike looked Dr. Shapiro up and down, trying to decide how to respond. *I'm not talking to any shrink.* Mike gave Dr. Shapiro his most intimidating glare in hopes that he might scare him off. No luck.

"Ah, I heard you were going to be a tough one, you," said Jason, wagging a finger in Mike's direction. "That's okay. You've had a tough go of it. Notice I referred to you as my *partner* and not my patient? That's because we're in this thing together! Don't worry, I'm in no hurry."

Easy for you to say. You may not be in much of a hurry, but I sure as hell am.

"Do you mind if I sit down?"

Mike simply stared. Jason stared back. Something about his eyes caught Mike off guard. He had seen the look before, many times before. *Shrink hell, this guys' a toughie. Probably smack me around if I don't go along with the program. Maybe loosen the brakes on my wheelchair.*

Mike took the dry-erase pen and board and wrote, "Don't need a counselor, therapist, psychologist, or buddy. Just want to get stronger and get the hell out of here." Mike accentuated the period with a loud pop. Jason read the board and smiled.

"I got a call from your boss, a Ms. Jackson. She said you'd be a little resistant, to say the least." Jason rotated his hand back and forth in the universal sign of uncertainty.

"Mr. O'Shea, err, may I call you Michael or Mike?"

Mike gave a uninterested shrug.

"Mike, if you can convince some poor schnook to come pick you up or somehow get out of here under your own steam, you are certainly free to leave. This is no prison, and you're no inmate," Jason said quietly. "You start your physical therapy in a few days, and they really work you here. But for you to be returned whole, you have to strengthen your body *and* mind."

Mike looked away. *Why is this guy still here?*

"I'm pooped. Think I'll finish up some case notes and call it a day. Hey, I heard you're a former fighter. There's a good fight on channel 9 tonight."

Mike wrote, "Thanks" on the board.

"You know, Mike, pardon my French, but this is a pretty fucked-up mess you've found yourself in. I may be able to help you make some sense of it. We're a couple of big city guys. Me from New York, you from Oakland. I think we'll get along good. Think it over."

*****

Over the next few days Mike was examined, poked, probed, and observed by a team of physical therapists, nurses, and the facility's medical director, Dr. Lionel Bettencourt. Bettencourt's days were primarily spent in his office sending out resumés to far more prestigious hospitals than Pacific Dunes and gorging himself on an impressive supply of junk food sequestered in a large desk drawer. Early on, Mike decided he despised Bettencourt intensely. As a fitness devotee, Mike had little use for doctors who put themselves in charge of the health of others but couldn't manage their own.

Dr. Bettencourt attempted to camouflage his impressive girth with a wide array of tailor-made suits and a year-round tan courtesy of a tube of bronzing cream recommended by his hairstylist. The same stylist colored his hair biweekly with "autumn chestnut," a ridiculously bright hue designed to mask even a hint of his premature gray. Dr. Bettencourt's nose, eyes, and mouth appeared two sizes too small, giving him a baby face, which was endearing as a youngster but presently gave him the appearance of one whose head was loitering around with little to do, waiting for his face to catch up.

Despite his girth, Bettencourt moved with surprising grace and ease. Pacific Dunes staff often commented on his impressive way of dropping in on conversations quietly and with no notice, a skill made easier by the soft soles of Bettencourt's $500 Italian loafers. In fact, were it not for the daily liberal dousing of a noxious cologne, he would have the stealth of Hawkeye in Longfellow's classic *Last of the Mohicans*.

During their first meeting, Bettencourt bluntly told Mike that his prognosis was bleak and that in all probability, his next stop would be a specialized care home where Mike could "finish up," a euphemism for decay and die.

"I see you suffer from chronic traumatic encephalopathy because of brain trauma brought on by boxing, rugby, and employment-related injuries," said Bettencourt.

"I was never the sports type in school, too busy getting several degrees. You know how it is."

I wonder if I could get my hands on a steak knife and poke my eye out. It'd be less painful than listening to this pompous ass.

"You are, should I say were, a probation officer," said Bettencourt. The way he said *probation officer* dripped with disdain for anyone who would waste their life working with the unwashed masses. He might as well have said, "I see you scrape the dried turds out of portable toilets for a living."

"Twenty-seven years," Mike wrote on his board.

"Interesting. Do you have to have a college education for a job like that?" asked Bettencourt.

Mike stared in disbelief and slowly grabbed the board. "I have a master's degree in English from the University of California at Berkeley, you ass wipe. Where did you go to school?" wrote Mike.

"No need to get huffy, Mr. O'Shea. I went to school back east. You haven't heard of the university, I'm sure. Very elite," Bettencourt responded as he wrote furiously in Mike's file. Dr. Bettencourt had attended the prestigious Medical School of Aruba, a small institute of higher learning on the Caribbean Island known for accepting low-grade dullards who couldn't get into legitimate medical schools in the United States.

"I sense we've gotten off on the wrong foot. Listen, bud, we've got to work together so we can get you back on your feet and go out and catch the bad guys!" Bettencourt said.

"I've got your lunch and dinner menus, Mr. O'Shea. I think you're going to really like dinner," said Jean DeFord, standing at the door. Mike looked away from Bettencourt and smiled. Jean was dressed in the same colorful hospital scrubs worn the day before, except running shoes replaced the sensible slip-ons favored by most of the Pacific Dune's staff.

"Not now. we're not done here yet. Can't you see that?" Bettencourt snapped.

"I'm really sorry, Doctor. I just thought Mr. O'Shea might be hungry. He didn't eat much breakfast."

"Do you speak English?" Bettencourt dramatically pronounced the word *English* as if he were speaking to someone who actually didn't speak English.

"I'm really sorry, Doctor. I'll come back," said Jean on the verge of tears.

As she placed the menu at his side, Mike gently grabbed Jean's hand, looked up at her face, and winked. He grabbed the menu and studied it intently, anything to make his message to Bettencourt crystal clear. *I'm done with you.*

"I'm sorry, Mr. O'Shea. We have some more tests to complete," whined Bettencourt.

Mike grabbed the board and wrote, "Apologize." Jean shook her head. Bettencourt was furious. Mike raised an eyebrow and cocked his head toward the board.

"We're done for now, Mr. O'Shea. I hope you enjoy the rest of your day," Bettencourt said coolly.

Bettencourt packed up his notes and walked out, brushing past Jean and causing her to step back against a wall to make room for his large frame. The smell of the eye-watering cologne lingered in Mike's room.

"Mr. O'Shea, you didn't have to do that. Dr. Bettencourt doesn't like to be disturbed when he's with a patient. I should have waited, but I thought you'd want to see the menu."

Mike grabbed the writing board. "I did! I'm starved. Thanks."

CHAPTER 15

Three weeks later

"This is Dr. Bettencourt. How may I help you?" he crooned into the phone.

"Dr. Bettencourt, Ken Tallmadge with the California Department of Corrections and Rehabilitation. How are you today, sir?"

Ken Tallmadge had all the charm one would associate with a former county fair barker who spent his college summers hawking Japanese-made kitchen knives with a cheap microphone strapped to his face.

"I'm well, Mr. Tallmadge. What can I do for you?" said Bettencourt suspiciously. Rare was a call to a physician from a prison official.

"Well, I'd like to grab a minute or two of your valuable time. I have a proposal which could benefit both you and your fine facility as well as the State of California."

"I'm a *vitally* busy man, Mr. Talmadge. What exactly would be the subject of this meeting?"

"I'd like to discuss a new state program which could change the way you do business for some time to come," said Ken Talmadge.

Bettencourt sighed as he minimized the computer screen and brought up his calendar. "I am available next Wednesday morning, but as I said, I am a very busy man."

"Dr. Bettencourt, I will be there at 0800 next Wednesday with bells on. See you then!"

Ken Talmadge begun his career as a correctional officer at the infamous San Quentin Prison. His street smarts and gift of gab soon took him out of the San Quentin cellblocks into the dark political world of the California Department of Corrections and Rehabilitation. With his natural sales skills, Ken soon came to the attention of the head of the state prison system. He made Ken the special assistant to the director, an impressive title which allowed Ken to essentially dick around at state expense. Ken's big break came when he learned that a federal grant application he had written had been accepted. The Department of Justice had released almost $1,000,000 to fund employment projects for state prison parolees.

"Here's how it works, Doctor," said Ken in his slickest carney barker voice.

"The state pays half the salary *and* medical coverage of the parolee. Plus your hospital gets a big fat tax break for employing our guys. A sweetheart deal, if you ask me!"

"Let me make sure we're clear on this," said Bettencourt. "All I have to do is pay fifty percent of the salary of one of your miscreants, and the state pays the rest?" Talmadge smiled and nodded. "In addition, the hospital would enjoy a significant reduction of state tax. Is that correct?"

"Correct-O," squealed Ken Talmadge. *This is easier than hawking those crappy Ginsu knives!*

Bettencourt's devious mind was reeling. *This is too good to be true.* "What type of criminals would I need to hire? Can't have any hopheads and perverts around here, you know. This is a highly rated medical facility."

"Absolutely not!" said Ken Talmadge. For effect, he pronounced absolutely "ab-so-lute-ly."

Too good to be true. Just too good to be true. "Mr. Talmadge, I will be in touch," Bettencourt said as he struggled out of his chair.

The two shook hands, a simple act of friendliness regrettable to Talmadge, who realized that he would have to endure the smell of Bettencourt's cologne on his hands during the drive back to his office.

Following the departure of Ken Talmadge, Bettencourt opened his desk drawer, removed a Mars Bar, and consumed it in three bites. As he sat back enjoying the rush of the processed sugar pulsing through his veins and partially clogged arteries, he did some calculations in his head.

At $25,000 a year for low-level staff, I slice a little off the top for myself and who cares? As far as the board of directors knows, this little agreement with the state doesn't exist. Just create enough room to make it worth the risk. Must let a few people go, but it'll be a good time to get rid of some dead wood around here. And it's tax-free!

That night, Bettencourt barely slept. He was too stimulated with greedy anticipation. But he knew for the plan to work, he would have to eliminate any possible prying eyes and appoint himself the acting chief financial officer, in addition to his duties as the chief of medical services. Fortunately for Bettencourt, Pacific Dunes was owned by a faceless corporation based in Indianapolis. If expenses were down and admissions up, the parent corporation paid little interest.

Bettencourt waddled down the hallway toward the administrative wing and the office of Evie Rodgers, the hospital's chief financial officer. Evie was universally beloved by the hospital staff for her grandmotherly manner and dry wit. She had little use for Bettencourt and made her feelings for the man well-known, which further ingratiated her to her colleagues.

Bettencourt stood at an office door that was rarely closed.

"A moment, Evie?" asked Bettencourt in much more of a command than question.

"Sure, Dr. B. Come on in."

"Evie, why do you insist on doing that?" Bettencourt asked with a weary sigh.

"Doing what, Dr. B?"

"Refer to me by my last initial. My name is *Dr. Bettencourt*, not an initial or derivative or some cutesy nickname I *never* authorized you to use."

"I'm sorry, Dr. Bettencourt. It won't happen again."

Bettencourt closed the office door, lowered his rotund body into a chair in front of Evie's desk, and considered his next move.

"Evie, this is a very difficult conversation to have with you. You see, Pacific Dunes is a part of a large corporation based in the Midwest."

Evie stared back at Bettencourt pleasantly, but she knew instinctively what was coming next.

"Evie, with the internet, emailing, Zoom meetings, and online conferences, the world has changed from when you were a young accountant. The people back at the home office handle all our books and...well, there's really no reason for you to be here."

"I figured this day would come sooner or later, Dr. Bettencourt. Just give me a day or so to pack up my things and say my goodbyes and I'll be out of your hair."

Bettencourt smiled. *This is going to be easier than I planned.*

*****

Each day, Mike endured a series of sessions with an endless legion of physical therapists, all of whom seemed sincere in their desire to reteach him to do everything, from combing his hair and brushing his teeth to sitting up and walking. The sessions were brutal. Physically, Mike found himself struggling to perform even the simplest task. As difficult as his new physical regimen was, he also struggled psychologically.

Each afternoon, Dr. Jason Shapiro would wheel Mike out to a bench overlooking the water for discussions about the emotional impact of his stroke. The observations were one-sided, with Mike jotting down single-word responses to Jason's questions on his writing board.

On occasion, Jason let his guard down and shared with Mike his concerns that Dr. Bettencourt was trying to force him out in favor of a younger, less well-paid psychiatrist.

"Fuck fat boy ☺," Mike would write on his board just to see Jason grin. After their second session, Jason grew confident that Mike was clinically depressed and prescribed a low dose of an antidepressant. Mike resisted at first, but with some prodding, he agreed and had to admit that the little red pill he took every morning was helping sweeten his sour disposition.

Both Mike and Jason were dealing with the frustrations, anger, and fear many go through as they grow old in a youth-obsessed culture. This made them natural allies. But what really solidified the friendship was that as a native New Yorker raised in the Williamsburg neighborhood of Brooklyn, Jason was a fierce boxing fan.

"Braddock or Baer?" asked Jason. The two were in their customary spot on a bluff outside the hospital overlooking the water.

"Braddock, of course," Mike wrote.

"Hagler or Hearns?"

Mike rolled his eyes. "Hearns," he wrote.

"Okay, Mr. Smart Guy. Duran or Leonard?"

Mike smiled and wrote "no mas" on the board, as he remembered the once fierce Panamanian boxer Roberto Duran fail to answer the bell with a simple "no mas" in his legendary battle with American fighter Sugar Ray Leonard.

As much as Mike was starting to enjoy Jason's company, he wasn't quite sure how these chats overlooking the ocean were helping him. *Maybe they're not really for me. Maybe the poor guy's lonely and just wants to talk. Guess that's okay.*

Mike grabbed the board and wrote. "Need to get out of my room."

Jason looked at the board and let out a quiet sigh. "I don't blame you. I'd want to get out of this joint too, regardless of our sparkling conversation and my warm companionship," he said with a grin.

Mike shook his head from side to side and wrote, "Not out of hospital. Out of room. Bored. Want some freedom. Help me."

Jason read the board with a perplexed look. "Mike, I'm not sure what you mean. Where exactly do you want to go?"

"I want to get out of my room and roam around a little. Make my *own decisions!*"

"Ah, I get it. You want the freedom to leave your room from time to time and get the lay of the land, so to speak. Is that it?"

"Yes, help me," Mike wrote.

Jason considered Mike's request. He knew that the man in the wheelchair in front of him, a man with essentially one half of a previously well-functioning body, had been making his own decisions for a long time. On top of the physical challenges, Jason knew the psychological dangers of people who spent much time in hospitals. "The professional patient," he called them. They were people who became so accustomed to having things done for them that they simply stopped trying to do anything for themselves and lost all semblance of independence. He wanted to help Mike avoid that syndrome.

"I think it's a good idea, Mike. I'll talk with Dr. Bettencourt."

Mike sighed and shook his head. "You know that dumb fuck isn't going to help me out," he wrote.

"It's a reasonable request. Let me see what I can do," said Jason, trying to muffle a giggle.

A week later, Mike had his wish. Jason had convinced Bettencourt to grant Mike's request. "Convince" wasn't exactly accurate. Jason had waited until just before noon when he knew that Bettencourt would be in a rush to beat the lunch crowd and presented him with a small selection of forms requiring his signature. Without looking at what he was doing, Bettencourt signed his name to Mike's freedom ticket. At least freedom from his room from time to time.

"Mr. O'Shea is authorized to use a wheelchair to go on unescorted excursions around the interior of the facility only," read the form on hospital letterhead. Knowing that this was an unorthodox directive, Jason placed a copy in Mike's file and gave him the original to keep in his pocket.

"It's a hall pass of sorts. Have fun, and remember, these doors all have alarms on them."

"I'll be good. Thanks," Mike wrote on the board.

CHAPTER 16

Mike lay in bed staring at the ceiling. *Nice to have a private room. Iggy must have pulled some strings to keep me with no cellie.* He looked around. Tommy had plastered the wall directly in front of his bed with photos, newspaper articles, and other memorabilia from Mike's career with the probation department. Iggy had placed a framed photo of the two of them at a San Francisco Giants game so many years past. Iggy dressed like the tackiest of tacky tourists and Mike, a chagrined smile on his handsome young face, looked so optimistic as if he had the whole world at his door, which, of course, he did. Next to that photo was an old fight bill from one of Mike's early bouts in the Bay Area Golden Gloves tournament, announcing the appearance of "Irish Mike O'Shea." Little did the promoters know that Mike was a full-blooded Native American. Not an ounce of real Irish blood flowed through Irish Mike's veins. But the moniker looked good on the flyer.

The hospital itself seemed to be well-run. The food was exceptional, and the exercise facility rivaled any modern fitness club. The Pacific Dunes Rehabilitation Hospital was indeed on the Pacific, and Mike could hear the surf when his window was open. Like most buildings in the area, the facility had a modern Spanish-style look with terra-cotta roof tiles and an adobe-colored exterior. But as hard as they tried, it was still a hospital and smelled like any other hospital he had been in. *Piss and disinfectant.*

Mike continued to scan his room and saw something new on a small bulletin board next to his clothes closet. It looked like an ad from a newspaper someone had cut out and pinned on the board: "The Law Office of Shapiro, Shapiro, Shapiro, and Shapiro Proudly Announces the Grand Opening of Their New North County Office."

Shapiros' trying to drum up business for his kids. Rare was a conversation with Jason that didn't mention his late wife, Elise, and their four grown children, all attorneys. The law office of Shapiro, Shapiro, Shapiro, and Shapiro was legendary in the Serra legal community. The senior Shapiro missed his beloved wife, but his grief was blunted by his intense pride for his children's success.

"They're the one-stop shop of attorneys. One for crooks, one for corporations, another for wills and estates, and the last for taxes. How can you go wrong with such wonderful lawyers?" Jason would often ask with obvious pride.

Mike smiled and imagined his therapist pinning up the ad while he slept. *Time for a ride.* He went about the long and painful process of swinging his legs to one side of his bed and pulling himself upright with the help of what looked like a gymnastic bar mounted above his bed. Fortunately, Mike had retained much of his impressive upper body strength despite the stroke, which made the process of lowering himself into the chair difficult but possible. After two weeks of painful physical therapy, he had regained the ability to move his arms sufficiently to operate a manual wheelchair. Mike eased himself out of his room and turned right down the long hallway, nodding amiably to staff and patients along the way.

Shapiro's happy pills must be working. A few weeks ago, I wanted to kill them all.

As much as they tried to make Pacific Dunes palatable to visitors, Mike couldn't get beyond the incredibly sad shape of the other patients. All were either brain injured or stroke victims. Most were incontinent (something Mike had fortunately been able to avoid). Only a handful could walk without assistance, and some had lost complete cognitive functioning. Some nights, Mike lay awake with the television blaring just to drown out the moans and senseless meanderings of some of the patients. One poor soul, a Vietnam

War veteran named Nate assigned to the room across from Mike, was convinced that an ancient Filipino night custodian, Luis, was a North Vietnamese conscript, bound and determined to shove a Chinese-made grenade right up "Old Nate's ass." Nate had a habit of speaking in the third person, which Mike found endearing.

"Keep away from Nate, you commie motherfucker!" he would scream from his room, causing Mike to elevate the audio on his TV. *Hope Nate minds his Ps and Qs and doesn't try to shank Luis. What the hell's gonna happen to that poor fool? No way he's ever getting out of some type of hospital or care home. Sad.*

As Mike wheeled himself from his room, he saw Nate in a chair in the hallway screaming obscenities at anyone who would listen. Mike maintained a "live and let live" attitude as much as anyone, but even *he* thought some room time for Nate might be in order.

He looked over Nate's shoulder and saw Luis pushing a large red garbage can on a rolling platform down the hallway. Biohazard symbols on the can identified the contents as a variety of unpleasant items synonymous with any medical facility. Luis wore his constant smile and, despite the task of cleaning up after people who couldn't do the job for themselves, maintained a good-natured disposition. He had seen the boxing poster in Mike's room and often brought Mike copies of *Ring Magazine*. Luis was a rabid devotee of the Filipino fighter Manny Pacquiao and enjoyed regaling him with summaries of his past fights.

"Good to see you out of bed," Luis said. Mike smiled and gave the thumbs up with his right hand.

Nate turned toward Luis, a look of terror and intense hostility draped his face.

"Ah, Charlie fuckin' VC's here. Come outta of his rathole to murder, rape, and spread his commie sewage around, I see!"

Mike looked at Luis and winked. Luis smiled and went about his business. Mike wheeled over to Nate and stuck out his hand, which Nate accepted hesitantly.

"Gooks all over this fuckin' base, Marine. Stay alert," Nate warned.

Nate, you're possibly the most insane person I've ever met, and given my employment history, that's impressive.

This night, Nate's rants were especially loud and bizarre. In his twisted world, the Viet Cong had just forced the evacuation of the American embassy in Hanoi.

"The bastards left Nate in the jungle to live off rats!" he screamed.

Nate was back to his hijinks a few nights later. Out of a desire to get a break from Nate and take advantage of his newfound independence, Mike decided it was time for a "walk." He glanced at the side of his bed and, seeing that the wheelchair had been removed, rang a buzzer. Mike despised having his wheelchair removed from his room but also understood that it was unreasonable for the hospital to have a wheelchair for every patient. Despite the humiliation of once again being dependent on another, Mike had learned to be patient with delayed responses to his request.

Lots of people here way worse off than me. But on this evening, the wait seemed especially long. Feeling like a kid who gets his hopes up to go to the circus only to have the trip cancelled, he turned back to his TV and hoped Nate might settle down for the night.

"Whasup?" Mike looked toward the door and saw a young man in the white uniform of a hospital orderly. *Must be new. Looks like a bit of a hard ass. What's this guy's story?*

"I said whasup?" repeated the young man, now with a hard edge in his voice.

"What, you can't talk? Cat got your tongue?"

Yeah, that's it, you fuckin' retard. The cat's got my tongue. Where'd they get this winner? Mike asked himself.

He was about twenty-five, white, fair complexion, muscular build, brown hair. *Looks like he might have spent some time in a weight room.* His hair was shaved on the side and slicked back on top in an odd military style, although Mike doubted he had ever been near the military. A silver medallion of a dollar sign hung from a thick chain around his neck. *Classy.* His name tag said Simpson. Mike looked at his bare forearms, two tattoos on each. The initials WAN in Old English lettering was on his right arm. Mike immediately recognized it as signifying affiliation with the White Aryan Nation prison gang.

On his left, the happy/sad theater masks and the words Laugh Now, Cry Later beneath them. Just below his left eye were three small dots forming a triangle. All the tattoos were synonymous with one who has embraced a street gang lifestyle.

Fuck me. They got a gangster working here. Great. Where's Luis? He'll run this punk outta here. Hell with Luis. I'll tell ole Nate the kid's a VC spy and he'll do the dirty work for me.

"Hey, old-timer. If you ain't gonna talk, I ain't gonna stay." The orderly turned and left the room. Mike stared at the door in disbelief. *Work with criminals all my life, end up here, and it's like I'm back on the street.*

*****

Mike was deep in sleep, assisted by yet more of Jason's "happy pills." He had a strange sensation that his breathing wasn't normal, almost as if his nostrils were somehow clogged. As he slowly awoke and adjusted his eyes, he saw a familiar face a few inches from his. It was a large man with a sheen of oil on his face. His breath was foul, a combination of rum, cigarettes, coffee, and generally poor oral hygiene. As Mike's head cleared, he realized that the man had grabbed his nose and squeezed his nostrils shut. *What the hell?*

Mike grabbed the man's wrist and. with a twist, broke the grip on his nose. The man stood back with a cruel smile which seemed familiar. He was tall, looked to Mike to be six foot three and change, and over three hundred pounds, mostly flab but at one time perhaps something else. The most frightening thing about Mike's late night visitor was that he wore the uniform of a Pacific Dunes security guard. Mike tried to make sense of it all. Over the breast of his shiny black jacket with an artificial fur collar, Mike saw an embroidered patch and a name tag.

No…you gotta be shittin' me! The name on the tag brought clarity to the weird scene. It read "Troop." *Richard fuckin' Troop is a security guard in my hospital!*

Mike stared into Troop's bloodshot eyes, not sure whether to panic, cry, or laugh at the ironic course his life had suddenly taken.

146

Richard Troop is out of the joint and working in this hospital. Is this a sick joke, Lord?

"You don't look so happy to see me, O'Shea. What the hell happened to you?" he asked gleefully.

Mike attempted to order Troop out of his room, but all that came out were guttural murmurs.

"Yep, I got paroled last month, O'Shea. Paid my debt to society, and here I am!"

Mike wondered how difficult it might be to convince Tommy to bring his gun down from his apartment. Not much chance of that. *He'd think I'd use it on myself.*

"We're gonna have loads of fun, O'Shea. Every night I'll have something special for you." Troop sat on the side of Mike's bed like he owned *it* and the rest of the hospital.

"My parole agent got me this job thanks to the boss, Bettencourt. I hear he gets a sweet kickback for every parolee he hires, so don't get any stupid ideas about tryin' to get me canned. I'm like the boss's own little piggy bank!"

Troop flicked Mike's nose with his index finger. He waited until the timing was just right, opened his mouth, and clamped down on Troop's finger until he tasted blood. Troop tried to jerk his finger back and squealed. With his free hand, Troop balled his fist and, with the full force of his girth behind it, landed a punch on the tip of Mike's nose. An explosion of blood started to soak the bedsheets and Mike's T-shirt. He released Troop's finger and spit blood all over his former probationer's uniform.

"You fucker. I'll kill you!" Troop snarled and brought his fist back for a second blow. This one landed just above Mike's right eye. Fortunately, the hospital bed absorbed some of the blow but landed with sufficient force for Mike to lose consciousness. Troop leaned toward Mike, wondering if he was still alive.

"Sleep tight, my little bitch. I'll pay you another visit tomorrow night."

Troop grabbed a towel from a hook inside of the closet by Mike's bed and wrapped it around his finger. He looked at his watch. The face read two thirty in the morning. The hospital would be quiet, except for some nurses and Luis the janitor. He slowly opened the door and looked down the hallway. Nothing. Troop quietly slipped out, closing the door behind him. He walked quickly to a parallel corridor, putting as much distance between him and Mike's room as possible.

"Hey, babe, got a bandage for Big Richey?" Troop asked the nurse sitting at a computer workstation in the center of the corridor. "Went out to get some cigs from my ride and slammed my finger in the door. Can you believe it?"

Nurse Marina Santos, who, like almost every other member of the Pacific Dunes staff, had taken an instant dislike to Troop, eyed his bloody finger suspiciously. She took a step back to avoid his smell. *I've got to move to days. I can't stand working on the same shift with this pig.* Marina rose from her chair, ducked into a small closet, and returned with a roll of gauze and some adhesive tape.

"Fix it yourself, and no smoking in the hospital," Rebecca said, disgust dripping from each word. "And my name's Nurse Santos, not *babe*."

Troop sneered and grabbed the supplies. "No problem, babe. I'll be down in the security office if you need me." Troop started to walk away. He turned and looked back at Marina. "You know, babe, if you'd lose a few pounds off that fat ass of yours, maybe you could get a job in a real hospital instead of this dump. Just some career advice."

Marina stared in disbelief. She turned back to her computer clicked on "New," typed in the name of Holly Christie, the Pacific Dune's nursing supervisor, moved the cursor down to the topic line, and typed in, "Complaint—Inappropriate Comment."

*****

"Dr. Bettencourt, I am outraged," said Holly Christie, the hospital nursing director. "This security guard, Mr. Troop, has been here for not even a week, and he's making the most outrageous comments toward one of my nurses."

Bettencourt took the email from Holly's hand and read it. He was more than slightly intimidated by the head nurse, who stood defiantly before him and had to remind himself that *he* was the boss here.

"Well, I agree. This is a bit beyond the pale, isn't it?" stammered Bettencourt.

"Beyond the pale?" asked Holly with disbelief. "Are you kidding me?"

"Ms. Christie, I wish to point out that this is all hearsay. We have no witnesses, and in the interest of fairness, we must consider both sides here," said Bettencourt, regaining some of his bravado.

"Are you nuts? Rebecca's one of my most credible nurses. You're going to accept the word of that sleazy rent-a-cop over her?"

Bettencourt reread the email. *Need to handle this delicately.* "I agree, Ms. Christie. This is a very serious accusation. I will conduct a full investigation into Mr. Troop's alleged behavior."

Bettencourt was feeling his old arrogant self and enjoyed regaining command.

"Fine," said Holly with absolutely no confidence that Bettencourt would do anything. "May I ask to be advised of the outcome of your investigation?"

"Oh, you can ask all you want, but as you know...or should know, this is now a confidential personnel matter, and as such, you are not privy to the outcome," said Bettencourt, now back fully in control.

Holly stared into Bettencourt's chinless face. *Why is he trying to cover for this asshole?*

"Now, Ms. Christie," said Bettencourt. "We both have important tasks before us, and I suggest you return to work and allow me to get back to the business of running this hospital."

"Thank you for your time, Dr. Bettencourt," said Holly, feeling much worse leaving Bettencourt's office than she had entering.

CHAPTER 17

"My God, Michael, what happened to you?" asked Iggy, looking at Mike's swollen nose and black eye. The priest visited his surrogate son several times a week, usually bringing down a Danish from Mike's favorite bakery, a copy of the *Serra Tribune*, and mail from his apartment. Ordinarily, the trips were routine, but as soon as Iggy saw Mike's face, he knew something serious had happened.

Mike grabbed the dry-erase board. "Got out of bed last night and took a header goin' to pee. Look worse than I feel.☺"

"Listen to me, Michael. That's the same bullshit grin you use to try on me when you were a kid and got caught out screwin' around. Now what happened?" Iggy demanded.

"Told you. Fell on way to b-room…cool your jets, big guy," Mike wrote on the board. He and Iggy stared at each other for a moment. Both knew Mike was lying, both knowing the *other* knew Mike was lying. Iggy sighed and pulled the Danish from a small bag, which Mike devoured. He gave Iggy a thumbs up. Iggy had spent enough time on the streets of Oakland to know when he was being conned. He also knew that once Mike made up his mind to keep a secret, it was going to remain kept.

"Hey, did you see the Giants last night?" Iggy asked.

Mike grabbed his pen and wrote, "Fell asleep at the bottom of 7th. What was final?"

"Eight to nothing…swept the series. Always nice to beat the Dodgers," said Iggy.

Mike grabbed the board. "Spring me from this dump and we'll go up to SF for a game!"

"You know why that'll never happen, lad?" asked Iggy, grinning. "Because you would never allow yourself to be tormented by four hours of my *alleged* bad driving."

Mike pulled the sheet over his eyes and rotated his hands as if he was steering a car.

"Be nice to me, Michael, or I'll buy you discount diapers when you get out of here!"

Mike giggled and realized that it had been some time since he had laughed. Iggy took notice. *His laugh sounds like my Michael. How long until he's speaking? Small miracles*, Iggy thought.

"What's going on in here? A strategy session of my two favorite Papists?" came the booming voice of Jason Shapiro. Jason and Iggy had become swift friends, partially out of their common affection for Mike but also from the mutual admiration and respect that came from two learned men who had an equal part of intellect and street smarts. Jason walked over to Mike's bed and gasped.

"What the hell happened to you?"

Mike shrugged and tilted his head toward Iggy.

"Good question, Doc. Michael says he fell going to the head, but I'm suspicious," said Iggy.

Jason and Iggy stared at each other, knowing that there was more to the story but also understanding that knowing Mike, they would probably never hear it.

"Oh, I almost forgot. I got a letter for you, Mike," said Jason, fishing a small envelope from his pocket. "From your friend, Sylvia Almeida."

Mike took the envelope and noticed there were no postage markings. It had apparently been hand delivered. Sylvia had been to the hospital. *No way I'm gonna let her see me like this. Nope.*

Iggy snapped his fingers. "Hey, Mike. Forgot to mention to you that I met with Coach Almeida a few weeks ago. She came to the rectory looking for me. Wanted to know about your condition.

Said she's been writing, but you never wrote back. She said she drove down and tried to get in to see you but that you weren't allowed to have visitors."

Mike looked irritated. *She hasn't heard from me and won't until I'm home and back to normal. She comes here and I become her newest charity case.* Mike regretted the thought. He and Sylvia had been dating exclusively up until his stroke. He was touched by her unanswered letters and refused visits but was adamant that she not see him in his present condition.

"A love interest, eh?" said Jason. "Hmm, the plot of the Michael O'Shea story thickens."

"Jason, you don't know the half of it!" gushed Iggy. "Sylvia is a fantastic woman. Just the type to keep our boy here in his place. And as a bonus, she's a strong Catholic girl from Brazil, of all places!"

Mike looked at Jason and Iggy with disgust. *Just what I need. Two old geezers meddling in my love life.* Mike grabbed the whiteboard. "What did you tell her??"

"I told you, she came to the rectory wanting some information about you. We've been meeting for coffee and breakfast ever since," said Iggy. "Mike, she is a real peach. Just perfect for you, and she cares very deeply about your welfare…I can tell!"

Jason's eyes were as wide as Mike had ever seen them. "Well, this *is* getting interesting," he said.

"In fact," said Iggy, "she invited me to become the team chaplain for the women's volleyball team. Isn't that great?"

"Not really," Mike wrote on the white board. "Stay away from collegiate sports. All mob controlled and they'll end up wackin' my favorite priest!"

*****

Fortunately for Mike, he had been able to get through his last four months at Pacific Dunes without having to move to a double room. This would be a key component in the plan he had slowly developed following the attack by Troop. The plan started to solidify when Mike was out for his "evening rounds," as the staff called his slow walks around the hospital. Walking wasn't entirely accurate. With the assistance of a heavy-duty walker and the sweat and persistence of Mike and his team of physical therapists, the wheelchair had been scuttled, and he was now able to get around on foot. One step forward with his right foot and then a drag of his left. Fortunately, his upper body strength made the use of the walker relatively simple.

Hard work, but it beats the shit outta the wheelchair. Mike's workouts were showing dividends. His balance, coordination, and muscle tone were significantly improving.

As was his routine, Mike looked in on Nate, and if he was awake, he plopped down in the chair by his bed for a quick game of dominoes. His speech had made slower progress than the rest of his body, so the conversations were rather one-sided. Nate still warned Mike to "watch out for Charlie," but his new medication had made him more lucid and less paranoid.

Mike let out a slow and slurred "Night, Nate. See ya next day." *Next day* had become Mike's way of saying *tomorrow*, which, for reasons unknown to his speech therapist, was more difficult because of his brain trauma. He used this technique with other words he struggled with. *Probably* was another challenge, which became *good chance*, and *temperature* was *hot/cold time*. It frustrated Mike that he was unable to master *all* the words in his vocabulary, but he had learned to use his substitutions with relative ease, so most people just thought he had a slightly odd way of stringing words together.

From Nate's room, Mike shuffled along the corridor and past Luis, who, as always, gave Mike a high five as they passed. For variety, Mike tried to change his routine each evening, which had made him familiar with the nurses and orderlies throughout the hospital. Mike refused to allow the presence of Richard Troop alter his excursions through the hospital.

Not gonna live in fear of that serpent. One part of Pacific Dunes Mike hadn't yet visited was the "C" unit or Critical Care Unit. This ten-room section of the hospital housed the most debilitated patients and was generally off-limits to those more ambulatory. The double fire door with the prominent "Authorized Staff Only" sign was opened. Mike stared down the long corridor. *What the hell, I'll just say I was lost.*

As Mike slowly made his way down the corridor, he saw that most of the doors were closed except for one near the end of the hall. He peeked in and saw a single bed with the form of a young boy lying face up, with a ventilator and air mask attached to his face by small rubber straps. The boy, no more than thirteen or fourteen, had a serene expression that came from severe brain damage suffered in an accident riding an all-terrain vehicle at the nearby River Beach Dunes, a mecca for off-roaders from all over California. Mike stepped into the boy's room. "Vasquez, Jamie" was written on a board directly in front of the bed, along with a list of medications and directions to the nursing staff. He stepped closer. *My God, he's just a kid.*

Mike stared into Jamie's face. His eyes were open, looking straight ahead, and he had an upturned mouth suggesting a bit of a smile. He had no training in head trauma (despite his own impressive history), so he could only wonder what, if anything, Jamie was thinking.

Mike walked toward the door and peered into the hallway. He noticed that the door to the room directly across from the boy's room wasn't completely closed and was slowly beginning to open. *Shit, get back into the kid's room quick!* Mike grabbed the door handle as he took a few steps back and flattened himself against the wall. The door was open just enough for him to peek out. As he did, he saw a man step from the room and look up and down the hall.

The man didn't look like anyone who had any business being alone with a critical care patient. It was Simpson, the first of Bettencourt's cadre of parolee/employees Mike had met a few weeks earlier when he asked for a wheelchair. Simpson looked down the hallway to the right and then left, straightened his clothes, and walked quickly toward the main part of the hospital. As Simpson walked away, Mike poked his head out of the room just in time to see him pull up the zipper of his pants.

What the hell? When he was relatively sure Simpson was gone, Mike stepped across the hallway and quietly opened the door to the room Simpson had just emerged from. He stared in disbelief and then tried to swallow the bile which was trying to escape from his stomach. A lone bed was placed in the center of the room. On her back lay what appeared to be a woman in her eighties, the same blank stare on her face as Jamie Vasquez in the room next door.

CHAPTER 18

Five months later

Harold Lamar Davis was born in Paso Adobe, Serra County's second largest city to the north. His parents moved to the area after his father was discharged following World War II, where he served as a private first class in the Marine Corps and saw action in the Pacific Theater. Harold's father, Harold Sr., got a job as a porter on the Southern Pacific Railroad after being honorably discharged in 1946. He married and raised a family of five girls and one son while living in Paso Adobe's "Adobe Park," a low-income former military housing complex on the city's poor northeast side.

Harold thrived under his father's discipline and mother's natural inclination to spoil her "baby boy." His athletic prowess and academic achievements made him a blue-chip recruit to the University of California, Los Angeles, where he earned a bachelor of arts degree in criminal justice and was a member of the world-renowned UCLA track team.

Upon graduation, Harold was hired by the Los Angeles Police Department, where he graduated near the top of his academy class. In the fall of 1984, legendary Police Chief Daryl Gates pinned a Patrol Officer badge on Harold's chest. His parents and sisters were in the audience, proud beyond belief. Harold quickly established himself and was promoted up the ranks. Thirty-two years later, he found himself in the enviable position of being retirement age. Oddly, as his fellow retirees were planning their escapes to hunting and fishing lodges in places like Idaho and Montana, Harold just wasn't quite finished.

Harold had never married. He enjoyed being single, especially as a cop in Los Angeles, a town where being a police officer could still open social doors locked to the rest of the population. He tried retirement. But Harold Davis was bored and still yearned for the chase, maybe not quite as intense as the chases of his days as a young officer but something more than dipping a fishing line off the end of the Santa Monica Pier.

Harold had another problem. His five sisters. Despite their age, he was their little brother, and they obsessively focused on finding him a wife. Their mission stood a better chance of success, of course, if Harold lived closer to the family home in northern Serra County. Marjorie, the Davis oldest daughter, had a solution. The Mussel Shores Police Department had a vacancy. Harold was bored with his retirement in Los Angeles, and Mussel Shores was just a nudge away from Paso Adobe.

What the heck. Fill out the application and see what happens, Harold thought. Fortunately, the Mussel Shores Police Chief, like many Serra County police chiefs, had a historical connection to the LAPD and immediately recognized Harold's bona fides as a "real cop." Harold was hired on the spot.

At the chief's insistence, Harold was hired as a detective and not as an entry-level patrol officer in deference to his thirty-plus years in law enforcement. As part of a two-detective Bureau of Investigations, Harold shared a small windowless office with his partner, Rebecca Santiago. Rebecca was thirty-two, had never worked anywhere other than in Mussel Shores, and possessed an abundance of hubris. Despite her bravado and confidence, Harold had to admit that there was something endearing about Rebecca. While she refused to acknowledge that he had anything to teach her (in Rebecca's closed mind, she had learned virtually all there was to know about police work as a young officer in her twenties), from time to time, she caught Harold off guard by asking for his opinion.

Harold stared at the small stack of reports taken by patrol officers. They were screened and then referred for follow-up investigation. After reviewing the reports, they identified those they could work solo and those that required they work in tandem.

"Got a slight problem, Pops," said Rebecca. She had taken to calling Harold *Pops*, which he begrudgingly allowed. *Guess it's an improvement over Gramps*, Harold thought.

"Personal or professional?" Harold had also become Rebecca's confidant and adviser and often found himself providing her with advice in various areas, from her inability to find a decent partner to how to best plan for her retirement.

"Professional. But I *would* like to chat about this guy I met last weekend. Looks promising, but he has two daughters in their teens, and I'm not sure if I'm ready for that," said Rebecca.

Harold shook a spindly finger in Rebecca's direction. "Remember what I told you, young lady. No settling." Harold tapped his forehead. "You marry a single father of teens who takes fatherhood seriously and you'll always be on the second team, *always*."

"I know, I know," said Rebecca.

"Okay. Now the professional problem. What you got?" asked Harold.

"NTF op," said Rebecca. "Could take me outta circulation for a couple of weeks."

As the Mussel Shores Police Department's representative on the county Narcotics Task Force, Rebecca was often called upon to work with narcotics officers from other departments on a multiagency team.

Unlike most of his younger counterparts, Harold had little interest in the activities of the Narcotics Task Force. He had worked drug assignments extensively in Los Angeles and simply found the constant surveillance and wiretap monitoring a little tedious. But he appreciated that this kind of work was still new and exciting to young investigators like Rebecca and was happy to pick up the slack during her absences. The two made plans to get together later in the week, and Rebecca stood and opened an old filing cabinet in the corner of the office. She pulled out a black ballistic vest and made her way to the door.

"Sorry to leave you high and dry at the last minute like this," she said.

"No problem. Go have fun but be careful."

As Rebecca turned toward the door to leave, Harold called out, "Hey."

"If you really like this fella and choose to disregard my wise counsel and go out with him, you'd make a hell of a mom," said Harold.

"Thanks, Pops."

*****

Since his arrival six months earlier, Mike had begun living two lives as a Pacific Dunes patient. The first was that of a stroke victim, who, despite the attention of a top-notch team of physicians, physical therapists, and of course, Dr. Jason Shapiro, seemed to have plateaued with his progress. In fact, much to the confusion and dismay of his treatment team, Mike was deteriorating. Although his primary physician had initially noted in his file that Mike's prognosis was "Excellent," that had been amended to "Guarded," and then downgraded to "Poor." Up until recently, his strength and fitness level had increased to the point where the treatment team was beginning to discuss his discharge and return home.

But within weeks, Mike's condition dropped to a level *below* that of his admission. He was barely able to load a scoop of food onto the therapeutic spoon, which now needed to be strapped to his hand. Mike's evening strolls aided with a walker were a thing of the past. He had returned to a wheelchair and rarely got out of bed. In fact, Mike had all but given up on the rigorous physical therapy sessions he had come to enjoy and which would have given him the strength to ultimately return to his apartment and resume some semblance of normalcy. Progress made regaining his voice was all but gone. Iggy was a wreck and called Jason daily. Jason had begrudgingly become

Iggy's de facto therapist as he tried to cope with Mike's deteriorating condition.

Tommy Sagapalu could barely witness his best friend in such a state. Once a week, Tommy drove Iggy down to Pacific Dunes for a visit with Mike, only to sit in the car sobbing, unable to accompany Iggy. Sylvia Almeida had accepted Mike's rejection and immersed herself in coaching women's volleyball at Cal Coastal University. Chief Probation Officer Cheryl Jackson, to her credit, continued to be the emotional rock of the small group who made up Mike's "family." She dutifully visited Mike every other day and made a point to ask his advice on various aspects of departmental operation. Mike recognized what was going on and appreciated Cheryl's strategy to keep him linked to his pre-stroke life.

Mike had deteriorated in other ways. He had started soiling his bed, was wearing adult diapers, and needed help in washing himself. All in all, Mike's general physical state had gone all to hell...*during the day.*

Always a night owl, Mike only slightly adjusted his sleep patterns. For most of the day, he slept or dozed with the television on. The nursing staff woke Mike to feed and bathe him, and there was serious talk of moving him to a more acute care facility. But things were different after ten o'clock when the evening shift was replaced by the overnight shift. Mike had been a patient at Pacific Dunes long enough to realize that safety checks were conducted by the nurses on the half hour, meaning every thirty minutes, someone poked their head in his room and, with a small penlight, made sure he was safe and documented the visit on a dry-erase board which hung the door. These checks occurred like clockwork. A testament to the dedication of the Pacific Dunes staff.

All the better for me, Mike thought.

Mike tucked himself in and gave the impression of having fallen into a deep sleep a few minutes before eleven o'clock. As expected, a nurse checked on him soon after, noted that he was asleep, and moved on to the next patient. As soon as the nurse closed his door, Mike sat up, threw his legs to the side of the mattress, and slowly stood under his own power. He had learned that these first moments were critical. After lying in bed all day and into the evening, Mike had to grow accustomed to standing and moving around. *Got to remember I'm still a damn stroke patient.*

Mike slowly rotated his head from side to side and then in small circles to work out the kinks in his neck. *Feels good.*

Slowly, he lowered himself down to the floor on the side of the bed opposite the door. If the nurse unexpectedly came back, he would simply moan, giving the impression that he had fallen out of bed. Mike stared up at the ceiling, the outline of an overhead light barely distinguishable in the dark. For the next twenty-five minutes, he performed the same series of calisthenics (albeit modified) he had done since his days as one of Iggy's youth boxers. Sit-ups, push-ups, knee bends, and a variety of stretching exercises. At ten minutes until midnight, he stepped into the small bathroom and wiped the sweat from his torso. Then back into bed in time for the next nurse's check.

Mike had hidden two gallon jugs of distilled water in his closet. Squaring his feet, he began a series of upper body resistance exercises with the water jugs. Mike was nowhere near his pre-stroke level of fitness but was impressive, especially for a man who gave the impression he would need constant care for the rest of his life. This routine went on until three or four in the morning, until he wiped himself down for the last time and climbed back into bed.

*****

Once a week, his treatment team met to discuss his progress, or lack thereof. A physical therapist spoke up first.

"I'm really stumped. For the first few months, he attacked his PT like a madman...I mean, really dedicated. Now I'm getting nothing out of him. In fact, he's completely tanked," said the therapist. "Also, and this is really weird, his muscle tone has *increased* when it should have decreased. Mr. O'Shea is building muscle when what he has should be atrophied."

A staff physician stared at Mike's lab results, including a recent CT scan and a complete blood panel. "His lab work and CT scan shows increased functioning. If anything, he's improved to the point where we should be looking at transitional care and then home."

As always, Jason Shapiro waited to hear the input of the other team members and then spoke up.

"Okay, let me get this straight," said Jason in his thick Brooklyn accent. "We have a patient who suffers a stroke. Makes amazing progress just by the sheer will of his pain-in-the-ass personality, and then about two months ago, not only starts to decline but he's also in full retreat, right?"

The group nodded a collective yes.

After a prolonged silence, Jason simply said, "I guess we need to find out what happened two months ago."

*****

The use of a walker was out of the question, so Jason used the assistance of one of the burly Pacific Dunes orderlies to get Mike out of bed and into a wheelchair.

"Thanks. I'll take it from here," Jason told the orderly.

It was a picture-perfect midsummer day in Mussel Shores. A "Chamber of Commerce Day," the locals called it. The historically mild summer had passed, and it was, climatically speaking, smooth sailing until the rains of December. As he maneuvered the wheelchair down the corridor, Jason noticed that Mike was dramatically leaning to his left side, the side most impacted by the stroke. *That's something new.* Jason wheeled Mike into a small courtyard adjacent to the hospital dining hall.

"Nice out here, Mike. The sun will do you good," said Jason as he stared at Mike and tried to make some sense of his condition.

"Not gonna bullshit you, guy. You've really backslid, laid a giant turd right in the middle of your progress, and the powers that be can't figure out what's up," said Jason.

Mike just stared ahead blankly. Slowly, he allowed his head to veer to his left until it was almost parallel with the ground. Jason gently tried to bring him upright in his chair.

"You're listing to the port side there, skipper," Jason said nervously, not knowing what to make of his favorite patient's condition.

"Mike, the docs and the therapists can't figure out what the hell happened to you. You were the top star around here, and suddenly, you go south," said Jason with a touch of urgency in his voice.

Mike had shifted his upper body to the left, only now he started to slide completely out of the chair. *Ought to get an Academy Award for this*, he thought.

Jason jumped up and tried to position Mike upright, to no avail. Now he was leaning forward as if he had lost *all* control of his body. Jason grabbed Mike to keep him from falling completely out of his chair. Not sure what to do, perplexed despite his years of experience and training, Jason held him like a parent would hold a sick child. Mike felt bad for Jason.

The poor goof really cares about me. If I was gonna report what I've seen, it would probably be to him. Nope. I'll take this one alone, Doc.

CHAPTER 19

Harold had just tapped the snooze button on his alarm clock for the third time. *All my buddies from the LAPD are retired, living with their third or sometimes fourth wives, and working on their golf swing. Why am I still on the job?*

The answer was easy, of course. Harold had no wife or children, no grandchildren, no pets, not even a house plant. He never had the time to find a suitable spouse and had enjoyed the freedom of single life. Harold also had no *real* hobbies. He enjoyed walking on the beach (which was just a few blocks from his condo). He liked to watch sports on his massive big-screen TV, dabbled in Italian cooking, read historical fiction, and fantasized about opening a snow cone stand on the beach.

Every four months, Harold would drive to Las Vegas for a reunion with some of his old law enforcement colleagues referred to as the "Fuzz That Wuz." Other than that, his primary time consumer and the source of intellectual stimulation was as a police detective in the small beach town. He loved his sisters, of course, but tolerated them and their respective spouses in small doses. Harold enjoyed being a cop and being around other cops. With his pension from the LAPD, his salary as a part-time detective in Mussel Shoals was just his fun money.

Harold slowly slipped out of the sheets and, after sitting on the side of his bed, trudged to the bathroom. While the shower water warmed, he stared into the mirror above the sink. Harold's skin was without wrinkles despite his closing in on his sixty-second birthday. His hair was cropped short but still full, now sprinkled with gray. The most prominent feature of the detective's face was an impressive array of light brown freckles. *Must have been a damn Irishman in the family tree.* Just as he was about to step into the steaming shower, Harold heard the familiar tone of his cell phone.

"Davis," Harold spoke into the receiver.

"Pops, it's Rebecca."

"Good morning, young lady. How are you this fine day?"

"One-eighty-seven at Pacific Dunes Hospital last night. Staff member," said Rebecca, using the penal code section for a murder. Like most officers, Rebecca used a kind of "pigeon English" when talking about crime and criminals.

"Let me get dressed and I'll meet you at the hospital in thirty."

As usual, Harold was nattily dressed in soft leather loafers, slacks, a silk shirt, and sport coat. As a plainclothes detective, he resisted the khakis and polo shirt look of the younger officers. He pulled his truck into a visitor's spot in the sprawling parking lot and walked toward the main entrance. Hundreds of feet of crime scene tape blocked off entrances, and several uniformed officers stood nearby chatting quietly.

"Morning, fellas. Rebecca around?"

"Should be right inside the main door, Pops," replied one of the officers.

Harold strolled through the front door with all the ease and casualness of one of the many tourists he saw on the beach during his morning walks. Murder investigations were not unique to Harold. When he retired, the Los Angeles City Council presented him with a proclamation which, among other niceties, stated that during his thirty years of service, Harold had been involved in investigating over three hundred murder cases. Harold always questioned that figure. *But it's a nice round number, and why allow the facts to ruin a good proclamation?* he often thought.

Rebecca was talking to a front desk receptionist who was clearly shaken.

Harold waited for a lull in the conversation and strode over to Rebecca. "What you got?"

"Employee found this morning in a laundry room by a janitor. Strangulation. Maybe six to seven hours ago. Lab techs are with the body," said Rebecca in an even monotone.

Harold and Rebecca walked down the hall to the hospital laundry room. Crime scene investigators from the sheriff's office scurried around in green lab coats. Mussel Shoals was far too small a community to support their own crime scene investigations team, so like most cities in Serra County, they looked to the sheriff's office for logistical support and expertise. The techs were wearing surgical masks, and as soon as Harold got inside the laundry room, he understood why. Like most murder victims, this one had lost control of his bowels at or following the time of death, giving the room a ripe stench. Shelves full of bedding lined the walls. Two industrial-sized washing machines stood in a corner next to two smaller dryers. At the foot of the dryers lay the victim.

The victim was a White male, mid-twenties, muscular, head shaved on the side, longer on the top. He lay facedown, left untouched by the first responding officers and crime scene techs. His left arm folded under his torso and right hand behind his neck, clutched into a fist. Harold got down on his belly so that he was eye level with the victim's neck. A bright red stripe, no more than a sixteenth of an inch wide, made a perfect necklace around the man's neck. He was dressed in white medical scrubs and brown work boots.

"Twenty-four-year-old night shift orderly," reported Rebecca, staring at some notes attached to a clipboard.

"Worked here for about six months. Found this in his locker."

Rebecca handed Harold a small laminated card with the seal of the California Department of Corrections and Rehabilitation at the top. Below that were the words *Parolee Identification Card.* The photo on the card matched the victim. The card also included his name, date of birth, height and weight, race, and gender, along with a series of numbers and codes indicating the terms of his parole. This last bit of information would be useful to any law enforcement officers who encountered the parolee.

The fact that the victim was a criminal wasn't much of a surprise to Harold. Despite what was reported in the media, many murder victims were also criminals, an occupational hazard that came with associating with the wrong people. What surprised Harold was the fact that a parolee had somehow ended up as an orderly in a private hospital.

Harold stepped over the body, jockeyed around a pair of crime scene technicians who were taking what would end up being hundreds of photos of the room, and sat down in a folding metal chair between the washers and dryers. He took a deep breath. Looking around the room, Harold tried to take in as many details, both small and obvious, as he could. Murders in Mussel Shores were rare, but Rebecca knew exactly what he was doing and left him undisturbed. From his chair, Harold could see the red strangulation marks on the victim's throat. Too red, too tightly concentrated to have been made by human hands. Harold knew that a garrote made of a very fine but strong material of some kind had been used.

For as long as he had been a police officer, Harold had a morbid fascination of murder weapons, and indeed this had helped him solve some of the murders touted in his inflated retirement proclamation. As he sat staring at the increasingly puffy face of the man on the floor, Harold started to play a familiar game he called "Why not?" *A garrote. Why not a knife? Too messy? Hard to conceal?* Harold stood and walked over to a clear plastic bag with the contents of a wastepaper basket, which had been tagged for identification by one of the crime technicians. All the contents would be processed into an evidence room at the sheriff's office. Harold put the bag down and returned to his perch in the corner of the room. *If not a knife, why not a gun? Too tough to buy? Too noisy? No way of getting ahold of a silencer?* Harold pulled his cell phone out and absentmindedly checked the score of the Los Angeles Dodgers game the previous evening. He looked back at the body. *If not a knife or a gun, why not a club? Takes too much strength? Sometimes we use the tool most available to us. But a garrote takes some strength and the element of surprise.* After almost an hour on the chair, Harold had slipped into a near trance.

"We're about ready to take him back to our place, Detective. That okay by you?" asked an investigator with the County Coroner's Office.

"Yeah, that'd be fine," answered Harold. "When will you do the cut?" he asked, referring to the obligatory autopsy following a murder.

"Got a guy out, and we're kind of backed up, but we'll put him at the front of the line. How about tomorrow afternoon?"

"Sounds good," said Harold as he left the laundry room.

Harold deeply sucked in the rich ocean air and looked out past the cliffs guarding Pacific Dunes from the surf below. The Mussel Shores police chief and the public information officer from the sheriff's office were giving a joint impromptu briefing to a handful of media members.

"Okay, Pops," said Rebecca, who was standing on the periphery of the media brief. "What do ya think?"

"I think, young lady, that I've been cooped up with a dead man who soiled his trousers for the last four hours, and I'd like to get some late breakfast. Follow me. I'm buying," said Harold with his usual unaffected grace.

Rebecca and Harold sat in a corner booth of Pat's Café, a local favorite on Dana Street in downtown Mussel Shores. Between bites of an egg white omelet, Rebecca poured over her notes. Harold nibbled on a slice of wheat toast and stared at the young surfers walking past Pat's to and from the beach a block away.

"I'd like you to do a couple of things, if you would. First, get some people from patrol into the hospital. I want all the staff and patients' hands looked at. Let me know if they find signs of fresh abrasions or cuts in their palms," said Harold in more of a casual comment than a directive.

"Got it," said Rebecca as she scribbled in a notebook. She knew that she was about to learn more about investigating a murder than she could ever pick up in a police academy classroom and welcomed the chance to assist Harold.

"Next, let's bring Zavalla in on this."

Dave Zavalla was a local parole agent who had reached legendary status when, on a hunch, he arrested one of his parolees on a technical violation. The parolee turned out to have been responsible for the kidnapping, rape, and murder of two local college students. Harold knew that with a dead parolee, Zavalla's input would be a key component in his investigation.

"Next, let's catalog a list of all the staff and patients at the hospital," said Harold.

"What about the hospital trash bins?" asked Rebecca. "It would take a small army to go through that stuff, and it'd be nasty. Can't imagine what kind of things they throw out."

Harold thought about Rebecca's question. In a perfect world, he would have unlimited resources a phone call away, but this was small-town policing, so the search of a murder weapon in the hospital trash wasn't feasible. Besides, he agreed with Rebecca. He could only imagine what kind of material would have to be sifted through.

The next day, Harold and Rebecca stood in the corner of a windowless room near the Serra Regional Airport. They wore protective surgical masks over their mouths and noses, plastic face visors attached to their foreheads, and thick vinyl aprons. With notebooks in hand, the detectives watched the medical examiner begin to carve into the lifeless body of David Lee Simpson, now laying face up on a shiny stainless-steel table.

"Dude looks like a wood," said Rebecca.

Harold nodded in agreement. *Wood* was short for peckerwood, a common term used to refer to a White supremacist within the California prison system. In addition to gang-related tattoos on his arms and hands, a Nazi-style *SS* was scored into Simpson's chest by a tattoo gun made in prison. The device was put together with a lancet procured from the prison dispensary by a diabetic inmate, a pen stolen from the prison library by another inmate, and the small motor of an ancient cassette tape player smuggled in by a prison janitor making a little side money.

Harold looked away from the lifeless eyes of David Lee Simpson, which had curiously opened since his body had been moved from Pacific Dunes.

"Find anything in the valley?" asked Harold, referring to the deep gap cut into the skin of David Lee's throat.

The medical examiner grabbed tweezers from a stainless-steel tray and held out thin strands of what looked like green fibers. "We'll need to wait for lab confirmation, but it looks like dental floss."

"Hmmm. Rebecca, if it's dental floss, let's make a note to see if it's the same brand provided to the patients," said Harold.

*****

Harold had known many tough guys. The nondescript man in front of him belonged to this exclusive club. Parole Agent Dave Zavalla had grown up in California's Salinas Valley, America's salad bowl. Zavalla enjoyed working with felons. He had entertained many opportunities to become a police officer or sheriff's deputy, even a high school teacher and basketball coach, but had balked, not wanting to give up working with the "fellas," as he referred to his charges. Harold liked Zavalla's no-nonsense demeanor. On several occasions during Harold's tenure with the Mussel Shores Police Department, a simple call to Zavalla had led to the solving of some serious crimes.

"David, tell us about this gentleman," invited Harold. He, Zavalla, and Rebecca had met in a conference room at the Mussel Shores Police Department to discuss David Lee Simpson's social and criminal history.

"Real shit bird," said Zavalla as he took a thick file from a battered state-issued briefcase. "Did seven years at Soledad for runnin' a meth cook and trying to kill his baby momma when he caught her with someone else."

"How did this piece of shit end up working in a hospital?" asked Rebecca.

"Good question," said Zavalla. "State employment program for parolees. Only they're not supposed to be workin' in anything that requires a security clearance," said Zavalla as he pulled a sheet from his file. "He was livin' with another winner. Parolee, name of Richard Troop. I'd have to double-check, but I'm pretty sure Troop works in the same hospital. Might want to check him out."

The parole agent closed his file and asked, "So what do you got on this deal? Anything?"

"A garrote made out of what looks to be dental floss and a very efficient killer," said Harold with a sigh.

"Plenty of people wanted this guy dead. Good luck. Call me if you need anything." Zavalla packed up his file, shook hands with the two detectives, and left the interview room.

*****

Harold had quickly grown weary of the silly cat and mouse game the rotund hospital administrator was playing. Dr. Lionel Bettencourt had left a message on Harold's voice mail at the police department in the middle of the night requesting an extension in getting Harold a list of names for both patients and staff in the facility the night of David Lee Simpson's murder.

Enough is enough doctor. I'll just get a warrant. With no clear suspect, Harold knew he would need to eliminate names, starting with the least likely—the patients in the care of the hospital who cognitively or physically lacked the ability to strangle a man.

Harold was an expert at writing warrants, something Rebecca had realized soon after he arrived from Los Angeles. She enjoyed watching him work, explaining his strategies along the way, peppered with stories of the golden days of law enforcement. The warrant sailed through the Court Clerk's Office and was quickly signed by an available judge. Not all warrants went this smoothly. In fact, in a small county where judges and detectives become familiar, sometimes even chummy, Harold was well-respected, and his requests almost always passed quick judicial scrutiny.

As they left the county courthouse, signed warrant in hand, Rebecca and Harold stopped off for coffee at the Spilled Beans. Rebecca grabbed two empty seats on the patio while Harold waded through the scrum of attorneys, students, and an assortment of other customers waiting to be served. As he was waiting in line, his thoughts drifted to his future. Perhaps finally a future outside of law enforcement.

My sisters would be thrilled, but what the hell would I do? Snow cone stand is starting to sound better and better.

Harold had developed an almost pathological fear of dying within days of retirement. It wasn't death that frightened him. It was the pity his friends and family would shower over his memory and the untimeliness of his death.

"Poor schmuck didn't even get a chance to enjoy the fruits of his labor," Harold could hear his friends lament. This fear was rooted in the reality that more than a few law enforcement officers do die shortly following retirement.

"Good morning. Two coffees. Black, if you please," Harold asked the young barista behind the counter.

After paying for the coffee, Harold moved to a pickup counter. A large bulletin board covered a wall. A variety of snapshots of customers holding paper cups with the shop's logo had been taken at well-known tourist spots all over the world. It was a local custom to have a photo taken with a to-go cup from a downtown business and then post the picture on the wall of the business. A smiling young couple standing in front of one of the Great Pyramids, the familiar Spilled Beans cups in hand. The district attorney who doubled as an army reservist stood in front of an ancient mosque in Afghanistan, M16A2 assault rifle casually slung over a shoulder and a Spilled Beans cup in his hand.

Below the photos was a newspaper article cut out from the *Serra Tribune*. "Veteran Probation Officer Collapses During Chase." The story below the headline described a well-known local probation officer who had a stroke following an intense foot chase.

"O'Shea Gets His Man and Then Collapses," read the byline. Harold glimpsed at another photo below the article. It showed an older man in a tight T-shirt, biceps bulging and obviously in good condition, sitting at one of the corner tables in the same coffee shop. A young woman stood over his shoulder, both intently looking at a tattered paperback held by the man. Written on a small Post-it over the photo were the words "Get well, O'Shea. We love you. The morning staff at the Bean."

Harold grimaced. *Grand. Another fallen law enforcement guy who didn't get a chance to enjoy his retirement.* After reading the remainder of the article, Harold carried the cups out to a small table Rebecca had commandeered.

Harold wearily lowered himself into a chair opposite his younger colleague and stared absently out onto the street. Rebecca had known Harold long enough to embrace silence when he got a pensive look on his face. After a few minutes, she couldn't stand the anticipation.

"What's up, Pops? What are you thinkin' about?" she asked.

"What do you know about snow cones, young lady?"

"Well, I used to love 'em as a kid. My grandpap bought me one whenever we would go to the zoo. Other than that, haven't given 'em much thought, I guess. What's up?"

"Let's face it, Detective. I'm going to be sixty-three years old in January. Isn't that a little long in the tooth to be a police officer?" asked Harold.

"Fuck no!" blurted Rebecca incredulously. Harold winced.

"Sorry," said Rebecca, knowing Harold's sensitivity to females and crude language.

"Harold, we were a bunch of hodads here when you arrived. When you retired from LAPD and moved up here, it was like Derek Jeter comin' out of retirement and signing with the Toledo Mud Hens," said Rebecca.

"Harold, you're the big time, the real deal. The cop we all want to be but know, in this small town, probably never will be." Harold thought he detected a hint of emotion in the usually overconfident detective's voice.

"I appreciate that, Rebecca. I surely do," remarked Harold.

After a few moments of silence, Rebecca asked, "So why the fuck *are* you asking about snow cones?"

Harold smiled. "Can't do this forever. I like the ocean, like people, need to keep busy when the time for my second retirement comes," said Harold. "Furthermore, is it quite possible for you to eliminate that unfortunate word *fuck* from your lexicon?"

"Still don't get it."

Harold looked around as if making sure no one was listening. In a conspiratorial tone, he said, "Keep this 10-36, but I've submitted a license application to open a snow cone stand in Clam Shell Bay."

Number 10-36 was police radio speak for confidential information, and Clam Shell Bay was a small resort town tucked away on the coast between Serra and Mussel Shores.

Rebecca thought for a while, realizing Harold was serious. "It'll never happen, Pops. You like the hunt too much!" said Rebecca.

"You might be right, but I have a suspicion I could get awfully used to it, young lady," said Harold.

"Well, now that we've plotted out the next chapter of the Harold Davis story, can we talk about David Lee?" asked Rebecca.

"Certainly," replied Harold. "Let's head to the Pacific Dunes Hospital and, to use your crude vernacular, really fuck up Dr. Bettencourt's day."

CHAPTER 20

No need to give this fool a heads-up I'm coming, Harold thought as he made his way into the Pacific Dunes main entrance. Rebecca followed close behind.

"Good morning, madame," he said cheerily as he breezed past the front desk receptionist, who started to object but thought better of it.

Harold and Rebecca walked through the labyrinth of hallways to Bettencourt's mahogany office door, a stark contrast to the battered institutional metal doors allocated to the rest of the staff. Harold didn't bother knocking. He turned the doorknob and, finding it unlocked, threw it open. Early in his career, Harold had learned the importance of the art of theater in police work and was enjoying himself.

Bettencourt was seated behind his desk, back to the door. He turned to Harold, a startled look on his fleshy face. Harold immediately saw the bottle of Crown Royal whiskey in his right hand, pouring a healthy shot into a coffee cup.

"Dr. Bettencourt, I'm mortified!" said Harold. "A man of letters such as yourself nipping at the barleycorn at this hour. Isn't there law mandating sobriety among members of our medical community?"

"Detective, you have absolutely no business disturbing me! I shall be filing a report with the city administrator posthaste," replied

Bettencourt. Apparently, the whiskey had taken effect because the word *absolutely* came out "akisliply" and *filing* "fickeling."

"Feel free to contact the city administrator, Doctor, and show him a copy of this search warrant commanding you to make available certain documents to me," Harold said, lightly waving the warrant.

Rebecca pulled down the sunglasses perched on the top of her head and pretended to wipe off a smudge as she stifled a giggle.

After directing his administrative staff to cooperate fully with the detectives, Dr. Bettencourt determined that he had "quite the day" and decided to head for his palatial home high above the Pacific. Appearing a tad unsteady on his feet, Harold turned to Rebecca with a knowing nod. In turn, Rebecca looked like a lioness about to pounce on the weakest antelope of the herd. As she followed Bettencourt to his Mercedes, Rebecca called in a patrol unit to pull him over on suspicion of driving while intoxicated just as he pulled out of the Pacific Dunes parking lot.

Harold had organized a small storeroom adjacent to the hospital lobby into a de facto office. One of the hospital custodians had brought in a small table and chair. Spread out on the table in neat piles were the admission files of the Pacific Dune patients who were there the night of David Lee's murder. With the assistance of one of the hospital's nurses, Harold had arranged the files based upon the patient's mobility and whether they were even conscious. Other than Dr. Bettencourt's stonewalling, Harold found the staff to be more than helpful. In fact, they seemed to be eager to help him with his investigation. Every now and then, a nurse or secretary would poke their head into Harold's impromptu office and, with a smile, offer to refresh his coffee or ask him if the temperature in the room was comfortable. The head of the dietary services department had come in with a menu and asked Harold for his favorite dishes, which he was assured would be the kitchen staff's pleasure to prepare. *These people want me here. Seem relieved that I'm here. Bettencourt, on the other hand, curses the day we met. Something's' up.*

Harold got up the next morning, threw on his satiny track suit purchased in 1986, and drove to Clam Shell Bay for a brisk walk. From Front Street, he crossed a promenade where vendors were assigned spaces. Artists, jewelry makers, and a sole hot dog concessionaire were all given an area to do business. He looked around and spotted an empty space near the stairs leading down to the beach.

That's it. That's where I will become Officer Snowcone! What flavor would you like, young lady? A little extra cherry syrup? What can I getcha, sonny?

A blanket of coastal fog was beginning to burn off. The waves were perfect, Harold thought. Large enough to give the kids on "boogie boards" a ride but not so large that the local lifeguards had much more to do than reunite lost children with their frantic parents.

After his walk and a quick shower, Harold was at his desk in an office in the rear of the police department. Rebecca had been pulled off the Pacific Dunes murder and assigned to a drug case involving a suspected heroin connection between Fresno and the coast. Harold didn't mind. In fact, he enjoyed the solitude. A clerk had run the names of the Pacific Dunes employees through the state criminal database. He opened a file with the names and was impressed with the generally law-abiding nature of the Pacific Dunes employees. *Maybe David Lee was an anomaly.*

That all changed with employee number 12, Richard Troop. Harold stared at the nine-page criminal record of the night security guard and David Lee's coworker and roommate. Troop's impressive record spoke for itself. Harold knew that private security officers with criminal records sometimes slithered through poorly conducted criminal background checks, but Troop's record was quite astounding.

How did these two parolees end up working in the same hospital? One as a security guard? If nothing else, Harold now had a suspect.

*****

"You're up to something, Marine."

Mike was startled awake from his now regular late afternoon nap. Nate had wheeled himself into his room and, after manipulating his wheelchair close to the bed, was now mere inches from Mike's nose.

"What r u talking about, you lunatic?" Mike wrote on his dry-erase board.

"What, you think Nate's a dummy?" Nate said in a low voice. "Nate *knows* somethin's up around this camp, jarhead." Nate had, in recent weeks, taken to calling everyone he actually liked "jarhead," which referenced the standard Marine-issued crew cut.

"Does Charlie know?" Mike wrote on the board. Obviously, despite having his medication increased, Nate was now completely delusional and fancied himself back in a North Vietnamese prisoner of war camp.

"Fuck, no!" Nate screamed.

"Okay, Marine, keep it down. Those VC guards ain't deaf!" Mike wrote on his board. *Got to keep this loon calm. Could complicate things.*

"They dragged a gook puke outta here in a body bag a couple weeks ago. You know it, Nate knows it, and the lieutenant knows it," said Nate, calmer now. "Nate thinks one of our guys greased 'em."

"Do you trust me, Marine?" wrote Mike.

"Fuck-n-a, Nate trust ya," he hissed.

"I will get us out of here, I promise. Just keep your trap shut!" wrote Mike.

Mike looked at the old Marine, whose chin was now quivering. *Don't do that, Nate, c'mon!* Mike grabbed the old vet by the shoulder and was surprised by his still taunt muscles.

"Stay close, Marine," said Nate as he grabbed the toggle on the armrest of his chair and expertly reversed himself and rolled out of Mike's room. *Can't let crazy Nate screw up crazy Mike's plan.*

Mike glanced at the clock on the wall. Nine thirty. He looked down at the green beans and apple sauce intentionally smeared on his hospital-issued pajamas during dinner. *Got to keep up a good front. The more of a mess they think I am, the less of a suspect.*

Feigning sleep, out of the corner of his eye, Mike saw the on-duty nurse come into his room and turn off the TV. After changing Mike's soiled shirt, the nurse turned down the night-light and quietly left. As soon as Mike was alone, he lowered himself down to the floor for his nightly workout. He was up to two hundred modified push-ups, ten sets of twenty. After a brief rest, two hundred more sit-ups, and finally, after scooting under the bed and grabbing the steel mattress supports, two hundred modified chest pull-ups. Mike knew he had made significant progress in his covert fitness plan. *Kind of feeling like my old self again.*

"Where are you, fuckface? Where are you, you sorry piece of shit, O'Shea?" Troop's unmistakable voice whispered as he closed the door to Mike's room.

Mike remained still and tried to control his breathing. He turned his head slightly to the left and saw Troop's massive boots. Troop had spent nearly all his first paycheck on a sparkling new private security officer uniform at a local law enforcement supply shop. Ironic for someone who had spent much of his life evading or resisting the police, often both. Troop slowly rounded Mike's bed and looked down at his motionless form on the floor.

"You fall outta bed, you sorry-ass cripple? Not such a tough guy now, are you, *Officer* O'Shea?" Troop snarled. "You know what, O'Shea, you stink. In fact, I can smell your funky ass from here," said Troop.

With his size 15 tactical boot, Troop kicked Mike in the head, sending searing pain from one ear to another. Mike absorbed the kick and remained motionless. *Don't move or you'll screw this whole thing up. Not much longer.*

Troop bent down to make sure he was still breathing. All he needed was for Mike to die, which would disrupt one of the few forms of recreation Troop still enjoyed. Convinced Mike had just fallen from his bed and knocked himself unconscious, Troop relaxed. Slowly, he unzipped his pants. Troop looked up at the door to Mike's room to make sure they remained alone.

"You stink bad, O'Shea. I think I'll give you a little shower."

Mike prepared for what he knew was coming next. If he had ever questioned his plan for the late David Lee Simpson and now Mr. Richard Troop, feeling urine cover his head sealed the deal. Warm liquid fell onto Mike's face, a few drops seeping into his mouth. Mike bit down on his tongue to keep from throwing up. *Stay strong. Don't move.*

Troop giggled and admired his handiwork. He zipped up his pants and slowly poked his head out into the hallway to make sure no one saw him leave. The light in the room opposite Mike's was dark. Still, Troop could make out the form of Nate, in his wheelchair, looking at him with a disjointed stare. Troop looked both ways down the hall, and when he was confident no one was watching, he stepped into Nate's room and shut the door.

"Listen, you fuckin' idiot. You saw nothing, got it?" Troop hissed at Nate.

"I know what you're up to, Charlie. Standby. First Cav'll be here by daybreak. Gonna rain all hell down on this camp," said Nate calmly.

Troop stared at Nate, trying to figure out what he was talking about. Possessing marginal intellect, Troop had no clue that Nate had, in fact, been held in a North Vietnamese prisoner of war camp. In fact, Troop was only vaguely aware that there was a major conflict in Southeast Asia that had indirectly led to Nate's current predicament. Troop strutted down the hall to the security office as though he owned the place, which, between the hours of eleven o'clock at night and seven o'clock in the morning, he essentially did.

The next morning, Mike lay in bed staring at a sports report on the TV, trying to figure out the next step in his plan. David Lee had been surprisingly easy. Mike had fashioned a garrote out of dental floss and two pieces of wood he had been able to pry out of the frame in the rear of his closet. He found David Lee asleep on duty, of course, and was able to get the crude murder weapon around his neck before he awoke. With his right hand, Mike had tightened the garrote with a few turns of his wrist. Eventually, David Lee awoke, and Mike held on using his own weight as leverage in tightening the garrote. Once he was convinced David Lee was no longer among the living, Mike slid back onto his wheelchair and was able to return to his room undetected by the night staff.

Killing David Lee was one thing. Getting rid of the murder weapon was another. Mike assumed the police would make finding the weapon a priority, and if he was ever even a marginal suspect, they would turn his room inside and then out. He had feigned enough perceived "accidents" and now required adult diapers full-time. While he hated to admit it, Mike was enjoying the freedom of just letting go whenever he had to relieve himself, avoiding the inconvenience of getting to the toilet. *What a sicko. You need to get outta here.*

After wrapping the garrote in a tight mass of toilet paper, Mike waited until he had an impressively large bowel movement. He removed the diaper in the bathroom and placed the garrote in the middle of his feces. Mike wrapped the diaper up, fastened the adhesive, and threw it in the waste can labeled BIOHAZARD, which sat by the door. He knew the cans were emptied daily and doubted even the most conscience of police detectives would be willing to search through diapers for the murder weapon. Yes, David Lee's death had been easier than Mike had anticipated. *But that was a dumbass who was sound asleep. Troop's going to be different.*

*****

Like most people drawn to a career in law enforcement, Mike had a very strong and at times a rigid sense of justice. Killing was a necessary evil if one were to survive. *Murder* was different. His conversations with Iggy about the church's position on just war, after his first officer-involved shooting, clarified that and brought Mike some peace. While he was reasonably sure David Lee had committed unspeakable acts against the comatose patient, Mike really had only circumstantial evidence. A parolee emerging from her room with his zipper down.

We got the truth, and we have the facts, Mike remembered from a presentation by a retired judge during his academy.

"The truth is nice, but what we need for justice to be done are the facts," the judge had said.

Bullshit. I know the punk was messing with the old lady. Either that or just zippin' up his pants after using her bathroom. You are on a very slippery slope, my friend.

Mike was shaken out of his internal morality inquest by Nate's gravelly voice.

"You awake, Marine?" Nate whispered as he wheeled over to Mike's bed.

Mike looked over at Nate, smiled, and motioned for him to come closer. Nate seemed to have an air of desperation well beyond his usual nuttiness. Mike took the ever-present dry-erase board. "How ya doing, Sarge?"

"The question, Marine, is how are *you* doin'?" asked Nate. "Saw Charlie leavin' your cell last night. Stay strong, Marine. First Cav's gonna blow this place all to hell!"

Mike was no expert in the science of mental health, but in his layman's opinion, Nate was even more unhinged than usual. He grabbed the dry-erase board. "What do you know, Sarge?"

Nate looked around suspiciously as though a North Vietnamese Army regular might be hiding in the closet.

"I saw death in Charlie's eye, Marine. We need to make a move before he greases us both. That's what I know!" Nate whispered.

Mike looked into Nate's eyes and wondered if he had ever been truly sane, or was Nate's condition the natural outcome of a far too young and naive eighteen-year-old from the sticks of eastern San Diego County sent off to war two weeks after his senior prom? By age default, Mike had missed the Vietnam War, but over the years, he had several Vietnam War vets on his caseload. He had also encountered more than a few frauds who tried to fabricate military experience to garner leniency from their sentencing judge. Some of the legitimate vets Mike supervised had succumbed to drugs or alcohol or both.

Mike considered Nate's prophetic statement. If he didn't act soon, would Troop indeed kill him? Would he then take out Nate? Was Troop also forcing himself on comatose patients as did his associate David Lee? Given Troop's increasingly violent and deviant treatment, Mike suspected that Nate's prediction might be on target. *Or am I just trying to justify murdering people? Thought I was one of the good guys? Who died and made you the judge, jury, and executioner? Have to deal with that later.*

Two o'clock in the morning was an especially lonely time in any hospital. Staff struggled to stay awake, and if sleep for the patients came at all, it was usually restless. For those who couldn't sleep, thoughts of home, family, friends, and life before whatever happened to land them in a rehabilitation hospital drifted into their thoughts. For Mike, the time had arrived to put into place the final act of the play he had plotted during similarly long nights lying in bed and staring at his television. Despite his theatrics indicating otherwise, Mike had forced his body to recover from his stroke with an equal amount of stealth and sheer will. He would never fully recover, but Mike had regained much of the strength and stamina that made a debilitating stroke so difficult to accept. He had also regained the ability to speak but continued to use the little whiteboard to communicate, adding an additional layer of symptoms to his repertoire.

Despite his improvement, for the last portion of his plan to succeed, Mike would remain wheelchair-bound. He lowered himself into the chair and wheeled out to the corridor.

"How you doing, Luis?" Mike wrote on the dry-erase board resting on his lap. The night custodian was pushing a cart with an impressive collection of cleaning supplies toward Mike's room.

"Just fine, Mike. No sleep tonight?" asked Luis.

"Don't tell the dietitians, but I got a sweet tooth!" Mike wrote on the board. "Could sure use a little ice cream."

"Well, I happen to have a key to the kitchen," said Luis with a kind smile. "I won't tell if you don't."

"Hey, that'd be great. Thanks!" Mike wrote on the board. *Geez. This guys' such a sweetheart. I hate to get him involved but got to get into the kitchen.*

Luis pulled a key attached to a thin wire from his belt and opened the door. Mike marveled at the size and cleanliness of the kitchen. He watched Luis open a large walk-in freezer and emerge with two single-serve containers of vanilla ice cream and two flat wooden spoons. As they ate, Mike nodded enthusiastically as Luis pulled photos of his family from his wallet. The first was of a beaming Luis, surrounded by his wife and four children, holding a certificate of citizenship the day he became "official," as Luis referred to his citizenship. Others included his children taken at high school and college graduation ceremonies.

A pang of guilt shot through Mike. *If this goes to shit, got to somehow get word to Luis to keep his mouth shut and let me go down for it.*

Luis took Mike's now empty ice cream container and tossed it in a garbage can. For the first time since David Lee's murder, Mike had considered the very distinct possibility that if he got caught, he would spend the rest of his life in prison.

Wouldn't be a bad gig. Three hots and a cot. Got a couple of English degrees. Could become a reading tutor. Might be more productive in prison than retirement.

"Thanks, Luis. That was great. Think I'll sleep okay now," Mike wrote on the board.

Luis gave him a thumbs up and started for the door to the corridor. As he held the door open, Mike reached out for the doorjambs with both hands and pulled himself through, carefully placing a piece of medical adhesive tape acquired on one of his "walks" across the locking mechanism. Following Mike out of the kitchen, Luis allowed the self-locking door to close quietly. Perhaps it was hopeful thinking, but Mike thought he failed to detect the subtle sound of the lock engaging.

Hope this works. Better come up with a backup plan, which should be of no concern given the devious sociopath I've apparently become.

With an enthusiastic wave, Mike wheeled himself back into his room, and when he was assured that Luis had disappeared down the hallway, he returned to the kitchen, where the door had indeed failed to lock.

Need something long, sharp, and thin. Mike peered over the chrome drawer at a collection of kitchen implements from ladles to spatulas. He pulled out what looked like a long fork with tiny prongs. *Length is good. Looks sturdy. But I'd have to sharpen it myself, and that'll take time.*

He quietly placed the implement back in the drawer. Startled by what sounded like small balls pouring into a metal box, Mike jerked his head to the left. Against the wall stood an industrial-sized ice machine. What appeared to be a wooden dowel, approximately five inches long, lay on top. Mike wheeled over for a closer look. He reached for the dowel, which was a wooden handle. Attached to the handle was a long piece of metal, the end sharpened to a fine point. Ice makers are quirky appliances. Sometimes they experience temperature variances, and the ice cubes begin to melt and meld together into one large piece of ice. When this takes place, a sharp tool is needed to break the ice up into manageable chunks.

Mike had discovered an ice pick.

*****

He slowly lowered himself down to the floor and crawled to the door leading out into the hallway. After nudging the door open a foot or so, Mike positioned his body so only the top of his head stuck out. If he saw anyone coming, he could quickly pull himself back into the room and quietly close the door. Mike lay in this position for what seemed like hours. At one point, he dozed off. Luckily, the loud boisterous voice of Security Officer Troop announcing his arrival on his unit shook Mike from his brief nap. As Troop's unmistakable hulk lumbered down the corridor, Mike slowly pulled himself out in the hallway.

Just my luck the sadist will just walk by and leave me here. Mike heard Troop's boot steps become closer until he sensed he was standing above him.

"O'Shea," Troop whispered. "What are you doing on the floor again, you worthless cripple?"

Mike braced for what he knew was coming. With surprising speed and efficiency for a three-hundred-pound man, Troop slammed the toe of his boot into the side of Mike's head, knocking him into the doorjamb. Mike groaned quietly.

"I'll tell you what, O'Shea. I'm gonna pick your sorry ass up and put ya back to beddy-bye."

Do not do this! You can simply ask Shapiro to call the PD and Troop's gone. You're not God. You might skate on one but pop two, and you're heading for big trouble, big trouble, mister! Do it now or Troop kills you. You'll be doin' society a favor. Mike could almost feel the weight of the proverbial angel and devil on his shoulders.

Troop bent down and hefted Mike up onto his shoulders, walked a few steps across the room, and unceremoniously dumped him onto the bed. He walked to the door and slowly peeked his head outside, making sure that no one was coming. When he was reasonably sure that his night's deviant recreation wouldn't be interrupted, he slowly closed the door and turned back toward Mike's bed.

That's it. Get over here. Troop stood to the right of Mike's bed. With an immense hand, he grabbed Mike's crotch and squeezed his testicles like a vice. Mike clamped his eyes shut, seeing nothing but bright stars as the pain seared through his body, doing all he could to stifle a scream. Finally, Troop let go and brought his mouth up to Mike's face, the stench bringing Mike to the verge of retching.

"That's what I thought, little man, little dick, O'Shea. Now I'm gonna show you what we did to punk-ass faggots like you in the joint."

Mike could hear the unmistakable sound of Troop pulling down his zipper. *Sorry, Troop. Gonna have to draw the line at rape. This ends now.*

With speed, agility, and strength having returned during his covert late night workouts, Mike grabbed Troop's collar, bringing their heads inches apart.

Richard Troop was a stupid man. Years of steroid use had severely damaged the frontal lobe of his brain. Unfortunately for Troop and society in general, the frontal lobe dictates such functions as impulse control and judgment. But for all his intellectual deficiencies, Troop knew immediately something was wrong. He stared into Mike's dark eyes, seeing nothing but hate and violence. Instinctively knowing that something was now definitely wrong, Troop tried to pull away. Mike's grasp on his collar only tightened, and Troop found himself lifting Mike up off his bed as he attempted to pull away. He grabbed Mike's left hand and tried to pry it from his collar without success.

Mike brought his right hand up and jammed the ice pick into Troops ear. He rotated his wrist and scrambled the outer portion of his brain. His eyes bulged and body stiffened as though reacting to an electric jolt. After a few seconds, Troop collapsed in a heap on top of Mike. After a final violent seizure, he inhaled his last breath.

Mike groped Troop's throat and found no pulse. He slipped out from under his victim, grabbed his feet, and slowly, with incredible labor, pulled Troop off the bed. His head made a dull thud as it struck the floor. Despite an improved physical state, Mike was still a stroke victim with limited use of his left side, making the task more difficult. He removed his sweat socks, hoping his bare feet would provide more traction.

Mike knew he needed to put as much space between him and Troop's body as possible. He dragged him as far down the corridor as he dared and into an empty room. As he shut the door, Mike realized that he had dumped Troop's body in a room next to Nate's. It might raise suspicion, but Mike had no time to find a second dumping ground. If Nate was ever considered a legitimate suspect, there would be no forensic evidence to connect the two.

Don't worry about Nate. Get your ass back to your room.

CHAPTER 21

Harold had been up late the night before, not investigating crimes or chasing ne'er-do-wells around Mussel Shores. He had a date. One of Harold's meddling but well-meaning sisters had fixed him up with a woman from the only Baptist church serving the African American community in Serra County.

"A lovely woman," his sister Maxine gushed. "And from a fine Atlanta family!"

Harold was accustomed to his sister's attempts to marry off their confirmed bachelor brother. But he reluctantly agreed to call Chief Probation Officer Cheryl Jackson after seeing her at an event honoring law enforcement dispatchers.

Harold had initially asked Cheryl to dinner. However, she balked and suggested a quiet dinner at Harold's place. The next night, Harold tried valiantly to operate a fresh pasta maker one of his sisters had given him for Christmas while a homemade marinara sauce simmered. Cheryl arrived on time. She wore tight white Capri pants and a green Cal Coastal sweatshirt. It was the perfect ensemble for a first date with a gentleman who Cheryl knew would want to avoid stuffiness at all costs.

I'll be lucky if he even bothers to clean his bathroom and I get anything other than cold takeout, Cheryl thought as she tried to force her BMW convertible into a small parking space in front of Harold's condominium complex.

Harold was a traditionalist when it came to romance and attire. He wore wool slacks, silk shirt, and an imported tie (yet another Christmas gift from a sister). Slightly embarrassed and feeling completely overdressed when he opened the door and saw Cheryl, dressed casually elegant, he darted into his bedroom as he mumbled a fib about just getting off work.

Now in jeans and a polo shirt, a tumbler of scotch in one hand and a stirring spoon in the other, Harold felt much more relaxed as he played host. Cheryl made the conversation easy, talking about everything from sports to politics to the history of the civil rights movement, one of her favorite topics. Harold cooked, laughed, and was thoroughly enjoying Cheryl's company while she sipped a cabernet and sliced vegetables for a salad.

As much as both tried, the topic of work was unavoidable. After dinner, Harold lent Cheryl a coat, and the pair took a walk on the Mussel Shores Pier. The Pacific Dunes Hospital was behind them, bathed in orange light from the sun over the horizon, merging ocean with sky. She pointed to the hospital and asked if Harold was involved in the murder investigation of an orderly.

"I am indeed. The deceased had no shortage of enemies, so my suspect list has become a bit unmanageable," Harold said as he picked up a shell from the sand and dropped it in his pocket. He had a glass jar on his kitchen counter, and this addition would go nicely with the others.

"I know," said Cheryl. "He was one of ours. A sex offender," said Cheryl.

"Yes, Mr. Simpson was a bad actor, as we used to say," replied Harold.

"Past victim out to get some revenge?" Cheryl asked.

"My gut tells me no, but my gut isn't really telling me anything else," said Harold.

"One of my officers is there, you know," said Cheryl, a look of sadness creeping into her sparkling eyes.

"At Pacific Dunes? Is he a patient?" Harold asked.

"Yes, and has been for months now. Michael O'Shea," said Cheryl. "The toughest night of my career, I can tell you, was getting the call that he had suffered a stroke."

"I read about it," said Harold. "Very tough break. I understand O'Shea was kind of a local legend."

"Michael was a lot of things…is a lot of things," said Cheryl. "Yes, a definite legend, a good friend, my best officer, and at times a real pain in my rump, and now he's sitting up there," Cheryl said as her voice cracked, pointing to the hospital on the cliff.

Harold could tell Cheryl was self-conscious about her display of emotion, so he deftly switched the direction of the conversation to track-and-field, a sport both had excelled in as collegiate athletes. Once they were back in front of Harold's condo, he invited Cheryl up for coffee, but she declined. Harold tried to hide his disappointment and wondered if he had moved too quickly with the preacher's daughter from Atlanta. He was reassured when Cheryl asked if he would be interested in accompanying her to a wine tasting fundraiser the following weekend. Harold quickly accepted, and Cheryl climbed into her BMW and drove off.

Got to thank my sister. For once, she got it right.

The next morning, Harold skipped his daily walk on the beach and slept in, at least by his standards. As he sipped coffee and watched the local news, the doorbell rang, and Harold saw two uniformed police officers through the peephole. *Something's up.*

"Morning, fellas. Everything okay?"

"Morning, Detective. Sorry to bother you at home, but we couldn't get you on your cell," said the older of the two officers.

Ah, shit. "The damn thing's been acting up," Harold ad-libbed, knowing he had turned it off the night before so as not to have his date interrupted. "What's up?" asked Harold.

"Another 187 at Pacific Dunes. Body is still there," said the officer.

"Patient?" asked Harold, reaching for his sport coat.

"Nope. Night security guard."

"Hmm." *This case just went from interesting to fascinating.*

*****

It had been three weeks since Security Officer Richard Troop had been laid to rest. His former wives, a rogue's gallery of local hoodlums, thugs, gym rats, parolees, and of course, Richard's beloved mother, Darla, were all in attendance. Darla Macklin was married to her fourth husband and possessed an anti-social personality equal to her sons. Her poorly died platinum hair and flashy thrift shop ensemble made a bold statement. In between smacking bubblegum, smoking Kools, and sipping from a mysterious brown liquid in a plastic sports bottle, Darla wept, cursed the system, and made vague reference to a lawsuit which would finally bring justice to her "Sweet Richey."

Harold had quickly grown to abhor her. Darla called daily and demanded updates on the Mussel Shores Police Department's efforts to find her "baby's" killer. She even went so far as to call the chief of police and demand that the "colored boy" be taken off the case and it be given to a "real cop." Appropriately, the chief of police now refused to take any calls from this "piece of shit mother of that piece of shit son of hers" and suggested Harold do the same. But Harold kept Darla Macklin engaged in hopes that she might provide some insight into possible leads. He also recruited Rebecca Santiago to park a surveillance van across the street from the cemetery and take photos of the funeral attendees. Harold explained to Rebecca that it wasn't unheard of for murderers to show up at the funerals of their victims.

As usual, Harold had been present for Troop's autopsy. Ultimately, the cause of death had been ruled a hemorrhage of the brain brought on by the piercing of the left lobe by an extremely sharp and long implement. It took a while for the medical examiner (ME) to determine the cause of death. Upon close examination of Troop's head, the ME had seen the small droplets of dried blood in his outer ear. After slicing open Troop's massive skull, the ME discovered the cause of death. A small wound through the ear into the outer regions of the brain, where the implement was twirled, creating additional damage.

Sitting in his office, Harold stared at a large dry-erase board he was using to chart out his investigation, which had now expanded to two parolees with extensive criminal and prison records. Starting at the beginning, Harold had written on the board, "How did Vs end up at Pacific Dunes?" It galled Harold to consider either Troop or David Lee Simpson as "victims," but technically, he mused, that's what they were. Now with clear access to all the Pacific Dunes records thanks to a superior court judge who trusted him implicitly and signed a search warrant, Harold had seized the personnel records of Troop and David Lee and spread them over his desk. The job applications for both were illegible. Given that David Lee was functionally illiterate and Troop a simpleton in a behemoth's body, it wasn't a surprise. Both applications had been filled out in the same blue ink in almost childlike script. In the sections listing work experience and criminal records, someone had written in clearly different handwriting and a different pen the words *Not Applicable.* Harold surmised that someone at Pacific Dunes with the authority to hire didn't particularly care whether the two men had any experience or criminal records. Harold leaned back and thought of the words of an ancient instructor at the LAPD academy who taught his basic investigations course: "There's no such thing as a coincidence, chase anomalies and deviations with fervent aggressiveness."

*****

"Mr. Talmadge, this is Detective Davis with the Mussel Shores Police Department. Do you have a minute, sir?" Harold asked.

"Hey, guy! How are things in Mussel Shores?" asked the Department of Corrections and Rehabilitation official with far too much enthusiasm.

"Mr. Talmadge, I'm handling the investigations of two CDC&R parolees by the names of David Lee Simpson and Richard Troop, and I understand you're familiar with both," said Harold.

"Yes, a terrible tragedy, Detective," said Agent Talmadge, his voice now draped in feigned sorrow.

"Mr. Talmadge, I'm trying to understand just how these two came to be employed at the Pacific Dunes facility," said Harold.

"Great question. Both shit-birds...err...the decedents had extensive criminal records."

Harold glanced at the criminal histories of both: attempted murder, extortion, drug possession and sales, assaults, rape, child molestations, intimidating witnesses, and a variety of less serious offenses.

"So," asked Harold, "how did these gentlemen end up in a medical facility with patients, many of whom are unable to care for themselves?"

"Easy," replied Agent Talmadge casually. "FTW. Freedom Through Work, state-funded vocational program for prison releases."

"I'm sorry?" said Harold.

Ken Talmadge went on to explain the State of California Department of Corrections and Rehabilitation took the "rehabilitation" portion seriously. So seriously, in fact, that the CDC&R went out and found jobs for parolees with the understanding that the state would pay 50 percent of their salary, including insurance and benefits. In turn, the employer would pay the remaining 50 percent of their salary and receive significant tax benefits.

This is a scam! Harold thought. *Bet dollars to donuts Bettencourt was getting something shady out of this.*

Harold marched into the Pacific Dunes lobby the next day and greeted the receptionist, with whom he had become friendly. He walked down the main hallway, and as was now his custom, he opened the large mahogany door of Dr. Lionel Bettencourt with no notice or announcement. Harold stood at the door and observed the massive frame of Dr. Bettencourt eagerly perusing the internet for the least expensive flights to countries with no extradition treaties with the United States.

"You know, Detective, these intrusions are becoming rather tiresome," said Bettencourt, not bothering to look up from his computer screen. Harold stared directly at Bettencourt, just long enough to make the big man squirm.

"Tell me about your involvement in the State Department of Corrections and Rehabilitation Freedom Through Work Program, Doctor," ordered Harold.

"I'm sorry?" replied Bettencourt meekly.

"Freedom Through Work, Doctor. The funded work program for parolees. Both your dead employees were involved in it," said Harold.

"Oh right, right, right," said Bettencourt. "Great program. Just swell that I was able to help those fellows get back on their feet."

"I've procured a sample of your handwriting, Doctor," said Harold flatly.

"Why?" squeaked Bettencourt.

Harold drew the applications from his briefcase and pointed to words "Not Applicable."

"To confirm it matches these."

"But I had nothing to do with their deaths!" blurted out Bettencourt, now visibly shaking.

"No, but you may have been criminally negligent when you hired two violent criminals to work around dependent and comatose patients, Doctor," said Harold with a smile.

"I will not stand for this *harassment,* Detective!" said Bettencourt with far too much bravado for a man on the verge of soiling his $300 slacks. "I demand to speak with my attorney."

"Probably a good call, Doc," said Harold as he slid the applications back in his briefcase. "You have until end of business tomorrow to have your attorney contact me. Also, we'll be keeping an eye on you, so stay put, and no traveling out of the county. Understood?"

Bettencourt tried to say something, but his throat cinched shut. A slight nod was all he could muster.

CHAPTER 22

Harold handed the pending case of the *State of California vs. Dr. Lionel Bettencourt* off to another detective, which allowed him to focus all his attention on the Pacific Dunes murders.

As a career detective, he had learned that sometimes crimes were solved not by identifying the most likely suspects but by first eliminating the least. First, Harold made a list of the Pacific Dunes patients who had been at the hospital during the murders and for the six-month period preceding. He had a clerk run those names through the CLETS system, which was a state-wide criminal database. Harold went back even further than the murders in case the victims had made some enemies of former patients who had returned to settle a grudge, entirely possible given the profiles of Simpson and Troop. Other than a sprinkling of low-level crimes committed decades before, the Pacific Dunes patients proved to be a relatively law-abiding group.

He asked a now slightly irritated police clerk to run the names through yet another set of systems to determine if any of the patients were either ex-military or ex-law enforcement members, or maybe both. This search proved more successful than the first two. During the six months leading up to the murders, there were three veterans, one retired sheriff's lieutenant, and the probation officer he and Cheryl had discussed. He wrote the five names down on a lined sheet of paper and made his way down the hall to a large room with a cluster of cubicles that housed the Mussel Shores Police Department's administrative staff. Harold knew that when taxing the patience of administrative staff, it was always best to "bring on the sugar," as his mother was fond of saying, and have a conversation versus dropping the request off in an "in box."

"Mrs. LeCount, how are you this fine morning?" asked Harold in his sweetest tone.

"Detective, are you going to give me another of your damn lists?" Barbara Anne LeCount had been a police clerk for forty-plus years. She had a sharp tongue, but her competence was unparalleled, Harold quickly realized upon his arrival, so he made it his mission to make Barbara LeCount an ally.

"Mrs. LeCount, before we discuss my unpleasantness, let's talk about that fine grandson of yours," Harold said, pointing to a large photo of a graduating senior at nearby Arroyo Berros High School.

Barbara Anne was immensely proud of all six of her grandchildren, but no more so than Seth, the youngster in the photo. Almost instantly, Barbara Anne's demeanor changed, her face softened, and it was clear that Harold had touched upon a soft spot.

"Oh, Detective!" she squealed. "He just got his acceptance letter into UCLA. He's gonna be a Bruin!"

"Congratulations, Mrs. L!" said Harold with sincerity. "Did you know that I graduated from UCLA?" asked Harold.

"Detective, would you talk to him? You know, give him some pointers? His parents and I are so nervous about sending him off to the big city."

Harold smiled. "Mrs. L, I would love to chat with the boy, and I'll do you one better. I'll give him my old UCLA pennant for his dorm room."

"Oh, Detective, you're a dear. Just a dear!" said Barbara Anne. "Now how can I help you?"

"Yes, ma'am. Just a short one this time. I've got a list of some patients residing at Pacific Dunes. An army veteran, retired sheriff's deputy, and a current probation officer. Looking for discharge status for the veteran, any disciplinary issues for the sheriff's lieutenant and the probation officer, and most importantly, their training records."

Harold had used highlighters to separate out the groups on his sheet of paper.

"Dealing with the military will be tough," Barbara Anne said with a look of worry. "Can I have a week or so?"

"You may, and thank you, ma'am," replied Harold.

Harold rose early, and after his customary walk on the beach, he treated himself to an omelet at Pat's Café. He bit into an English muffin as he perused his case notes. Harold wrote his notes in an entirely indecipherable script that was unreadable to anyone other than himself. Unlike his younger peers, Harold eschewed the use of a computer and still used a small lined notebook. He knew that if, God forbid, the book was ever lost, the finder would probably toss it in the nearest trash can since the pages were filled with squiggly lines and gibberish. But in the back of Harold's mind, he also knew that if a clever defense lawyer ever subpoenaed his notes, he could present them with his own special spin. A sip of orange juice and a bite of omelet and Harold's attention turned back to his notes.

At the bottom of the last page was a sentence that was again unreadable to anyone other than the writer. *What was B's scam, and was B capable of murder?* B, of course, was Bettencourt. Harold was fascinated by the arrangement Bettencourt had made with the Department of Corrections and Rehabilitation. Lionel Bettencourt hadn't struck Harold as a particularly socially conscious individual or someone with an interest in reforming parolees. *There has to be something in it for him.*

On his way to Pacific Dunes, Harold stopped by the Beach Cities Cinnamon Rolls a block up from the water and picked up a box of ridiculously rich cinnamon rolls covered in raisins and walnuts with a delightful coating of sour cream sauce. He greeted the chief of security at the reception desk, a distinguished-looking retiree from the Salinas Police Department by the name of Hugo Sanchez. Like many law enforcement retirees, Sanchez just couldn't let go of his professional roots and continuously peppered Harold with questions about his investigation.

"Chief Sanchez, greetings!" Harold bellowed as he strolled into the Pacific Dunes lobby.

"Detective, as always, I am at your service," said Sanchez earnestly.

"Chief Sanchez, a little something for you and your security force," said Harold as he handed over the box of cinnamon rolls. Harold always referred to the Pacific Dunes security officers under Sanchez's supervision as his "security force" and couldn't help but notice Sanchez's chest puff slightly at the reference.

Sanchez beamed at the gesture and Harold's sign of respect. He bowed slightly as though welcoming royalty and said, "We are, as always, honored to host you, Detective. How may I be of service?"

"I hear that Dr. Bettencourt has taken a leave of absence. Who's the majordomo around here now?" Harold whispered conspiratorially.

"Dr. Shapiro is the acting chief of staff. A solid man, in my estimation. Would you like to meet him?" asked Sanchez.

"Yes, sir, I would if you have the time." Sanchez led Harold down the hall to the cluttered office of Dr. Jason Shapiro.

"Dr. Shapiro, with honor, I introduce Detective Harold Davis of the Mussel Shores Police Department," said Sanchez with a ceremonial bow and a light tap of his left breast with his right fist. *Oh, brother*, thought Harold, a bit embarrassed.

"I will leave you two alone," said Sanchez as he dramatically backed out of the room and gave one final bow before he exited.

"Give me a minute, Detective, would ya'?" asked the psychiatrist in his thick East Coast accent.

Dr. Shapiro was listening to his voice mail, and by the long list of scribbled notes in front of him, Harold knew he was dealing with a busy man. Industriousness was not an attribute he would have given Dr. Shapiro's predecessor, Bettencourt. Dr. Shapiro listened to one last message, finished up his notes, and got out of his chair to greet Harold.

"Jason Shapiro. How are ya?" asked Jason, sticking out his hand.

"Sorry for the interruption, Doctor. You look like a busy man," said Harold.

"Well, up until Bettencourt left, I was busy. Now I'm damn frantic trying to keep this place going," said Jason.

"I've been assigned to investigate the Simpson and Troop murders, and I thought you might be able to offer some insight regarding some of your patients."

"Got some confidentiality issues as far as specific medical conditions, but I'll do my best," said Jason. "Hey, I've been stuffed in this office all day. Do you mind if we walk and talk? Maybe eat street?" asked Jason.

"Beg your pardon, Doctor?" asked Harold.

"Oh, you're not from my neck of the woods, are you, Detective?" asked Jason, waving his finger and smiling. "Eat street. It means to grab lunch from a street vendor and eat as you stroll. One of my favorite pastimes back in New York," he said, patting his ample waist.

Jason led Harold to a small hot dog stand a half mile from Pacific Dunes.

"Manny, you silly son of a bitch. How are ya?" Jason screamed at an older balding man working the cart.

The man looked up and smiled. It was obvious to Harold that Jason was a regular customer, and he enjoyed watching him and the cart owner spar amicably. With a large kosher hot dog smothered in onions and sauerkraut in one hand and a bottle of soda in the other, Jason led Harold down a path to the beach.

Harold was satisfied with a bottle of seltzer water and a bag of salt-free chips. The two sat on a rickety wooden bench a few yards from the sand. Jason let out a sigh of someone who enjoyed getting away from his office from time to time. They discussed sports, the weather, the joys of living on California's Central Coast, and how each had arrived at their respective stations in life. Harold waited for a natural pause in the conversation then asked the first of a set of questions he had prepared in his mind.

"As you may know, Doctor, the decedents had a rather *colorful* history," said Harold.

"Detective, we're not going to get far unless you drop the Doctor mumbo jumbo. Call me Jason, please."

"You got it, Jason," said Harold with a bashful nod.

"Those two bums were real pieces of work, I'll tell you that," said Jason. "I tried to get Bettencourt to give them the boot many times, but he was locked into those two for some reason."

"I have to tell you, Jason, the staff at your hospital have been nothing but professional and courteous. Is it accurate to say the victims just didn't fit in?"

"Hah! That's an understatement," said Jason with a laugh. "The majority of the staff *are* good people. Knowing Bettencourt as I do, if you dig deep enough, I bet you'll find he was getting some kind of kickback from the state for those two."

"Why do you think that?" asked Harold.

Jason stared at Harold and then looked away, obviously uncomfortable with the turn of the conversation.

"Detective, I can't prove this, but after I got the call from the corporate office appointing me as the acting chief of staff, I took a look at the books…such as they were," said Jason.

"Anomalies?" asked Harold.

"Only if you call *two* sets of books anomalies. I know the hospital got a tax break, and I think the state covered a portion of their salary and benefits, but I'll bet Bettencourt was getting something more out of the deal."

Harold made a mental note to have the detectives working on the Bettencourt side of the case contact Jason.

"Jason, if you don't mind, I'd like you to discuss that with some of my colleagues looking into Dr. Bettencourt's activities here at the hospital," said Harold.

"Sure thing. Bettencourt is a bad guy, Detective, and I'll help any way I can."

"I appreciate that. Now getting back to the murders. Plenty of people wanted to see those two dead. I think you've already figured that out," said Harold.

Jason nodded as he took a sip of his soda water.

"But I need to start some place, so the natural first look would be people who were at the hospital the night of the murders," said Harold.

Harold took a sheet of yellow legal paper from the pocket of his sport coat, unfolded it, and handed it to Jason.

"Jason, this is a list of staff and patients who were physically in the hospital the night of the murders. Any of them have any conflicts with the victims?" asked Harold.

Jason took the sheet and studied it closely. Like any seasoned investigator, Harold studied Jason's possible responses as he read the list. After a few minutes, he took a pen from his shirt pocket and started scribbling notes on the paper.

"Those two punks fancied themselves real lady's men. The names with check marks are nurses and secretaries they hit on, offended, or otherwise gave a bad time to," said Jason.

"Was anything done about it?" asked Harold.

"Nah," said Jason. "People complained to Bettencourt, and he gave them the regular goatshit about not tolerating a hostile work environment, but nothing of any substance was done."

"How do you know nothing was done?" asked Harold.

"Can't say for sure. I confronted Bettencourt at a staff meeting once, and he assured us he had acted but cited some foolishness about the confidentiality of the punks. Nothing was done because they stayed, even after the complaints," said Jason with slight agitation in his voice.

Harold looked at the list. Jason had checked off seven names of female employees. In the margin by three of the names, he had written, "Left."

"Why did they leave?" asked Harold.

"Come on, guy! Wouldn't you leave if you were a human pincushion to those bums?" asked Jason, no longer trying to hide his agitation.

Harold took a second sheet of paper from his pocket. This one included a list of names of patients who were present the night of the murders. He handed it to Jason, who once again studied the list closely.

"I know you can't tell me who could have *physically* committed the murders, Jason, but anyone on that list stick out as someone who may have had a motive?" asked Harold.

GARY L. JORALEMON

"You have to understand the nature of the patients here, Detective. Many are noncommunicative. Those who can speak, for the most part, have some cognitive impairments. Like this fellow," said Jason, pointing to Nate's name.

"What's his story?" asked Harold/

"Severe PTSD from the Vietnam War and then a stroke, which compounded his paranoia. For all intents and purposes, he's still in Vietnam, and it's still 1968," said Jason.

"Could he commit murder?" asked Harold.

"Oh, most certainly," said Jason. "But I'd bet he didn't."

"Why not?" asked Harold.

"Nate's a talker. If his paranoia became so out of control—and it has not, by the way—that he *was* to commit murder, he wouldn't be able to stop talking about. He would see it as his duty, so why cover it up?" said Jason. "Nate sees all those who he dislikes as North Vietnamese Army regulars. If he were to take one out, ya couldn't shut the poor schnook up."

Harold led the way back up the path to the sidewalk and up the hill to Pacific Dunes. The sun was starting to lower just enough to make the water twinkle. He thought of Cheryl and promised himself he would call her. He had been slightly remiss in his pursuit of Chief Jackson, and the view made him wistful to spend it with someone other than the colorful New York psychiatrist.

"Just one more question, Doctor," asked Harold. "With all the patients you've worked with here, does one stand out more than others? Your most memorable patient, so to speak," asked Harold.

"You bet," answered Jason with a slight grin. "Fascinating fellow. Former amateur fighter with a master's degree in English from Cal. As a boxing fan, we clicked immediately. Although if he could speak, he'd probably tell you I'm a bit of a pain in the tuchus. You two have something in common."

"And what would that be?" asked Harold.

"You're both in law enforcement."

CHAPTER 23

Harold was trying vainly to enjoy a peaceful Sunday morning. *Amazing what a good night's rest, strong cup of coffee, and Sunday paper does for the soul*, he thought. The sound of his cell phone ringing jostled Harold from his state of contentment.

"Davis," said Harold.

"Sorry to bug ya on a Sunday morning, Pops, but I have some info from the coroner's I thought you might find interesting," said Rebecca Santiago.

"All ears, Rebecca," Harold said.

"Three things," said Rebecca. "First, the fibers found around Simpson's throat were consistent with the same dental floss the patients at Pacific Dunes are given."

"Go on," said Harold, now jotting down notes on a pad of paper.

"Simpson had a really nasty case of gonorrhea. Don't know if that helps, but it kind of jumped out at me."

"Interesting," said Harold. "The floss is pertinent and supports an inside job. Let's put the VD on the back burner. At this point, it's not relevant, but that could always change."

After spending his Sunday walking on the beach, shopping for groceries, and taking a long nap, Harold warmed a plate of home-made raviolis he had been trying to perfect. Following dinner, he poured a small scotch and called Cheryl Jackson.

"Oh, hello, Detective," said Cheryl coolly.

Harold knew he was remiss for not calling sooner. He also knew that a woman like Cheryl Jackson did not pursue suitors. She was far too accustomed to *being* pursued and could afford to be discerning.

"Cheryl, I am truly sorry. This mess at Pacific Dunes has been very time-consuming," said Harold.

After a rather uncomfortable pause, Cheryl responded, "I understand how busy you must be and assumed as much when I heard about the second murder."

"Let me make it up to you. Cal Coastal plays UC Santa Barbara Friday night. How about it?" asked Harold hopefully. More uncomfortable silence.

"Well, unfortunately, Detective, I have other plans Friday night. I *will* be on campus, but not for a sporting event. I have a fundraiser at the Performing Arts Center. Would you care to join me?" asked Cheryl in her sweetest Southern drawl.

Harold squinted his eyes and grimaced. The last thing he wanted to do was go to a fundraiser with a gaggle of snobs and pseudo-intellectuals, or "fake smart guys," his father was fond of saying. He could picture himself standing among stuffy corduroy-clad professors in the campus Performing Arts Center while hearing the faint sound of the crowd next door in the basketball gym.

"I would love to, ma'am. Dress code please."

"Dressy casual would be wonderful, Harold. Pick me up at my place at seven, please," Cheryl said in a commanding tone.

"See you then."

She played basketball in college, for Pete's sake. Why pick a fundraiser over a game? Harold took a sip of scotch, pulled two sheets of paper from his pocket, and stared at Shapiro's handiwork. Halfway down the second sheet, he gazed at the now familiar name of Michael O'Shea. *A probation officer before he landed in Pacific Dunes. Cheryl's probation officer. A former boxer. The guy in the newspaper article on the coffee shop bulletin board.*

Harold sat down in a second bedroom he had converted into a home office and turned on his computer. *If we had Google when I was a young cop, I might have lived up to the three hundred murder inves-*

tigations nonsense in my retirement proclamation. When the familiar Google page appeared, he typed in "Deputy Probation Officer
Michael O'Shea."

After fifteen minutes of reading articles from the *Serra Tribune*,
Los Angeles Times, *San Francisco Chronicle*, and several online news
sources, Harold shut down his computer and stared out his window.
From his office, he could see a slice of the Pacific a few blocks away,
just enough to know the evening fog was rolling in. As a career police
officer, much of that as a detective, Harold knew he might have found
his first viable suspect to the murders and probably should have been
pouring a second and possibly celebratory scotch. But all he felt was a
small icy knot in the pit of his stomach, and as the evening went on,
the knot grew larger and colder.

*****

"Detective Davis, Mussel Shores PD here to see Investigator
Mowry, please," Harold announced at the window of the district
attorney's office on the third floor of the courthouse.

A clerk sitting behind a ballistic window examined Harold's
shield and identification and picked up her phone.

"Diana will be right up," the clerk said.

Diana Mowry was the assistant chief investigator for the district
attorney's office and a fellow transplant from the Los Angeles Police
Department. She and Harold, both "defectors," as they called themselves, had crossed paths in Los Angeles and occasionally bumped
into each other when they settled into their new agencies to the north.

"You look good, Pops," said Diana good-naturedly.

"I feel even better, young lady, and greatly appreciate your assistance," said Harold. "By the by, how did you hear about that unfortunate nickname?"

"Rebecca Santiago and I are on the same beach volleyball team.
She raves about you."

"Hmmm" was all Harold could offer in response.

Diana and Harold exchanged pleasantries and caught up on
gossip about their former colleagues with the LAPD. She led Harold

to a "soft" interview room in the rear of the DA's large office complex. The room was enclosed with no windows or natural light. But the mauve color chosen for the walls, soft tones of the overstuffed chairs, and lighting gave it a cozy feeling. The ambiance was intentional, which came in handy for interviewing victims and witnesses, many of whom were traumatized and frightened children. A decade earlier, Michael O'Shea had been interviewed in the same room following the first of his two officer-involved shootings. Conversely, down the hall were several "hard rooms." Bare walls, harsh lighting, a one-way mirror with a video camera on the other side, and furniture manufactured by inmates in a nearby prison were reserved for the guilty or suspected guilty, thus designed to motivate the subject to fess up and get the hell out of that dungeon as soon as possible.

"Okay, here the files of your victims," said Diana. "Stay as long as you need, but of course, no copies, and no removals."

"Thanks, Diana. Greatly appreciated," said Harold.

Harold sat down at a small table in the corner of the room and looked at two large stacks of manila files. Yellow Post-it notes identified one stack "Troop" and the other "Simpson." He shed his sport coat and made himself comfortable. The size of the files suggested accurately that he would spend the rest of the day in the small room. Harold drew a notebook from his briefcase and, in his indecipherable script, began taking notes about the lives of what he soon found were indeed two very bad men.

Harold began with David Lee Simpson. He recognized a common thread, similar to what he had observed dealing with hundreds of criminals over his career. A fatherless child raised by a grandmother who turned him over to Child Protective Services when he became too big and aggressive for an elderly lady to contain. Placement in a series of eleven foster homes accomplished little other than exposing the youngster to other delinquents. David Lee was severely beaten by one foster mother and molested by the boyfriend of another. He experienced frequent juvenile hall commitments and, ultimately, a six-year sentence in the California Youth Authority facility in Paso Adobe for voluntary manslaughter, the latter earned after stabbing a drug addict twice his age for failing to pay his drug tab. Upon release from the Youth Authority, David Lee's criminal education was complete. He drifted throughout the Western United States, landing in local jails along the way. David Lee had at least three former wives (that he could recall) and several children he had nothing to do with. Harold almost felt sorry for him.

Poor fool never really had a chance. This pity subsided when Harold read that David Lee's most recent offense was sexually molesting a developmentally delayed nineteen-year-old boy he met in a homeless shelter.

Now let's see what Mr. Troop has to say. Harold removed the thick rubber bands binding together a total of six thick files which told the tale of Richard Troop. Harold grew to despise Troop after only reading the first few pages of the first file. An almost comical lack of common sense paired with unparalleled arrogance and narcissism. Troop was the perfect sociopath, Harold thought, with two glaring exceptions. He was legitimately stupid and entirely dislikeable. Most of the sociopaths Harold had come into contact with had been both highly intelligent and quite charming. *Which is why Washington, DC, and boardrooms all over the country are full of them,* he thought.

Midway through the second Troop file, Harold took off his reading glasses and rubbed his eyes. The clock on the wall and his rumbling stomach indicated it was lunchtime. He walked out of the courthouse and into a spectacular Central Coast day. *Ah, this is the real reason why I moved here. Just don't mention that to the sisters.* He hadn't spent much time in the city of Serra since he lived and worked to the south near the beach. But every time he walked around the downtown area, Harold wondered why he didn't come up to the college town more often. He jogged across Cuesta Avenue, past an art-deco theater in the classical style of Hollywood's glory days, and down into the heart of the city's original Chinatown. It was no longer much of a Chinatown, as Harold soon discovered. An old two-story brick building stood on the corner. Originally, the building was a dry goods store which was once the social and commercial hub of a formerly thriving Chinese community. Across the street, the smells from a restaurant drew Harold in.

An old-fashioned chime above the door to Wong's Original Chinese Cafe announced Harold's arrival. As liberal as Serrans liked to think of themselves, the sight of a six-foot-four Black man still drew stares. Harold eased his lanky frame into one of the few vacant seats at the stainless-steel counter and glanced over the lunch menu. As always, Wong's was doing a brisk lunch business. Whoever Wong was, he had staffed the place well, and the service was prompt. He ordered a large bowl of wonton soup and some egg rolls from a woman of about twenty wearing a pink Cal Coastal sweatshirt. Harold looked around the now crowded dining room. The walls were covered with framed prints of exotic ports in what Harold assumed was China and photos of Mr. and Mrs. Wong posing with local dignitaries. To his right, he noticed a narrow stairway leading to a second floor. Just above the first step, Harold saw another framed photo. The entire Wong clan stood around a stocky man in a weathered blue and white letterman jacket. His waitress was in the middle of the photo wearing the same pink sweatshirt. Most of the adults held glasses and appeared to be in various stages of inebriation as they toasted someone's apparent good fortune. *Something about that fella. Know him from somewhere.*

Harold looked down and realized that his order had been placed on the counter in front of him. Still trying to place the Caucasian among a Chinese family in the photo, he quickly consumed his lunch.

"How was it?" asked the waitress.

"Perfect. Thank you for asking," Harold responded. "Young lady, may I ask you a question?"

"Sure," the waitress said with a smile.

"Would you mind telling me who the gentleman in the middle of that photo is?" he asked, pointing toward the picture.

"You mean O'Shea?"

"O'Shea?" asked Harold.

"Yeah, we just call him O'Shea. He lives in the apartment upstairs. My aunt and uncle have rented to him since I was little."

"My name is Harold, by the way. What's yours?

"Heather Wong. My family owns this restaurant."

"Well, Heather, is he a friend of yours?" asked Harold, attempting to appear as casual as he could.

"Well, he's pretty much a family member. Kind of like an uncle to me, I guess. My aunt and uncle call him Gad Sen, which means Godson in Mandarin," said Heather.

"Is Mr. O'Shea still living upstairs?" asked Harold.

"My aunt and uncle say this will always be his home, but he got hurt and is in a hospital down in Mussel Shores. Hope he comes back soon. I miss O'Shea," said Heather. "Wants people to think he's a tough guy, but he's just a sweetheart. An old boyfriend was hassling me a few years ago. O'Shea spoke with him, and we've never seen the jerk since." Heather giggled. "We joke that O'Shea buried him out in the dunes somewhere."

Harold thought he saw tears welling up in Heather's eyes and knew not to push the conversation any further.

"Heather, it's been a pleasure," said Harold, extending his hand. "I hope your friend is well and on the mend."

After paying his bill, including a generous tip for the proprietor's niece, Harold stood and walked by the photo at the foot of the stairs. *This is all getting spooky.*

After a brisk walk around town, Harold resisted the urge to grab a newspaper and relax in the Spilled Beans on Cuesta Street and returned to the courthouse. Starting where he had left off, he moved from Troop's stint as a local delinquent to his adult criminal career. Harold laughed out loud as he read of Troop's cockamamie scheme to build a strip club in his girlfriend's garage. He reviewed the first of a total of nineteen probation violation reports, each one more serious and bizarre. Harold had seen Troop's type before. *If he had put all that effort toward honest work, this imbecile would be president.*

It wasn't until Harold got to Troop's final probation report recommending a significant time behind the bars of a state prison that the reading got interesting. In the final file, Harold read under the "Summary of Offense" segment a tale that impressed even an experienced law enforcement officer. Troop had attacked his probation officer, not once but twice. The first incident took place in the probation department's office, a second in the parking lot of a local hospital. The victim, if you could call the winner of a street fight a victim, was an officer by the name of Michael Ignatius O'Shea.

Well, I'll be. We just moved from spooky to damned spooky. Victim is murdered in a hospital. Victim's former probation officer is a patient in the hospital. Probation officer appears to be a bit of a ruffian himself and previously hospitalized the victim when the victim resisted arrest.

Harold leaned back in his chair and tried to absorb this new tidbit of information. He updated his notes and closed the last of Troop's criminal files. *O'Shea is now officially my only suspect.*

CHAPTER 24

Harold stepped out of the shower and stared blankly into his closet. As a creature of habit and confirmed bachelor, he had struggled mightily when his sisters had covertly and slowly given away most of his comfortable clothes upon his arrival from Los Angeles several years earlier. Harold's sisters were both a curse and blessing, but that was another story.

Dressy casual. What's that mean? Tell me again why you're going to a stuffy-ass fundraiser and missing a college basketball game? Harold knew the answer, of course. He was sixty-two years old, in good health, and had a family who loved him. He was financially secure and still professionally relevant. *What more could I ask for?* The answer was relatively simple. Harold got lonely at night.

He reluctantly skipped a pair of jeans and sweatshirt and opted for a pair of gray wool slacks, black leather loafers with some foreign writing on the soles, a black silk T-shirt which Harold hated because he had to spend twelve bucks to have it dry cleaned every time he wore it, and a gray cashmere sport coat. He dabbed some cologne on his hands and ran them through his thinning salt-and-pepper hair. Harold gave himself one final examination in the mirror. *Not bad, Detective.*

Cheryl owned a two-story townhouse in a gated development high above the small coastal town of Clam Shell Beach. *Being a chief probation officer must pay damn well,* Harold thought as he drove up to a large iron gate and pressed a small silver button on the call box.

"Is that you, Detective Davis?" asked Cheryl sweetly.

"It is, indeed, ma'am. Looking forward to the basketball game," Harold said, grinning to himself.

"Hilarious, Detective. Absolutely precious, that sense of humor of yours. Second building on your left."

Harold watched the gate swing open. He followed her directions and parked his Chevrolet Silverado pickup truck in a spot a few steps from Cheryl's front door. Marveling at the butterflies in his belly and unaccustomed to the excitement of a fresh romance, Harold pressed Cheryl's doorbell and waited patiently.

"Good evening, Harold," said Cheryl as she opened the door to her townhouse.

"Good evening to you, Cheryl. You look very nice," Harold responded.

"As do you. Come on in. May I take your coat?" asked Cheryl.

"Yes, please," said Harold, taking off his sport coat.

Cheryl's home was tastefully decorated in soft colors accentuated by strategically placed lamps and recessed lights. A baby grand piano stood in a corner by a large window looking over the beach. Antique frames holding photos were placed on top of the piano. The largest was a dated photo of a very young-looking Cheryl and her parents, with mother and father looking like the proper and prominent Atlanta couple they were and Cheryl, a massive mane of hair tucked under a graduation cap.

"That's my mom, dad, and me the day I graduated from Howard University," said Cheryl.

"What was your major?" asked Harold.

"Music!" answered Cheryl with a smile. "I think Daddy had a dream that I would become the music director in his church, but I got the bug to move to California and was fortunate enough to get a postgraduate scholarship to Stanford to study early childhood development."

"Ever regret not sticking with music?" asked Harold.

"Not a bit. I still play now and then, but I've had a great career in public service, so no regrets."

Harold caught himself staring into Cheryl's eyes longer than he probably should have. "Well, guess we should head into town," he said, glancing at his watch.

"Actually, the fundraiser doesn't start for an hour or so, and the first part is a silent auction, so we have plenty of time. Would you like a drink before we leave? A glass of wine, perhaps?" asked Cheryl.

"A glass of wine would be nice, but a cold beer would be even better," said Harold. Cheryl was finding Harold's lack of pretensions increasingly attractive.

"A beer it is, Detective. Make yourself comfortable and I'll be right back," said Cheryl.

Harold watched Cheryl walk into a small kitchen off the living room and admired her rear end. She was wearing a tight skirt and matching blouse. *Perfect. Sexy but classy.* From speakers came the familiar sounds of the song "Sweet Love" by the Commodores. Both had been raised on seventies soul music, and Lionel Richie's deep voice made Harold nostalgic for his days at UCLA. Cheryl returned with a chardonnay and handed Harold a frosted mug of imported beer, much more high-flying than the Pabst Blue Ribbon perched on the top shelf of his refrigerator at home.

Cheryl sat down next to Harold on an overstuffed couch. He enjoyed the closeness and started devising a way to skip the fundraiser and spend the rest of the evening in Cheryl's townhouse. From the drawer of a side table, Cheryl pulled out a small remote control and turned on the gas flames of her fireplace.

Harold grinned. *This is getting cozy.* The two talked easily about music and their lives growing up, she in Atlanta, the daughter of a prominent preacher, and he in Paso Adobe, the son of a railroad worker. Their respective mothers had been known as housewives, whom both agreed ruled their homes with velvet gloves which concealed iron fists. Harold enjoyed the way Cheryl laughed easily at his attempts at humor and slightly touched his arm when she tried to make a point. Harold sneaked a glance at his watch and realized that the fundraiser had just started.

"Can I get you another beer, Harold?"' asked Cheryl.

"That would be very nice, thank you," said Harold, hoping against hope that this was a harbinger that the fundraiser was off and a pleasant evening overlooking the Pacific was on. He was pleasantly surprised to see that Cheryl had changed into a pair of white sweatpants and sweatshirt with the Greek letters of her college sorority embroidered on the front.

"You know, Harold, it's getting stormy out, and if I recall, the Lakers are on tonight. Would you mind too much if we stayed in and watched the game?" asked Cheryl.

"Only if you promise to take me to the next charity fundraiser and I can take my shoes off?" *I may have found the perfect female.*

As the evening progressed, Harold became increasingly comfortable and smitten. His shoes were now off, and he had untucked his shirt. Cheryl's massive plasma television and matching stadium sound system blasted the sights and sounds of the Los Angeles Lakers. Her taunts and cheers were spot on, making it obvious that she knew the game. Harold pictured a younger Cheryl Jackson, Howard University point guard commanding the other four players like she now commanded her probation officers. Cheryl had pulled a pizza from her freezer and "doctored" it up with fresh mushrooms, chopped basil, and olives. Before eating, Harold excused himself to use the bathroom. He made his way down a long hallway, walls filled with photos documenting Cheryl's life and career. One picture caught Harold's eye. Cheryl was professionally dressed and standing on a stage. Equally well-attired dignitaries were gathered around the foreground. Cheryl smiled as she handed a framed document to a stocky dark-haired man.

Looks as though he could handle himself in a squabble. Despite the solemnity of the event, whatever it was, the fellow was dressed in jeans, a flannel shirt, and a tattered college letterman's jacket, blue with faded and cracked white leather sleeves. A knit tie apparently from another era was noosed around his thick neck, almost as if at the last minute, someone influential had convinced this brute to spruce up a bit. Harold immediately recognized Michael O'Shea from the photos at the Spilled Beans and Wong's Café.

"Did you fall in?" Cheryl asked as she turned the corner toward the bathroom.

"Did I fall in? That's what my mom used to ask when my daddy spent too much time in the bathroom," Harold said with a giggle. "Not exactly. I was admiring your pictures," said Harold.

Cheryl gave Harold a brief explanation of each photo.

"This is an interesting-looking fellow," said Harold, pointing to the photo of Cheryl and Mike.

"That's O'Shea. I think I told you about him. One of my officers. Head trauma finally caught up with him, and he had a stroke chasing a gang member. He's the gentleman at Pacific Dunes." She glanced sideways at him. "Are you still working the case?"

"I am, and as soon as I use your facility, I'd like to ask you about that," said Harold.

He stood staring into a mirror placed directly at eye level above the toilet in Cheryl's bathroom. Harold marveled at the décor and wondered if Cheryl had hired a decorator or handled that task herself. He guessed the latter. After washing up, he rejoined Cheryl on the couch. The basketball game had ended, and music was back on, this time a ballad by Bill Withers.

"Cheryl, I hope you'll let me know if I'm overstepping my boundaries here."

Cheryl looked at Harold apprehensively. *Probably wondering why I'm ruining a perfectly nice evening talking shop.*

"Yes?" Cheryl said, sounding like a grade schoolteacher daring a mischievous student to explain him or herself for some act of malfeasance.

"Full disclosure, Cheryl. You know I'm working the Pacific Dunes murders. I have no suspects to speak of, so in that context, everyone associated with the hospital is a suspect," said Harold.

"My God, Harold! You're saying that you suspect Michael O'Shea of killing those two men?"

Harold was impressed with the speed with which Cheryl had jumped off the couch and now stood directly in front of him in what was tantamount to a combat stance. *Wow, kitten to lioness.* He was equally impressed with how swiftly she had reached a conclusion that Michael O'Shea was a suspect. *Maybe she has her own suspicions.*

"One of the victims was a probationer. Went to prison for assaulting your officer…although from what I read, Officer O'Shea got the better of him in the fight," said Harold almost apologetically.

"Large muscle-bound man? Stupid looking?" asked Cheryl, calmer now.

"Well, the last time I saw the gentleman, he was on a coroner's table, but yes, I'd say that's an accurate description," replied Harold with a chuckle.

Cheryl slowly sat in a large chair adjacent to the couch and tucked her legs under her. She looked pensive, and Harold knew he had clicked on a switch in her memory.

"I was there that day, and yes, O'Shea certainly emerged the victor in that particular altercation," said Cheryl quietly. "I hadn't put the two together. Are you sure about this?"

"It's all in the file," said Harold.

"You have to understand. Michael is a wonderful man and a close friend. At least as close as you can be with a subordinate," said Cheryl. "But he's a very violent man. I can't tell you how many times the county has been sued for his beatings."

"His *beatings*?" asked Harold, surprise in his voice. "How did he keep his job?"

"Very good question, Detective," said Cheryl. "He kept his job because all of his use of force incidents, and there are far too many to recall, sailed through the scrutiny of all investigative bodies responsible for examining these things.

"Well, it's really a moot point…I mean, have you ever met O'Shea?" asked Cheryl.

"Nope. Never met him," said Harold.

"Harold, there's no way he could have killed those men. He can barely get out of bed. The stroke almost killed him," said Cheryl.

"Can he speak?" asked Harold.

"Not well," Cheryl said, shaking her head from side to side. "For the most part, he communicates using a small writing board."

Harold folded his arms and looked down. Looking back at Cheryl, he said, "Cheryl, is it possible that O'Shea might be able to offer me at least some insight into what was going on in the hospital leading up to the murders?"

"Possibly. He's also probably clinically paranoid, so he might not talk to you at all."

"What's he got to be paranoid about?" asked Harold.

"Well, perhaps paranoid is too harsh a term. How about highly suspicious?" said Cheryl.

"I'd like some more background on this fellow before we meet. Other than you, who else knows him well?" asked Harold.

Cheryl smiled. "When was the last time you were in a Catholic church, Detective?"

CHAPTER 25

Weeks passed before Cheryl and Harold saw each other again. Cheryl's father had suffered a mild heart attack, and she flew back to Atlanta to help her mother with his recovery and care. Even though they were apart, Harold and Cheryl continued their courting via email. In the evening, she would help herself to a tumbler of her mother's peach brandy, the only liquor allowed in the Jackson home, and retire to her old bedroom to write long emails to Harold. Harold looked forward to doing the same. At some point, she insisted that Harold state his intentions. After turning off his computer and taking a long late-night stroll along the beach boardwalk, Harold returned to his condo and responded:

Good evening, Cheryl

Regarding your inquiry as to my intentions, must admit, it's been a while since I've been "involved" with anyone, and I've discovered I've missed it! I like you, Cheryl, and I think we have a great deal in common. As you know, I have been a bachelor for a *very* long time, and I am a bit set in my ways. I don't shave on the weekends, I am prone to drinking out of the milk carton, don't always flush, and have been known to demonstrate a propensity for profanity, especially when my Lakers are down! Having said all that, if you are game, I would propose that we become "exclusive" (a term youngsters use for "going steady"). This seems to be a good place to start, to me at least. Hope all is well with your folks and look forward to your return to the Sunshine State.

Fondly,
H

Cheryl read Harold's email and smiled. He was astute enough to be current but traditional enough to be formal and even courtly. *Believe I will take Detective Davis up on his kind offer.*

The following Saturday evening, Harold picked Cheryl up at Serra's small regional airport. She looked great as always in knee-length shorts and a matching top, comfortable travel clothes which allowed Harold to admire her long legs as they walked to his car. Although she had been gone for less than three weeks, Cheryl had packed four matching pieces of luggage, which Harold schlepped down the winding path from the terminal to the airport parking lot.

The now *couple* of Cheryl Jackson and Harold Davis held hands in comfortable silence as they drove the back roads from the airport to Clam Shell Beach. Harold dragged the luggage into Cheryl's bedroom and realized that he had never been this deep into her townhouse. He set down the luggage in a corner of the bedroom and turned to make a smart crack about the weight of her suitcases. Cheryl was standing inches from him and gently ran her finger across his cheek.

"Detective, you shaved for me even though it's a weekend," she purred.

They spent the evening whispering and giggling in bed like a couple of adolescents. Cheryl announced she was thirsty and half jogged to the kitchen to work out some of the kinks from a long flight. She cracked open a bottle of home-brewed root beer made by her father in the basement of the family home. After pouring the brown liquid into two glasses of ice, Cheryl returned to the bedroom, only to find Harold curled around one of her large pillows, snoring blissfully. She covered him up with a blanket, turned off the bedside lamp, and quietly closed the door behind her.

After catching up on her emails, Cheryl crafted one of the more awkward correspondences she could recall. She understood Harold's interest in Mike, possibly someone who could be a source of information since he *was* the former probation officer of one of the victims. But Cheryl was savvy enough to know that Harold's seemingly innocent delving into Mike's background wasn't *entirely* innocent. Under any other circumstances, Mike would have made a stellar suspect. His connection to one of the victims was obvious, and as far as she knew, he was the only trained and proven killer in the hospital the night of the murders.

Cheryl knew she needed to tread lightly. She and Harold, the lead investigator on the case, were now "involved." It was important that she not say or do *anything* which crossed personal or professional boundaries. After staring at the screen of her computer, she wrote:

Good evening, Father De la Rosa,

I hope this note finds you well and in good health. Of the many sources of sadness that came with Michael's illness was feeling that I have lost track of one of my favorite people. Let's not allow that to occur! I have been out of town visiting my folks in Atlanta, so I haven't seen Michael recently, but I plan on going down to Pacific Dunes over the next few days. While he seems slightly agitated with my visits, seeing him certainly buoys *my* spirits, so they shall continue!

On another issue, I have made acquaintance with Detective Harold Davis of the Mussel Shores Police Department. He is the lead investigator in the Pacific Dunes murders, and assuming he has not already done so, I believe he may contact you to get some background information on Michael. Just a "heads-up," as they say. Let's do our best to get together for lunch next week if you are available. I miss you Father. Take good care.

Cheryl

Confident that she had retained an appropriate personal and professional boundary with Harold while extending a courtesy to Iggy, Cheryl clicked send. As she walked toward her bedroom, she stopped in the hallway and stared at the photo of herself with Mike.

The man's an invalid. He can barely walk, let alone murder two people. Stop this nonsense, she thought.

*****

Harold parked his city-issued vehicle in the four-story parking structure on Pacific Street in downtown Serra. Serra was busy with shoppers and people with a variety of business near the government center, so he had to search for a parking space, finally locating one on the top level of the structure.

Harold walked down Pacific Street past Chinatown and Wong's Cafe. He thought back on his lunch of egg rolls and wonton soup while he took a break from looking at the files of the Pacific Dunes victims and inhaled sweet aromas wafting from the kitchen. *Hell with this goofy diet Cheryl has apparently put me on. I'm stopping in for some lunch after my meeting.*

Harold smiled as he thought of how quickly his courtship with Cheryl had progressed. She started accepting invitations to a variety of social events on their behalf and had suggested that he limit fats and carbohydrates in his diet. Harold noticed that when Cheryl shopped, she shopped for two and had stocked her refrigerator with his favorite beer. He also noticed that she had prominently displayed the Lakers' schedule on her refrigerator and, as an act of supreme consideration, refused to schedule anything on the nights the Lakers played. He further noticed that Cheryl had bought some formfitting Laker T-shirts which she had taken to wearing while watching games. As a final act of hospitality, she purchased a new toothbrush and bathrobe for Harold, which now hung on a hook in the bathroom. *Boy, is she workin' you.*

"Good morning, ma'am. I'm Detective Harold Davis with the Mussel Shores Police Department. Is Father De la Rosa in? I believe he's expecting me," Harold announced to the elderly housekeeper employed by the parish to keep the rectory tidy and cook for Father Iggy and the other priest assigned to the church.

The housekeeper took a minute or two to inspect Harold's badge and identification card, much longer than was necessary. Harold grinned. *You never know when an imposter cop is going to walk in and take advantage of an elderly priest.*

"Father's not in, but he is expecting you and should return momentarily," the housekeeper said in a thick accent Harold pegged as Northern European. "You may wait in his study."

The housekeeper led Harold up a staircase and down a long hallway into a large office overlooking the street. Harold looked around and realized that he was standing in one of the older parts of the church complex. The walls were made of a beige material that he assumed was adobe. Roughhewn oak beams ran lengthwise across the ceiling. In the corner of the office was a large desk, also made of thick oak. A sturdy-looking bookcase sat behind the desk. Harold wondered how many of the priests in the church's nearly two-hundred-year history had occupied this office. Several acknowledgments to modern technology were evident. A flat-screen television was mounted on the wall directly in front of an antique sofa, and a small laptop was placed on top of the desk.

On one of the walls hung photographs of various sizes and frame styles documenting the life and career of the occupant, Father Ignatius Sean De la Rosa. A young man in boxing shoes and trunks assumed a classic fighter's stance in one photo with the caption "Iggy De la Rosa, 1969 Golden Gloves Champion, San Francisco,

California." The young fighter bore a striking resemblance to Robert De Niro in the film *Taxi Driver*, Harold thought.

There were several photos of Iggy in gray sweats, standing next to a dark-haired youngster at a variety of boxing events. One caught Harold's attention. It was a grainy eight-by-ten black-and-white photo taken by a sportswriter who doubled as a photographer with the *San Francisco Chronicle*. In the photo was a young Michael, eighteen or so, in white boxing shorts, face bloodied and bruised, arms casually hanging from the ropes of a boxing ring. Father Iggy held an ice pack on his neck while whispering something intently in the fighter's ear. *Certainly, more than a priest to the kid.*

"Hey! What the hell are you doin' in here?" bellowed Iggy from the door.

Harold identified the man as the occupant of the office from the wall of photos. He appeared older but no less fit. Before Harold had a chance to respond the man repeated his question.

"I *said*, what the hell are you doing in here?"

"Detective Harold Davis. You must be Father De la Rosa. I believe we have an appointment," Harold said meekly.

Iggy assumed an aggressive stance—hands balled into fists tucked into his hips, feet shoulders length apart. His gray sweats were stained with perspiration.

"Ha! I got ya!" yelled Iggy as he stuck out his right hand. "Just can't pass up the chance to stick it to a good cop. I was the chaplain for the Oakland PD for about a hundred years, ya know."

"I didn't know, Father, but I'm pleased to make your acquaintance," said Harold with a tone of relief.

"Sit down, sit down, Detective. Can I get you anything? Water, coffee, a pop maybe?" asked Iggy in a far friendlier voice.

"No, thank you, Father. I'm fine," said Harold.

"I hope you don't mind my little stab at humor, Detective. I'm old, and the one thing I dislike about other old people is that they lose their ability to *laugh*," said Iggy.

"I appreciate your humor and you seeing me. Hope I didn't disturb you," said Harold, motioning to Iggy's attire.

223

"Not at all, and I apologize for not being here when you arrived. I just got back from my morning workout up at the college and lost track of time."

"Really?" asked Harold, impressed, given the priest's apparent age.

"Yeah, be seventy-four next month and get up to campus a few days a week," said Iggy proudly.

"What exactly do you *do* there, Father?"

"Ah. I have found God's Fountain of Youth in a college stadium, Detective. Let me show you," said Iggy, motioning Harold over to more photographs.

Harold couldn't help but notice the natural athleticism in Iggy's gait as he walked across the room.

"Here's a picture I took of Michael when he was in high school at Edward's Field up at Cal," said Iggy.

Harold looked at a photo of young Michael O'Shea running up steep cement stadium steps. Sweat drenched the almost identical outfit as this priest's standing before him.

"Kids are funny, Detective. You never know what they're going to pick up on. For me and Michael, it was running those damn stadium steps. Been doing it for years. Of course, my knees gave out a while back, so now it's more of a soft stroll, considering becoming a crawl," said Iggy with a laugh. "I cycle as well, but nothing gives me the zing of runnin' the steps."

"What exactly is your relationship with Officer O'Shea?" asked Harold.

"I'll only answer that question if you agree to call me Iggy. Okay, Detective?"

"It's a deal, Iggy. If you agree to call me Harold."

"Deal!" said Iggy.

Iggy walked over to his desk and grabbed a pair of reading glasses. He returned to the wall of photos and searched for one in particular.

"Here we go," Iggy said under his breath. He pointed to a picture of Mike as an infant, held by a tall muscular man in an ill-fitting suit, a pretty blond woman next to him, and Iggy to their right in a gold and white hassock.

"I knew Michael's father, Emile, when he was a cop with the OPD. His mom was my housekeeper up at Saint Mary's in Oakland. I introduced 'em!" said Iggy with pride.

"So you've known Officer O'Shea all of his life?" asked Harold.

"I have. When his dad was killed, I kind of became his surrogate father," said Iggy with a tinge of emotion in his voice.

"Killed on the job?' Harold asked.

"Yeah," replied Iggy in almost a whisper. "On Michael's first birthday."

"What about his mother?" asked Harold.

"Died of cancer when he was a senior at Cal. After that, I guess I was the only family he had," said Iggy. "He had some nutjob aunts and uncles, but for all intent and purposes, I was it for the kid."

Iggy led Harold over to a chair in front of the oak desk. He took off his glasses while loosening the laces of his sneakers.

"As you know, Iggy, Officer O'Shea was a patient in the Pacific Dunes Rehabilitative Hospital the nights of the two murders I'm investigating," said Harold.

"I was in Texas, visiting my aunt and uncle the day JFK was assassinated, Detective. Does that mean I killed the president?" Iggy asked in a soothing voice reserved for grooms with cold feet.

"Not at all, Father. I'm just trying to gather background information on the hospital patients who were in the facility the evenings of the murders. Frankly, I don't have much else to go on," said Harold with a shrug.

Iggy gave Harold an icy glare. Harold looked away, not wanting to agitate the priest by exposing what appeared to be a two-hundred-pound nerve by the name of Michael O'Shea.

"Father, I'd like to ask you a question. Would you consider Officer O'Shea to be a violent man?" asked Harold. *He's already got me pegged as unfriendly. Might as well throw the dice*, thought Harold.

Iggy rose from his chair, walked to the door of his office, and called out, "Helga, could we have a couple of beers please?"

Harold knew instinctively that Iggy had something profound to say and wanted to buy some time. The housekeeper, who was conveniently listening to the conversation as best she could through the thick oak door, quickly grabbed two bottles of beer and mugs, placed them on a tray, and delivered them to Iggy's office as directed. Iggy accepted the tray and placed it on his desk. He carefully poured the beer into the mugs, offered one to Harold, and grabbed one for himself.

"Michael O'Shea is a very complex man, Detective," said Iggy, taking a sip from the mug.

"On that we can certainly agree, Father," said Harold, relieved that the priest had assumed a more conciliatory tone.

"It's no coincidence that he was named after St. Michael, God's enforcer."

Iggy put his glasses back on, stood, and walked again toward the wall of photos. He scanned the frames until he found the right photo and motioned Harold over.

"See that one?" asked Iggy, motioning to a black-and-white picture of Mike, standing on one side of a boxing referee wearing short-sleeved white shirt, black slacks, and a black bow tie in the style worn by boxing officials during the sport's golden years. Another young fighter stood opposite the referee. The referee held Mike's right hand aloft in victory. His opponent's hand was limp to his side. The opponent's manager stood behind his young fighter, one hand around his waist, holding him up after a savage beating.

"Look at that poor kid," said Iggy, quietly pointing a finger to the other fighter. "It was the 1979 AAU semifinal fight in Denver. Michael's opponent was hospitalized for almost a *month* following that fight. Brain hemorrhage, broken nose, broken eye socket," said Iggy sadly.

"Why didn't the referee stop the fight sooner?" asked Harold.

"That's the point, Harold. The fight *was* stopped early. Ninety seconds into the *first* round, in fact. Michael inflicted that amount of damage in about a minute and a half," replied Iggy. "And it wasn't a gross mismatch. The other kid was quite good. But he ran into a buzz saw that day."

Harold looked at photos he had missed before. A dozen or so with a much younger Iggy standing to the side of a collection of youngsters, mostly Black and Latino, a few White, all in ill-fitting boxing shorts and tank tops. Documentation of Iggy's career as a boxing coach in the basement of St. Mary's Church.

On an adjacent shelf, Harold noticed a larger photo of Iggy and Mike on the sidelines of one of Mike's rugby matches. Mike, hands on his knees and trying to catch his breath, and Iggy, leaning in to provide some words of encouragement. It was one of those priceless candid photos that perfectly reflected the moment. Harold noticed that both of Iggy's hands were bandaged.

"Almost looks like you were on the field that day, Iggy," said Harold, pointing to Iggy's hands in the photo.

"I'm not sure why I'm going to tell you this, Harold, but I feel like I can trust you, and I'm a pretty good judge of character."

Harold smiled and nodded at the compliment.

"My hands were bandaged because a few days before that picture was taken, I beat a young monk senseless. Almost killed him, actually."

Harold looked at Iggy, then again at the photo, and back to Iggy. Iggy proceeded to describe Brother William, his arrival at the St. Mary's rectory, and finally the morning Iggy stumbled upon William's stash of pornography.

An astonished Harold stared again at the photo, trying to imagine Mike trying to pull Iggy off the unconscious monk's body.

"Beg your pardon, Iggy, but your actions were, well, they were justified, in my opinion."

"Not sure I can agree with you, Harold. Guess someday I'll find out," Iggy said with a sad smile. "Even though Michael was a grown man by then, he was a *young* man and still impressionable. I don't think I set the best example of restraint and emotional maturity that day."

"Thank you for sharing that with me."

"I don't talk about it much, and Michael and I have never discussed it since." Iggy took a deep breath of relief. "I have to say it was a bit cathartic. Thanks for listening."

Iggy walked back to his desk and took a sip of beer. "Well, you're not here to hear an old priest's confession. Let's get back to Mike."

Harold chose his words carefully. "It appears that Mike was a very good fighter, perhaps professional level. Why did he stop fighting?" asked Harold.

"There's a question," said Iggy with a chuckle. "You said you haven't met Michael yet, Harold, but when you do, look at those specs of his. They look like they were crafted from Coke bottles. Got to tell ya, between the glasses and those cauliflowers he calls ears... well, let's just say I've never quite understood why the ladies seem to fawn all over the guy."

"Eye damage?" asked Harold.

Iggy smiled sadly. "Detached retinae. Would have gone blind in his left eye if he had kept fighting. Hearing the news from a doctor was one of the more traumatic days of the kid's life. Mine too, for that matter. Speaking as objectively as I can, had it not been for Michael's eye injury, I believe he could have become an Olympian and then fought professionally and reached deeply into the top rankings of the light heavyweight division...perhaps even gone all the way if you consider the top light heavies at the time."

Harold looked down and imagined an eighteen-year-old boxer with bright aspirations, sitting in a doctor's office, stunned, consoled by his coach and surrogate father (an image Iggy would have found surprisingly accurate).

"I don't know how many concussions Mike suffered fighting. We didn't really think about that back then, but I suspect at least a few," said Iggy. "Then he joined the rugby club at Cal, which, if you know anything about rugby, surely didn't help things."

Iggy returned to the wall of photos. "Look at this one," he said to Harold.

"Oh my gosh...what a picture," Harold said, recoiling from the framed photo of Mike at a rugby match.

The photo was of a much younger Michael O'Shea in a rugby kit, soaked in mud and sweat. Two burly teammates held him upright as another teammate, who happened to be an emergency room physician, stitched up a large gash just above Mike's left eye. What made the photo striking was that the photographer clicked her camera just as the skin above Mike's eye was pulled away from his head by the rugby-playing doctor's suture. The photo appeared in the *Berkeley Gazette* and was picked up by the Associated Press, where it appeared in sports pages throughout the country.

"Michael was drawn to violent sports, wasn't he?" asked Harold.

"Absolutely," said Iggy. "Great home, loving parents, no abuse of any kind. But for some reason, the kid was just hardwired for violence." *Watch yourself. Might be a little too candid,* Iggy thought.

Iggy stood and walked to the office door. "Helga, a couple of more beers, if you please," he called out. "I am by no means a trained psychologist," said Iggy, taking his seat at the desk. "But I have had sufficient training and experience in the human condition to have formulated a theory that might help you understand Michael." *Why are you helping this guy? You know where's he's headed,* Iggy said to himself.

Harold listened intently. Not only was the priest a wealth of background information, but he was also finding the story of Michael O'Shea compelling.

"Michael's conception and the conception of others like him are one of the great ironies of the universe," said Iggy. "Despite his Irish-Catholic upbringing, he is full Native American adopted by Bridgette and Emile. His birth mother was a very young runaway from a tribe over in the San Joaquin Valley. Michael was not conceived under the best circumstances. From what little we know, his mother was raped by Michael's biological father, a member of the same tribe as the mother."

Iggy took a deep breath as if reliving the pain of the story himself. "The mother found herself hooking in Oakland and was severely beaten by her pimp, hoping to end her pregnancy himself. Mike's birth was an *incredibly* violent experience, one in which his mother died shortly after giving birth. He came about out of the love of God, but certainly not the love of his birth parents. Do you understand the magnitude of that?"

Harold squirmed, slightly uncomfortable engaging in a conversation about faith with a priest. In Harold's Baptist upbringing, these conversations simply didn't occur.

"So your statement that Mike was hardwired for violence makes sense."

"A miraculous and wonderful thing happens when the Lord brings a man and a woman together," said Iggy. "But when that conception is founded on hate and violence, how can the child, deep within his mother's womb, *not* be impacted by those horrible emotions?"

After a pause, Iggy went on. "Don't get me wrong, Harold. Michael survived those experiences wonderfully. He graduated with two degrees in English from a prestigious university and had a terrific career in law enforcement. But he simply approaches violence differently that the rest of us."

"How so?" asked Harold

"Mike was never a brawler. A sweet-natured kid. No yanking the wings off butterflies like some of the other sad cases I've seen. But he is very *efficient* in using violence to resolve problems, *if* in his own mind there are no other reasonable alternatives."

"Not uncommon in law enforcement to find men like that," Harold said with a slight nod.

"Agreed. In Mike's case, God has placed him in some very difficult situations over the years, clearly giving him the opportunity to engage in lawful and justified violence. To put it bluntly, if you delve further, you will find that Michael is a bit of what the lads up in the Oakland PD would refer to as a shit magnet," Iggy said with a giggle.

Iggy stared at Harold and asked, "During a long career, Detective, how many people have you killed?"

"None, thank God. Like to keep it that way," said Harold.

"Michael has killed two times in the line of duty, Harold, and one additional nonfatal shooting. I tell you that knowing you would have eventually found out, if in fact you don't already know. But as scripture tells us, there is a difference between killing and murder. Michael will kill if he has to, but he is not a murderer," said Iggy.

"From what I know of the hospital deaths, they were murders, not killings."

Harold said, "That they were."

"You know, Harold, I suspect I know the real reason you came here today," said Iggy.

"Just trying to get some perspective," said Harold, beginning to feel uneasy with the directness of the priest.

"The real reason you're here is to ask me if Michael has confessed to the murders to me as his priest. That's the real reason I suspect."

Harold looked down, wondering if this meeting was the best idea. "I've kind of put you in a jam here, haven't I?"

Iggy gave a noncommittal smile. "Hey, you feel like a walk? There's an ice cream place around the corner."

CHAPTER 26

Harold thanked the priest for his time and candor and politely declined Iggy's ice cream offer. Alone in his office, Iggy picked up the old photo of him and Mike and returned it to his wall of memories. Harold was right. Iggy's bandaged hands suggested that *he* had competed in the ring.

Rough day. Don't know if I've talked about it since it happened. I don't even think about it. Haven't talked about it with Mike. Wonder if he ever goes back to that day? A very "un-priest-like" response, fella.

Thirty-four years earlier

A few lonely weeks after his mother's funeral, Mike began the arduous task of going through her things with the help of some of the women in the parish. As was Bridgette's wishes, the house she raised a son in as a single mother was sold with half the proceeds going to the church and the other to Mike, leaving him without a place to stay until he plotted out his future. With a few boxes in hand, he crossed the street and knocked on the rectory door one bright December morning. Iggy opened the door. Dark stains dominated his sweatshirt from an hour workout in the basement boxing gym.

"Hey, Mike. Come on in," said Iggy, pleased to see Mike so early.

The two walked into the rectory kitchen, and Iggy poured them both coffee and got out the fixings for scrambled eggs. After a quick breakfast, Mike admitted to Iggy that with all the stress and activity of his mother's death, he really hadn't planned on where to stay when the house sold.

"Want a roomie, Father?" asked Mike with a smile.

Iggy looked down as if in deep thought. "Well, son. You know we have a haircut standard around here. Not sure you cut the mustard with that mop of yours."

Mike grinned sheepishly. His hair indeed hung well below his ears and collar. "Yeah, I know. It's just that I kind of get tired of people starin' at the ears." Years of boxing and rugby had rendered his ears disfigured with what is known as "cauliflower ears."

Iggy pointed to his own equally unique ears. "You're preaching to the choir, son."

"If it's a hassle, I totally understand...no problem," said Mike.

"Of course, Michael, you know you're always welcome here. I want you to think of this as your home."

"I appreciate that, Iggy," said Mike. "I could move back into the basement of the sorority house where I was working in the kitchen or stay with some of my rugby buddies, but let's face it, I'm just a little too old for the college scene."

"So what are you going to do with your life, lad?" asked Iggy in a tone lighter than the solemnity of the question.

"Well, I've got my job at McDuff's tending bar, and I'm going to play rugby with the Old Blues."

The Old Blues was the Cal alumni rugby team and was almost as well-known in the rugby community as the university's team. Many Old Blues went on to play for the American national team, the Eagles.

"Also enrolled in a couple of grad classes," Mike added.

"Grad classes?" said Iggy in surprise.

"Oh yeah, forgot to tell you. In a fit of desperation, the University of California, Berkeley, accepted me into their master's program in English," said Mike sheepishly.

In response to his godson's failure to share this bit of good news, Iggy simply shut his eyes and shook his head.

Iggy's smile affirmed for Mike that his short-term plan was acceptable, at least for the time being.

"I won't be here long, Iggy. Just till I kind of figure things out, and I want to pay rent."

"No rent, Mike. Just clean up after yourself, and you can help with the youth boxing program when I need you. And *no girls*, Michael. Got that?" Mike smiled. Iggy did not.

"I'm not fooling around, son. The bishop finds out my roommate is some kind of playboy and I've got big problems, big problems, mister. Got it?"

Mike nodded solemnly. *Guy's killin' me. Weird enough I'm living with my priest. Does he really think I'm gonna try and sneak chicks in here?*

After a day of rugby, a graduate class, and the closing shift at McDuff's, Mike trudged up the stairs of the rectory to his room down the hall from Iggy. Despite the hour, he could see light under the door leading into Iggy's bedroom and office. Mike knocked on the door lightly and heard Iggy's voice call, "Come on in." Iggy sat at his desk, a copy of a biography of St. Ignatius de Loyola, his namesake, in one hand, a small tumbler of scotch in the other. Mike fell into a chair near the desk and took off his shoes.

"You look like you could use a drink, lad," said Iggy.

"Too pooped," mumbled Mike, sitting back in the chair and closing his eyes.

"Hey, I'm glad you came in. I want to talk to you about something. We have a guest."

"What's her name?" asked Mike with a smile, eyes still closed.

"It's a *he*, not a she, funny guy," replied Iggy. "Brother William O'Connor is his name, and he'll be bunking in the extra room downstairs."

"That's nice," Mike said in a dreamy voice as he stretched out in the chair. "What's his story?"

"Well, I'll tell you what I know, which isn't much. Salinan brother from the monastery up in Napa. Young kid, just got out of the seminary." Iggy paused to compose his next sentence. "There was some trouble involving William up in Napa. The diocese wasn't entirely clear what happened, but someone in a high place thinks some time here at St. Mary's would be good for him."

Mike looked half asleep and completely uninterested. "I'll take him to rugby practice tomorrow. We can always use another tackling dummy."

Brother William O'Connor was indeed young. At twenty-one, he was one of the youngest novitiates to ever enter the Brothers of Aquinas, an order of teaching monks based in California's Napa Valley. He was an odd sort, with the baby fat and acne of an adolescent but a way of grinning that wasn't youthful at all. In fact, it was a little unsettling, Iggy thought when he greeted William at the door of the rectory. William was shy by nature and seemed devoid of any sense of humor. Mike took an immediate dislike to the young man and paid him little attention. On occasion, he'd ask Iggy, "Why is that guy here again?" To which Iggy would only give his standard reply that William had apparently experienced problems of some sort up at the Napa monastery and had been sent to St. Mary's for a "break." Iggy seemed as in the dark about the monk's presence as Mike.

William was an amateur photographer with an impressive array of cameras, lighting equipment, tripods, and various devices Mike and Iggy couldn't quite identify. With Iggy's permission, he established a small dark room in an empty closet off the rectory kitchen where he could develop his own photographs. Even though he and Mike were just a few years apart in age, both college educated, and came from the same faith, they had virtually nothing in common and no real desire to change that.

Their only verbal interaction was when Iggy introduced the two. After inspecting Mike's olive complexion, dark hair and eyes, and rather flat nose, he said, "You don't look Irish."

"He's not, William. Mike's biological parents were indigenous Indians, but he was adopted by wonderful Irish Catholic parents," Iggy said.

Sensing correctly that William lacked any real social skills, Mike decided to avoid his new housemate, and the two went about their business while staying out of one another's space.

William busied himself reading, eating Iggy out of house and home, napping, watching soap operas, and playing with his cameras. He took over altar server duties at mass each day, but other than that, Mike really wasn't sure what William did with his time and was still mystified *why* he was there.

*****

Mike had taken to referring to William as "the squatter," which, at first, brought a subtle smile to Iggy's face, but now he was just another irritant. Mike lay in bed one morning, having slept in after a late night working at McDuff's. He stared at the celling, one arm under his head, as he contemplated his future and how long before Iggy started referring to *him* as "the squatter."

Mike had to admit, as comfortable as his life had become, at twenty-four, living for free in a church rectory with his priest and strange little William was just pathetic. The fact that he was unable to enjoy the overnight company of females made a curious situation that much worse. *Yep, gotta make a move. Time to leave the roost.*

Mike's moment of self-reflection was disrupted by glass breaking and what sounded like the squealing of a child downstairs. Thinking that perhaps an intruder had broken into the rectory, Mike leaped out of bed, threw on a pair of gym shorts, and bolted from his room toward the staircase. As Mike ran into the rectory entryway, he heard what sounded like a bar brawl coming from William's bedroom. In a few steps, he was in front of William's bedroom and immediately saw that the thick oak door was half off its hinges. Wood from the doorjamb was splintered, and the doorknob was hanging by a few disengaged wood screws.

Mike peered into the bedroom and saw a scene which would remain etched in his memory forever. A newspaper was spread on the floor with a pair of Iggy's reading glasses now snapped in two. Camera equipment was strewn around the room in various forms of disrepair, as if someone had taken a baseball bat to them. On the floor in the center of the room was William, on his back, attempting with little success to deflect expertly thrown blows from a maniacal-looking Iggy. The priest was above William, legs straddling the young monk's shoulders.

"Help me, Mike! He's a crazy man!" William screeched.

Uh-oh, he's right. The damn priest has lost it. What the hell happened to Iggy? The blows continued, and now blood either from Iggy's fist or William's fleshy face was covering both.

"Iggy!" Mike yelled with no response, just more punches. "Iggy, stop!" Mike called again, with no reaction from Mike's mentor, friend, and surrogate father. *This can't be happening.* Just more punches. "*Father Ignatius*, get the fuck off him!" Mike commanded in a loud voice.

At the sound of his formal name and one Mike rarely if ever used, Iggy's violent spell was broken. Mike seized upon the pause, grabbed Iggy by the shirt collar, and lifted him off the now unconscious William.

"What the hell's the matter with you?" Mike demanded.

Mike heard the low whine of an ambulance close by. He surveyed the room and tried again to make sense of what had happened. Mike waded a few steps through broken camera equipment in the direction of William's bed, looked down, and froze.

"Oh my god," Mike said in a whisper. "Oh, God, no."

On William's bed was an opened medium-sized suitcase. Mike then realized what an amazing job his mother and Iggy had done sheltering him from life's evil and sickness. Never had he felt so completely innocent and ill prepared to deal with the pure darkness he saw on the bed. Strewn about were dozens of photos, both color and black-and-white. In each image, Mike saw the vacant look of children, appearing to be ten years and younger.

The children were mostly nude. In many of the photos were the larger forms of men, also nude. Mike realized what had driven Iggy to such rage. He had come upon, quite accidently, William's vast collection of child pornography. Mike felt nauseous. He looked around, found a trash can by the bed, and dropped to his knees as he heaved the contents of his stomach.

*****

The paramedics took William's vitals and assured Mike that despite "one bad ass kickin'," he would survive. He moaned as the paramedics loaded the gurney into the rear of the ambulance. William had gained consciousness but refused to make eye contact with Mike through his badly swollen eyes. A paramedic asked Mike what had happened. Out of an immediate desire to protect Iggy, Mike responded that he just wasn't sure.

"Better get ready to talk to the cops. This kid's in bad shape," replied the paramedic.

Mike found Iggy in his office. He remained silent and let Iggy explain in his own time what had caused him to apparently attempt murder. Iggy walked to a cabinet bolted to the wall behind his desk and pulled out a bottle of scotch and small tumbler. With shaking hands, he poured a stout portion of the reddish-brown liquid into the glass. Iggy took a sip, sat back in his chair, and closed his eyes. Mike eyed the bottle. *You know, I could use one of those too, Padre.*

"Knuckles are swollen," Iggy said almost absentmindedly.

"I can see that," said Mike. "Want to tell me what this is all about?"

Iggy abruptly stood and walked out of the office. Mike just stared at his empty chair. *Okay, this is just fuckin' nuts.* He gave out a sigh of relief when Iggy returned with his right hand wrapped in a plastic bag of ice.

Iggy began to explain that he had had concerns about William from the beginning and didn't appreciate, as he put it, a "royal diocesan dump job." The diocese was virtually mute on why William had been exited from the monastery. Calls to the monastery prefect went unreturned, a fact that infuriated Iggy.

Earlier that morning, Iggy returned to the rectory from his early morning workout. Still soaked in sweat, he walked into the kitchen and loaded the coffee maker. It was at that moment when he heard the muffled voice of a child coming from inside William's room. Iggy stood at William's door, listening intently and trying to make out both who was talking and what was being said. Iggy immediately recognized William's voice, and within a few seconds, he realized that the second voice was that of a young boy. Iggy tried the doorknob and found that it was locked. He began rapping on the door.

"William, open the door!" Iggy screamed. No answer. More pounding. "William, open the door, now!" The voices became quiet.

In one fluid motion, Iggy reared back his right foot and slammed it just above the doorknob. With surprising efficiency, the door gave way, and the wood surrounding the frame splintered. One final kick completed the job, and the door flew open, hanging off the hinges by a few slivers of wood and metal screws. Mike stared at Iggy still in disbelief. *Is he makin' this shit up?*

"You know Juan, one of my CYO kids?"

Mike nodded. "Yeah, good kid."

Once I made it into the bedroom, I saw little Juan and knew it wasn't good," said Iggy. "The poor kid looked terrified. He grabbed his clothes and bolted out the door before I could see if he was okay."

"Oh shit, he was naked?" asked Mike. Iggy slowly nodded.

Iggy paused and looked away. "Mike, I looked at the pictures spread out on William's bed and felt sick. I saw pure evil. It was as if Satan himself entered this home…this church."

Iggy slowly stood up and walked toward the window of his office looking out over the large garden that separated the church from the rectory.

"I just snapped, Mike," said Iggy. "The next thing I know, you're pulling me off him. You probably saved his life." Now wondering where exactly *he* had disappeared to, Iggy asked Mike, "Where the hell is William? What happened to him?"

"He's at the hospital, Iggy. You did quite a number on him," replied Mike flatly.

Deep down, Mike was proud of Iggy and wished he had saved a little of William for him. But he also knew that Iggy would scold him for this thought. Iggy and Mike remained silent, both trying to get their heads around the "William thing," as Iggy would come to refer to it.

The loud pounding on the front door startled them both. Mike slowly got up on wobbly feet and walked down the stairs to the living room. When he opened the front door, Mike saw the faces of two uniformed members of the Oakland Police Department. He recognized both officers as he did many members of the Oakland Police Department, either because he was the son of a slain cop or through Iggy's role as a police chaplain.

"Hiya, Mike. Got a minute?" asked the older of the two police officers casually.

Mike's mind was racing. He instinctively knew that as a priest, Iggy had far more to lose than he did. Mike's loyalty to Iggy kicked in, and he started to rub his fists and shoulder in an almost comically exaggerated manner.

"I really kicked the shit out of that kid, didn't I, fellas?" asked Mike. "Hey, can you give me the name of a good lawyer? Think I'm gonna need one," he said in a jovial voice.

"What are you talkin' about, Mike? We just took a statement, and he said Iggy beat him up," said one of the officers.

Mike tried to gather his thoughts and get behind his story. "Iggy? He's a priest, for shit's sake. I beat up the sick little deviant. So when do I get my rights read to me? Man, hope I don't get a bubba for a cellmate! Know what I mean, fellas?"

"Michael, knock it off," commanded Iggy, now standing in the doorway.

Mike looked at the police officers and tapped a finger to his forehead as if to say, "Don't listen to the priest. I'm the sane one here!"

"Boys, I'd be happy to talk to you. Come on into my office," said Iggy.

With Mike in tow like a small but obedient child, Iggy led the two uniformed men to his office and sat behind his desk. Mike leaned against a wall in the corner, thick arms crossed, staring intently at the floor as he heard Iggy provide a statement which Mike knew might end his life as a priest. *Damn, Iggy may end up sleeping on my couch.*

Following the interview, an older detective in a rumpled business suit approached Iggy and asked to speak with him outside.

"Father, that kid is in pretty bad shape, which is okay because he's a piece-of shit pervert. Excuse my language, Father."

Iggy took a deep breath and replied, "I had no reason to allow myself to lose control like that, Detective. I expect no special deals, believe me."

The detective looked away, trying to hide a slight grin. "Father, there's not a DA in the state that would touch this case. As far as we're concerned, you're a hero." Iggy looked almost insulted at this depiction. "We'll be in touch, Father. Take care of yourself."

CHAPTER 27

Chief of Security Hugo Sanchez stood erect at his post inside the Pacific Dunes lobby, eyeing the shift of morning workers as they filed in. Harold liked Sanchez. He respected his career as a former police officer in the tough Northern Californian town of Salinas and the professionalism with which he approached his job as a security officer.

"Good morning, Detective," Sanchez said.

"Chief Sanchez, my friend, good to see you well this morning," Harold responded with equal formality.

Sanchez looked around. "Any breaks in the case, if I might inquire?" he asked quietly.

Harold feigned a frustrated look. The same look he had assumed for decades as a detective. *It's easier for a smart man to play dumb than a dumb man to try to fool the world into thinking he knows what's going on.*

"No closer now than I was when this thing blew up," said Harold.

"I have a suspicion about the activity of at least one of the men," said Sanchez.

"What kind of suspicions?" asked Harold.

"Without corroboration, it would be mere speculation," said Sanchez.

Harold shot Sanchez a look as if to say, "C'mon, out with it."

"No solid proof, you must understand, but I believe the first victim *may*, and I underscore the word *may*, have been sexually abusing one of our comatose patients. I am unable to provide you with additional information. Chalk it up to hospital gossip."

The words *sexual* and *abusing* jolted Harold. "Well, if that was true, why in the hell didn't anyone do something about it?"

"In my opinion, and again, just speculation, I believe Dr. Bettencourt may have engaged in a cover-up regarding this matter," said Sanchez. "That bastard Bettencourt knew they were bad men and kept them around here anyway." Sanchez was now visibly angry.

Harold sighed. "Okay. Anything else?"

"Keep at it, Detective. I believe you are getting closer."

Harold knocked on Jason's office door.

"C'mon in," said Jason in his thick New York accent.

"Good morning, Doc. Am I disturbing you?" asked Harold.

"Harold! I'm glad to see you," said Jason. "Hey, I got a beef with youse."

Harold enjoyed the way true Easterners added an odd plural tone to the simple word *you.*

"I'm innocent," he said as he threw up his hands.

"I got a fuckin' parking ticket downtown last night. Had dinner at Mama's, the only place I can get pasta like it should be made, and when I came out, bam…a ticket!" Jason's intensity suggested Harold had personally written the citation.

"Well, *were* you illegally parked?" asked Harold.

Jason sat back in his chair and allowed a slight smile. "For eight minutes, *maybe* I was, but that's not the point, copper."

Harold sighed. "Send me the ticket and I'll see what I can do."

"Ha! I knew I could count on you, pally! Now, how can I help?"

"Understanding your confidentially limitations, is there anything you can tell me in general terms about Michael O'Shea's stay here?"

Jason removed his glasses, found a handkerchief in a desk drawer, and began to clean off what appeared to be an especially stubborn smudge. *Seems to be biding his time before he answers,* thought Harold.

"Admitted in fair shape," said Jason. "Very slow but steady progress, then plateaus, then tanks. I mean really tanks."

"How bad? And when?" asked Harold.

"Getting a little close to the line, Detective," said Jason.

Hmmm, a minute ago I was pally. *Now I'm* Detective. "Generally speaking."

"Pretty bad. Incontinent and close to comatose," said Jason flatly. "Then a few weeks later, makes a dramatic comeback close to his pre-stroke status."

Jason left the office, allowing Harold to his thoughts. *Bad shape when he arrives. Slight but steady improvement. Stops suddenly and seems to deteriorate, worse than when he arrived. Starts to soil his bed.*

Harold shuddered. He hated to hear anything about men his age becoming unable to care for themselves. His most prominent fear was of becoming incontinent. Becoming dependent on employees in a facility like Pacific Dunes was not how he envisioned his golden years. In Harold's case, in the event of a catastrophic health episode, he would be on his own or become a burden on Cheryl Jackson.

Harold stared at his notes. After deteriorating, Mike stabilized for a few weeks and then started making progress. Harold took a pen and scratch paper from his briefcase and sketched out a crude timeline. *What were you up to, Officer O'Shea? Bet you don't believe in coincidences either.*

Harold sat and glanced out the window of Jason's office, allowing himself to fall into a trance of sorts as he reviewed the distinct possibility that he had solved a double murder. The ramifications were immense. If he was correct, Mike might spend the rest of his life in prison and die in a hospital ward.

*****

"My probation officer said I needed to be here at eleven sharp to give a sample, and I need to pee like a racehorse!" Harold billowed in his deep baritone voice.

"Shhh! Get in here!" said Cheryl. She was at her desk in the probation department headquarters high above Serra.

"Okay, okay," said Harold, giggling.

Cheryl closed the door to her large office. "What are you doing here, Detective? Going to take me to lunch perhaps?" asked Cheryl with mock formality.

"How about a little sugar first?" said Harold with a giggle as he grabbed Cheryl around the waist.

"Detective, did you take one of those little blue pills I found in your medicine cabinet?" asked Cheryl with a grin.

"No, I'm entranced by your beauty, and I've always been excited by women in power," said Harold, nuzzling Cheryl's neck.

Cheryl pushed Harold away and held him at arm's length. "Harold, what *is* going on?" she asked, concern creeping into her voice. "Oh my God, is something wrong? Are you ill?"

"Oh, for goodness' sake, Cheryl. I'm fine," said Harold. "You've been working with criminals for too long."

Cheryl tilted her head and squinted. "You're up to something," she said with suspicion.

"I confess. I'm here to take the loveliest woman in Serra to lunch." Harold suggested Wong's Chinese Cafe.

"Perfect," Cheryl agreed.

They had successfully beaten the midday lunch crowd and secured a booth by the window. Harold led Cheryl to her seat and then sat across from her. After a few seconds, she got up and came over to Harold's side of the booth. Cheryl snuggled up next to him, grasping his arm and placing her head on Harold's shoulder.

"What a nice surprise to see you, Detective."

"The pleasure is all mine, ma'am," Harold responded. One of the things Cheryl loved about Harold was his courtliness. He had a very traditional way of treating her gallantly without coming off as condescending.

"I love this place," said Cheryl, looking around Wong's, now starting to fill up with the downtown lunch crowd. "You know, Michael O'Shea lived…lives in the apartment upstairs."

Harold nodded to the photograph of the Wong family and Mike hanging on the wall. "I did know that. The Wong family is very fond of your officer."

"I tried to get him to move to a more, how would you say, age-appropriate locale, but Michael never really grew out of his college stage, and well, this was perfect for him, I guess," she said with a touch of sadness in her voice.

"You miss him, don't you?" asked Harold, putting his hand over hers.

Cheryl sighed. "I do miss him. He was a royal pain in my backside, I will tell you. But he was my best officer, and while stalking around one another like a couple of jungle cats, he became a good friend."

"Have you heard any news about his condition?" asked Harold.

Cheryl's face brightened. "I have. I saw Father Ignatius at mass this week, and he said Michael's recovery really seems to have sped up."

"Mass? What's a nice Southern Baptist girl like you doing at mass on a Sunday morning?" asked Harold.

"I try to go every now and then whenever Father Iggy is preaching, or whatever they call it," said Cheryl. "Don't tell my parents, Detective," she whispered.

"Your secret is safe with me, but it won't be detective much longer," said Harold as he casually perused the menu.

Cheryl jerked her head toward Harold. "What?" she said with concern. "What's going on. You *are* ill!"

Harold thought she was about to burst into tears. "No, nothing like that," he said. "It's just that, well, I'm done."

Cheryl stared into his eyes. "What do you mean, done?"

"Cheryl, I've been a police officer for thirty-five years. Thirty with the LAPD and the last five here with Mussel Shores," Harold said quietly.

Cheryl sat back and stared into Harold's eyes. She reached up and brushed his graying hair. "You're tired, aren't you?" she asked.

"I've had a wonderful career. Done it all, as they say. Now it's time to let some of these fine young officers have their chance," said Harold. *Just don't have the courage to tell you I think your finest officer and BFF is a cold-blooded killer and that I don't want to be the one to have to put the silver bracelets on him.*

Cheryl examined her love's still smooth face. *He's holding out on me, but I'll get to the bottom of this.*

*****

After finishing up their lunch at Wong's, Harold and Cheryl walked through the El Camino Plaza surrounding the Our Lady Catholic Church. There was a cool onshore breeze blowing. Tourists of all ages scrambled around the old church complex, some with cameras, some carrying young children. A few people in business attire sat on benches and enjoyed their lunch breaks before they returned to the government center or any number of businesses in the downtown district. The place felt electric without being overcrowded.

Cheryl held Harold's hand and guided him over to a footbridge which crossed the Paso Creek, the main water source for the padres who had established their church two hundred years earlier. The long line of missions from San Diego in the south to San Francisco to the north had been strategically placed one day's journey apart. Today, the creek still meandered past the church, not quite as clean as it once was but still the center of the city.

"So, Harold, where does this big career change of yours leave *us*?" asked Cheryl.

"Well, I've thought about that," said Harold.

"And?" asked Cheryl suspiciously.

"Cheryl, you're way out of my league, in every way," said Harold quietly, his voice thick with emotion.

Cheryl looked away, sensing she was about to get the "You're just too good for me" send-off. Cheryl Jackson, at forty-nine years old, had never married. Her career had come first, and she was too old now to consider children, so marriage just seemed to be an inconvenience. Another reason Cheryl had remained single was that she had mastered what she called the "preemptive strike." Once she got even the slightest inkling that a man she was interested in didn't share her feelings, she cut him loose without mercy or ceremony, thus avoiding any unnecessary pain or messiness. But Harold was different. She had fallen in love with the lanky cop and confirmed bachelor. *Damn it, he's about to break my heart*, she thought.

Harold made a valiant attempt to compose himself. "Cheryl, you and I both know there are plenty of other fellas who could offer you much more than me."

"Are you out of your mind?" Cheryl demanded. She shoved Harold in the chest and stuck her jaw out like a boxer. Harold looked around, hoping the nearby tourists didn't make more of Cheryl's outburst than necessary.

"Either stay or leave, Harold Davis, but now's the time to make your intentions clear, sir," Cheryl stated with authority.

A slight smile crossed Harold's lips. He took a step back and admired Cheryl's beauty. Harold slipped his hand into the pocket of his sport jacket and pulled out a small box. He opened it slightly and feigned a look of surprise.

"Damn, they gave me the wrong one!" he said as he put the box back into his pocket. "Well, I guess we'll have to continue this conversation later."

"You moron, this is not even remotely funny," Cheryl hissed. "You better say something awfully impressive in the next ten seconds or I'm simply leaving, and don't consider attempting to contact me tomorrow. Or *ever*, for that matter."

Harold had always found himself to be an amusing man, but he knew that not everyone, especially the ladies in his life, fully concurred with his assessment. *Quit screwing around and get on with it.* With one hand, he reached into his pocket and brought out the box. With the other, he gently pulled Cheryl's hand to his and kissed it. Harold opened the box and produced a simple but elegantly impressive diamond engagement ring.

"Please forgive my nonsense. If you'll have me, I would like to marry you, Cheryl. I love you and hope you'll say yes," said Harold.

Sensing things were moving favorably in her direction, Cheryl smiled. Without even looking at the ring, she said, "It would be my pleasure, Harold Davis, and I love you back."

The next morning, Cheryl had left for work, but not before informing Harold that if he was under the impression that they would be "cohabitating" prior to their nuptials, he was dead wrong. She was still the daughter of a Baptist preacher from Atlanta and the highest-ranking female law enforcement officer in Serra County, and they would maintain separate residences until the day of the wedding. No exceptions. Although Harold suspected their current occasional sleepovers would be acceptable, but nothing more.

"I'll not be your trollop, sir," she informed him.

Harold replied with a simple and quiet "Yes, ma'am" and wondered how his life continued to be dominated by strong women. Between his own mother, sisters, and now Cheryl, he wondered if there was a viable reason not to opt for castration at this point and just speed up the inevitable.

Harold drove his pickup truck down to the Clam Shell Beach pier and walked toward the three hundred feet of lumber jutting out into the water. He needed to tie up some loose ends on the Pacific Dunes murder investigations. Harold was reasonably sure that Mike had killed both David Lee Simpson and Richard Troop. He was also unsure that a cogent case could be made against Mike. No murder weapon, the prime suspect a stroke victim (although Harold was now starting to question Mike's true medical condition), and two "victims" who had amassed an impressive collection of characterologically challenged associates who would have relished seeing both dead. In the unlikely event Mike were convicted, Serra remained a conservative law and order county, and public sentiment would demand the lightest sentence possible. Harold's instincts told him that at some point early in his stay at Pacific Dunes, Mike had somehow discovered that David Lee was up to some form of malfeasance and simply took matters into his own hands. As for Richard Troop, Harold suspected that the security guard had taken advantage of Mike's debilitated condition to settle old debts, and Mike simply grew tired of being a punching bag, or worse.

What public good will be done by locking up O'Shea? If he did it, and I'm pretty sure he did, we should give the bastard a medal. Harold bought a bag of popcorn from a vendor on the pier. He shared some with the seagulls who loitered nearby, benefiting from the generosity of fowl-loving pedestrians. *So that's it? Close the case and declare unsolved? No second opinion? No consultation with the district attorney's office? Very shady, Detective. Very shady indeed. If you're struggling with this, you don't deserve to carry a badge.*

Harold looked back toward the parking lot and away from the waves crashing into the pier. He turned up the collar of his windbreaker and shoved his hands into his pocket to ward off the morning chill. Harold felt a similar chill in the pit of his stomach. Never one to even accept a free cup of coffee and pastry offered simply because of his profession, Harold knew he was venturing into uncharted ethical waters.

CHAPTER 28

"How's it hangin', Mawine?" Mike asked the grizzled old veteran.

Mike's speech therapy hadn't progressed as well as his physical therapy, but that didn't bother him much. He had difficulty pronouncing his Rs, which came out as Ws. Marine became "Mawine," right became "wight." Slightly more frustrating was that cognitively, Mike knew what word to use but at times struggled with speaking the word aloud. He had developed a pattern of speech similar to someone with a stutter.

"It's hangin' just fine, boot. Why the hell you talk so funny?" Nate asked. "Charlie fucked with your tongue, didn't he? Fuckin' gooks got no honor!"

Mike chuckled. He never grew tired of Nate's mania and was fond of the old man. "Yeah, fuckin' Chawee." He walked over to Nate's chair, switched the cane to his left hand, and stuck out his right.

"What the fuck's this? You goin' somewheres?" asked Nate, slightly alarmed.

"Hey, what the fuck happen to your ears? They look like prunes!" Although Nate had seen Mike daily for months, he had apparently just noticed his distinctive cauliflower ears.

Mike smiled. *This is going to be rough.* "Shippin' out. Got my paperwork wight…" Mike was struggling with the word "here." He patted his shirt pocket as if it held transfer orders of some kind.

"Where are those fucks at HQ sending ya?" Nate asked in a whisper.

Mike was continually amused by Nate's ability to use the word *fuck* as a noun and not just an adjective or verb. In this case, "fucks" referred to the imaginary commanders assigned to the headquarters that existed only within the confines of his delusional mind.

"Stateside," said Mike, quietly trying to keep his own emotions in check.

"We're a little short, ya know. This is a damn small detachment to begin with! What the hell am I supposed to do?" asked Nate, now clearly agitated.

Mike shrugged and tried to look equally agitated. "Not much I can do, Sarge. I got the points, and I'm heading out on the p.m. flight."

"You says you got the points to go home?" asked Nate in a whisper, as if the Marines might have made a mistake in sending his comrade home.

"My wotation's up, Sarge. I'm goin' home," said Mike.

"Well, I'll be damned," said Nate. "You been a fuck of a good Marine. Now git goin'."

Nate took Mike's right hand in a tight grasp. Mike looked at the floor, not sure that he could maintain his composure much longer. He grabbed his cane and made the slow walk to the door. Mike turned toward Nate's empty chair. Nate, the old Marine, body and mind crippled with demons both physical and mental, was standing erect as though God had shoved a steel rod up his spine. His right hand slowly came up to his forehead in a sharp salute, forearm at a perfect forty-five-degree angle. Mike had never served in the military and was reasonably sure he had never saluted anyone, but on this occasion, he did his best and returned Nate's salute. As tears streamed down Nate's cheeks, he turned and walked down the hall.

Mike's final stop was the office of Jason Shapiro.

"What's this?" asked Jason.

"A cod. What the fuck you think it is?" replied Mike.

"A cod, like a fish?" asked Jason as he smelled the envelope.

"Ha, ha, funny man." said Mike.

"Well, you said it was a cod," said Jason as he opened Mike's card.

Jason read the card and looked up at Mike. "This is really touching, Michael."

Mike waved a hand dismissively. He stood and walked over to the far wall of Jason's office. A completely disorganized collection of photos, newspaper articles, promotional flyers for a variety of New York boxing events, and mementos from a career spent giving comfort to patients plastered the entire wall. Mike liked to look at Jason's wall and always saw something new and interesting. Up in a corner, he saw a photo of him and Jason having a sandwich at a nearby deli.

"Does this make me yo favwit patient?" asked Mike.

Jason walked over and stood by Mike looking at the wall. "I will tell you this, Mike. You have not only been my *favorite* patient but also my most *interesting*," he said, warmly grasping Mike's shoulder.

After a moment, Jason returned to his desk. "They warn us against allowing professional boundaries to break down with clients during our residency. I figured if it happened to me, it would be with an unhinged blond with enormous tatas, not a broken-down Indian," said Jason with a chuckle. "Anyway, none of this goodbye bullshit. Just because you're being discharged doesn't mean we're done!" Jason opened a drawer of his desk and shuffled through a mess of papers, pens, paperclips, and odds and ends. Finding what he was looking for, he pulled a small packet from the pile.

"You're not through with me, pally. Tickets to the Lakers and Boston Celtics at the Staple Center in a few weeks, remember?"

Mike smiled. Jason had set an artificial benchmark for Mike, and as a reward, he promised him Lakers tickets. *The man's good to his word, I'll give him that.*

"Who ahh the extra tickets faa?" asked Mike.

"Funny you should ask. I invited your boss, Cheryl Jackson, and her fiancé, Harold Davis," said Jason.

"My boss?" Mike asked in a bit of a whine.

"Yeah, a great gal, and her fiancé, Harold, and I have become pals. He handled the murder investigations here at the hospital," said Jason.

Mike shrugged. "Must of cost you a pwetty penny." *Not liking this at all. Either Detective What's-His-Name is incompetent or has his suspicions. Maybe he'll put the cuffs on me at halftime.*

Jason counted the tickets. "Oh, and I got one for Father Iggy. I get a kick outta that guy. I think he's trying to convert me," he said with a giggle.

After months "in custody," as Mike referred to the Pacific Dunes Hospital, a road trip sounded enticing, even if it was with his boss and her cop boyfriend who was probably on the verge of making the arrest of his life.

The title "boss" didn't exactly apply to Chief Cheryl Jackson. Former boss was more accurate. Mike's medical retirement case had snaked through a bureaucratic maze involving the County of Serra Human Resources Department, the State of California Department of Health and Human Services, and the local superior court. Petra Yablonsky had led the charge to have Mike medically retired with full and lifetime benefits, much of them tax-free.

Teams of doctors on both sides, the county's and Mike's, had conceded that during his career, he had suffered two major skull fractures and concussions, both of which had contributed to his stroke.

His official retirement hit Mike like one of the punches he absorbed during his fight days. He was no longer a probation officer. His badge would be retooled with a "Retired" ribbon below his previous title. If he wanted to carry a concealed firearm, he would need to go to the local shooting range where a kid, young enough to be his son, would lead him through a basic qualification course. Mike's name would start to blur among the law enforcement community until it was unknown to the next generation of cops and probation officers. There was a time, he recalled, when he would appear at a crime scene and those present would breathe either a figurative or often a literal sigh of relief that someone who knew what they were doing and could handle themselves in an emergency was on scene.

If I show up now, I'm just a cripple getting in the way. Just perfect.

*****

"Okay, take it easy now, Michael," cautioned Iggy, leading Mike up the stairs to his apartment.

As he had done since his childhood, Mike shrugged off Iggy's attempt to help and insisted on climbing the stairs on his own. With each step, he felt a wave of freedom wash over him. Mike had read about the adjustment struggles Vietnam War prisoners experienced when they returned home and empathized. He reached the top of the landing and peered around the corner into his living room. Cheryl had hired a cleaning crew to come in and make the place presentable, but Mike knew immediately he was home. The apartment smelled clean, but there was an unmistakable odor, a mixture of exotic scents wafting up from the restaurant below and the homey smell of an old building that brought Mike back to the day that he prepared for work as usual, not to return for over a year.

Mike turned and walked slowly toward his bedroom.

"Hey, don't forget this, Michael," said Iggy as he handed Mike his cane.

Mike looked at the cane and then back at Iggy. "Up heah, I'm okay. Out theah, I'll use it, I pwomise," he said with a smile.

Iggy followed Mike into his bedroom. On a hook inside a closet door hung his old Cal letterman's jacket. The blue felt material was faded, and the white leather sleeves cracked and dulled, but it remained the unmistakable jacket awarded to those select few who could refer to themselves as athletes of the University of California at Berkeley. Mike took the jacket down from the hook, brought it to his face, and breathed deeply. *Funny how smells take you back.*

Mike dug into the pocket of the jacket and produced a key. Iggy looked on with suspicion. He stepped to the rear of the closet and shoved aside an assortment of shirts, blue jeans, and sweatshirts.

Standing behind Mike, Iggy could see the faded outline of a small rectangle at the rear of the closet. Mike reached down and, with his fingernail, scraped away a small piece of masking tape that had been painted over with the same color as the walls of the closet. To the naked eye, the tape was merely an anomaly in the wall of an old apartment closet. After scraping off a corner of the tape, he pulled it back, exposing a keyhole. Mike inserted the key and slowly opened what turned out to be a small door, no more than five feet by three.

"This may be a felony in some states. Sure you want to stay?" Mike asked with a mischievous grin.

"For the love of God, Michael, what have you got in there?" asked Iggy.

Mike pulled the small door open, reached in, and pulled a chain dangling from above the opening. Over his shoulder, Iggy peered into a tiny closet within a closet. A bare light bulb hanging from the ceiling illuminated the interior. Mike groped around and pulled out an AR15 semiautomatic rifle. Shelves of ammunition lined the upper half of the small space. A tactical vest with the word *Probation* sat on a shelf in the corner. On a small hook hung a duty belt with several pouches and an empty holster. In the corner was a yellow Taser, shaped like a gun but bright yellow and much larger. Next to the Taser was a police radio and battery charger. Mike gently laid the assault rifle against the wall of the closet, turned toward Iggy, and winked. Next, he pulled out a Mossberg twelve-gauge shotgun. Finally, Mike reached in and pulled out a Glock 9 mm pistol. He slowly stood up and carried the two long guns out of the closet and laid them on his bed.

Mike looked over his shoulder and said, "Gwab the pistol, would ya, Iggy?"

Iggy looked mortified. "Will it go off?"

"It will if you pull the twigger," said Mike with a giggle.

Iggy obeyed and gingerly picked up the pistol as if it was a well-used baby's diaper.

"My God, Michael, you look like you're ready for a war," said Iggy.

After checking the weapons to ensure they were in good condition and fully loaded, Mike placed the Mossberg against a corner of the bedroom, the AR-15 behind the bathroom door, and the Glock in a drawer of a small table used as a nightstand. He turned to Iggy. No smile or wink this time.

"Iggy, met some bad men and women ovah the yeahs," he said slowly. "Some ah dead, some ah alive, and all of 'em have families that may twy and look me up. Just tryin' to even the playing field a little. You know about the threats."

"You know, Michael, when you became a probation officer, I was so excited for you!" Iggy said as he sat on a small stool in the corner of Mike's bedroom. "I thought it was a perfect fit. You know, former jock, a boxer at that, mentoring young toughs."

Mike smiled and remembered Iggy driving down from Oakland for his swearing-in ceremony. In his black jacket and priest's collar, with a massive camera hanging around his neck, Iggy could barely contain himself. He snapped dozens of photos commemorating the event and told Mike he was more excited than the day he was ordained a priest. After the ceremony in the county courthouse, Iggy treated Mike and some of his new friends at the probation department to pizza and beers, an expense the Jesuit couldn't afford but insisted upon.

"I figured you'd be, you know, kind of a big brother to these poor kids," said Iggy.

Mike smiled. *Yeah, me too.*

"I mean, for goodness' sake, Michael, you have English degrees from Cal Berkeley, and now look at you. You've become some kind of urban warrior."

Mike had experienced the same thought on several occasions. He had never planned on going into law enforcement like his father, but once the job began to change and the probationers became more violent, the accouterments seemed reasonable.

"Urban warriyah?" Mike said. "Come on, Iggy. This is Sehwa. Things can get dicey, but it's not Baghdad."

"I know, I know," said Iggy. "But I can't help but think that had I known what the job would evolve into, I could have somehow altered your life path, and then…well, maybe this wouldn't have happened to you." Iggy's voice became thick, and his eyes teared up.

Mike stared with a look of disappointment. "For shit's sake, Iggy, are you crwin'? Get a hold of yoself. Yoo always pweachin' about God's will. Well, my deal *was* His will. End of stowee."

Iggy wiped his eyes and took a deep breath. "Sorry, Michael. It's just that, well, you know."

"Yes, Father Ignatius. I know," said Mike with a smile.

"Well, now that you're settled in and have your arsenal all set up, how 'bout a cone?"

Iggy, still trying to bribe me with ice cream. "Deal if it includes beah and pizza!"

As promised, Iggy treated Mike to dinner at Trusendi's Pizzeria, a downtown Serra staple, and then ice cream at a shop on Cuesta Street. In the spirit of celebration for Mike's homecoming, the two ended the evening at a small nightclub on Toro Street. A well-stocked bar occupied the street level, with a second bar and small stage in the basement. A jazz trio was performing for the mostly older audience. The environment was a little too sedate for the college crowd. Mike ordered two drams of Glen Fiddich Scotch, which he and Iggy enjoyed as they listened to the cover band play classics from Vince Girardi and Dave Brubeck. Around midnight, they walked up Cuesta Avenue to Palm Street and the two-hundred-year-old mission Iggy called home. With Iggy safely tucked in, Mike walked the few blocks to his apartment. As he approached the stairs which led to the second floor of the old building, he saw three men in their mid-twenties, all in restaurant whites, enjoying cold beers near the rear entrance to Wong's. He recognized them as a busboy and Wong's two cooks.

"Hey, O'Shea!" called out the oldest of the three.

"Hectoo, que pasa?" asked Mike.

"Good to have you home, my man," said Hector Gomez, the Wong's front-line chef since he was in his teens.

"Good to be home, Hectoo. How warr you fellas?" asked Mike, nodding to Hector's companions.

A stocky busboy with tattoos lacing up his neck jumped to his feet. "O'Shea, you remember me, my homie?"

Mike eyed the young man, taking note of the tattoos. He knew immediately the busboy was a current or former gang member and probationer.

Mike had lived in Serra for almost thirty years and had assembled an eclectic assortment of friends and associates—criminals, cops, lawyers, poets, waitresses, professors, the homeless, and bartenders among them. Over the years, he had grown accustomed to bumping into people he found familiar but whose names he simply couldn't recall.

Mike grasped his hand in a firm grip and said quietly as he leaned in, "Give me a name, my man."

The busboy smiled. "Noah Dominguez, homie!"

Mike took a step back, releasing the man's hand. "Noah Dominguez, Oak Pawk Pwoject in Paso Adobe! I sent you to the joint, didn't I?"

"You sure as hell did, and that was pretty fucked up, homie," said Noah with sincere offense. "But you know what, homie, I learned to cook in prison!"

Mike nodded, knowing where the story was going. "And Mr. Wong, he hired me, homie, even though he knows I'm a parolee. He said he asked you about me, and you gave him the *green light.*"

"Mr. Wong is a good man," said Mike. *I remember sending this fool off on a state sabbatical, but for the life of me, I can't remember talkin' to Wong about him. Damn headshots.*

"O'Shea, remember the night you took me in? Remember, homie?"

Mike smiled. *I have no idea what he's talking about.* "Like it was yestooday," he said.

"Do you remember what you said to me, homie?" asked Noah, no smiles, all business now.

I hope nothing to piss you off. You look like you hit the weights pretty hard in the joint, and now that I'm an invalid, I got to be a little more cautious. "Tell me," said Mike quietly.

"You told me, 'Noah, I sense *greatness* in you.' Do you remember that, O'Shea?"

"I sure do, Noah," said Mike. *I don't know what the hell this kid is talking about. Just glad he's not tryin' to shank me.*

"And you know what, homie? I *hated* you for a long time." Noah's eyes squinted.

Let's keep things civil here, guy.

"I thought about finding you when I got out and *fucking* you up real bad, O'Shea," said Noah in almost a whisper.

This kid's killing my buzz. Good thing I have my Glock strapped to my ankle, although I have no idea if I could toss my cane aside and draw down. "Noah, it was just business," said Mike in his most conciliatory tone.

Hector, the busboy, sensing potential trouble, stood and took a few steps back. *Shit, I was hoping to just go to bed on my first night back.* Without warning and lighting quick speed, Noah grabbed Mike's right hand and yanked it to his own throat. "Feel that, homie?"

"Sure do, Noah. Fit as a fiddle," said Mike nervously.

"*Alive,* motherfucker," said Noah with a low hiss. "Alive because of you, homie." *Not sure where this is all going, but it's late, and I'm a stroke victim and slightly intoxicated,* thought Mike. "I thought you punked me, O'Shea, but you actually saved my life, homie."

Mike gave Noah a weak and confused smile. *Shit, this goof works below where I lay my head each night?*

"If you hadn't locked me up, O'Shea, I'd be dead right now, you know."

Relieved, Mike smiled and shrugged. *Tis nothing. Just another saved life.* Noah took his beefy right hand and grabbed the back of his head. He pulled Mike closer until their foreheads touched.

"I owe you my life, homie. I will protect you forever," said Noah, his voice cracking with emotion.

Two grown men in tears in the span of a few hours. First Iggy and now this jackass. Mike slowly disengaged from Noah's grasp. "Noah, I meant what I said. There *was* something special about you. I'm glad you made the most of pwison, and I'm glad I live above where you work. Stop by upstairs anytime." *Oh God, why did I say that? Please don't actually take me up on it.*

Noah took a few steps back and made a fist with his right hand and touched it to his chest. After a pause, he brought his fist to his lips where he kissed his hand and then saluted Mike with a two-fingered peace sign.

"I'm here for you, my homie," he said dramatically.

"Good to know," Mike said with a weak smile.

CHAPTER 29

Mike spent the next few days getting acclimated. His time at Pacific Dunes had been a prison of sorts. Highly scheduled and regulated, all decisions made by others in authority, and a dependence on the staff. Mike had supervised former state prison inmates and recognized the signs of institutionalization. A slow but definite process where the inmate—in his case, the patient—slowly ceases seeing themselves as an independent person, rather, a prisoner living within a highly regulated culture. Mike saw some of the signs in himself. During his first full day at home, he couldn't quite understand why he was so hungry. By three o'clock in the afternoon, he realized that he hadn't eaten all day. He was waiting for breakfast and lunch to be served and simply forgot that now *he* was the one who would decide when and what he ate. *Weird*, Mike thought as he inhaled a plate of rice and vegetables from Wong's.

His second night home, Mike woke up in a cold sweat after dreaming of killing Richard Troop and David Lee Simpson. *I guess that's to be expected but not much fun to relive.*

By day 3, he was a little bored and trying to grow accustomed to the fact that he was now retired and effectively unemployed. With plenty of money in the bank, a generous pension, and few expenses, Mike clearly didn't need to work but missed the excitement and the comradery of the other probation officers. Petra Yablonsky and Tommy Sagapalu had taken him out to breakfast, but having been off the job for over to a year, Mike felt a little irrelevant. *Old war stories can only get you so far, and then you just become pathetic. Not for me.* He knew that with his health stabilized, at some point he would need to find something interesting to occupy his time.

Day 4 was taken care of with Jason Shapiro's day trip to Los Angeles for a Lakers game. As promised, Jason arrived at Mike's apartment at eight o'clock in the morning in a large passenger van borrowed from the hospital.

Mike sat on the stoop of his building reading the sports page and enjoyed a cup of coffee from Spilled Beans, where he had been greeted like a conquering hero. Much to his surprise, Mike's recovery had sped up since his release, and he was now able to get around without the cane, and his speech continued to improve.

"You look marvelous, Michael!" said Jason. "Freedom agrees with you."

Mike shrugged and looked Jason up and down. "You look like shit, Doc. What the hell they doin' to you down theah?"

"Thanks for the supportive compliment, ya prick. They're working my poor New York ass to death!" said Jason. "All I want is for those lazy bums back at headquarters to hire my replacement so I can go back to treating patients, something I'm actually good at."

"Maybe they like you wunnin' the place. You got to be an impwovement oveah that cwook Bettencourt," said Mike.

"I'm trying to intentionally screw up the books a bit in hopes, you know, that I'd get a nice demotion and go back to my practice, but no, Mr. or Mrs. Big Shot back east won't budge," said Jason.

"Don't know what to tell ya," said Mike with a shrug and slightly crooked smile, a casualty of facial paralysis caused by his stroke. Mike looked at his watch. "Iggy will be heah any minute. You want a coffee? Thewer's a place down the stweet."

"No thanks. I'll be pissing all the way to LA. Actually, I'd like to see your place."

"You betcha. Come on up," said Mike as he slowly led the way up to the apartment.

"My humboo digs," said Mike as they reached the landing.

Jason stepped into the living room and looked around. "Cozy," he said with a smile. "Actually, it looks like a college kid's flat." Jason looked at Mike with something between confusion and admiration.

"Well, I've been livin' heah since I got out of college, so I guess it kind of is."

"Mike, why did you never settle down and marry?" asked Jason. "This ain't bad, but ya got to admit, it's a little, well, unorthodox for a fifty-two-year-old man. No offense."

Mike smiled. "Not sure why I nevoo settled down exactly other than being a pwobation officer is a petty crappy life for waisin' a family. Late nights, callouts, all that stuff. But the weal weason I guess is that I weally like my solitude...like being alone."

"Ever get close? To marrying, I mean," asked Jason.

"I've met a ton of gweat women in this town. Some a little... okay, a lot nutsy, but all gweat in they own way.

"But I nevoo met one I couldn't live without." Mike walked over to a photo of himself and his parents. "I think that's what they had. Didn't want to live without each othoo. If I don't find it, I pass and keep on livin' like I live," said Mike, waving one hand across his living room.

"Hey, what about the volleyball coach?" asked Jason. "Boy, she is one looker, I'll tell ya."

"That she is," said Mike. "I wouldn't let her visit me in the hospital, so who knows now."

Mike heard the unmistakable knock of Iggy on his street level door. Five quick knocks, a pause, then two more. "Come on up, Iggy!" yelled Mike.

Iggy appeared on the landing in full Los Angeles Lakers regalia. Baggy gold shorts, a bright purple game jersey over a gold Lakers T-shirt, and a weaved fedora with a Lakers hat band.

"Whewe'd you get this stuff?" asked Mike, obviously amused. "You look like Jack Nicholson dwopped some acid and went on a shopping swree."

"Ahh," Iggy said with a dismissive wave of the hand. "Jason, my friend, how are you?" asked Iggy with glee. It had been some time since he had seen the psychiatrist.

"I am well, Father," said Jason, extending his hand with a nod. "Michael and I were just having a fascinating conversation about his marital status."

Iggy gave a look of pure disgust. "Don't get me started, Doctor. My only hope for a grandchild is tied up in this aged frat boy."

Mike grabbed a sweatshirt from a closet by his front door and looked at Iggy. "You got a jacket? Might get cold down theah."

Iggy shrugged. Truth be told, he was afraid a jacket would cover his customized ensemble.

Mike reached into the closet and grabbed a second sweatshirt and handed it to Iggy. "Take it. You may need it." *Shit, is this what it's gonna be like? Me takin' care of Iggy. There's a switch.*

As the three emerged from Mike's apartment, a red BMW convertible drove up and parked in front of Wong's. Cheryl pressed a button on the dashboard, closing the top. Harold struggled to pry himself from the passenger side.

"C'mon, Detective, you're getting old," said Cheryl playfully.

"Good morning, gents," said Harold, walking over to Mike, Jason, and Iggy. Greetings and handshakes were exchanged.

Cheryl gave each of them a warm hug. She looked at Mike approvingly. "You look great, Michael. Absolutely fantastic." Mike bristled at both the compliment and the public display of affection from his former chief.

Despite their commonality, Harold and Mike had never met. Regardless, Harold felt that he knew Mike well, both as his future wife's favorite employee and the primary suspect in his recent murder investigation.

Mike grasped Harold's outstretched hand firmly, perhaps more firmly than was necessary given the circumstances.

"Good to know ya," Mike said, maintaining contact with Harold's eyes just long enough to make him a little uncomfortable. *Got to handle this guy just right. Don't give 'em a thing. In fact, let's see if we can rattle him a bit*, Mike thought.

Harold had known many potentially dangerous men. Some real, some in the twisted world of their own imaginations. He quickly assessed Mike and placed him firmly in the former column and knew exactly what Mike was up to. *He's trying to intimidate me.*

Jason fetched the van, and the group piled in. Iggy took the front passenger seat. Cheryl climbed into the second row of seats, and Mike headed for the third row, both to allow Cheryl to sit next to her fiancé and to give him a chance to stretch out.

Harold climbed in last and said to Cheryl, "Hey, sweat pea, you don't mind if I sit next to Mr. O'Shea, do you? It will give us a chance to get to know each other."

Mike looked slightly annoyed, which only made Harold believe it was an even better idea. *No, no, no, sit with the missus and stay in your lane, guy.*

"May I call you Mike?" asked Harold.

Mike, not quite sure how to handle what was surely going to turn into a very awkward conversation, responded with a neutral "You betcha."

Jason merged onto Highway 101 and headed south. Harold started out with small talk—sports, living in Serra, a few cute stories about himself and Cheryl, then their shared profession.

I don't want to like this guy, but I do, thought Mike. By Santa Barbara, they were swapping tales and laughing at the same irreverent humor like old comrades. Cheryl was occupied with a book on her reader, and Iggy and Jason were engaged in a spirited conversation about Iggy's namesake, St. Ignatius of Loyola.

By Ventura, Harold had concocted a way to bring up the topic of their mutual connection to the Pacific Dunes Rehabilitation Hospital. It was a competent attempt to lure Mike into a conversation about the murders, but Mike saw it coming. As the van passed through the affluent area of Thousand Oaks, Harold motioned to an upscale high school campus sitting on a hill above the highway and said, "My old partner at Mussel Shores PD graduated from Oaks Christian High School. Quite a sports powerhouse, I understand."

Mike gave a benign smile. *Sure it is, Detective. Why don't you just enjoy your retirement, take up a hobby, and leave me the hell alone?*

"In fact, you may have met her, Rebecca Santiago. She was one of the detectives who worked with me on the Pacific Dunes murders."

Mike had a nodding acquaintance with Rebecca Santiago but feigned racking his brain. "May have. Can't say for sure."

Harold was a wizard in the art of small talk and the follow-up question. "Tell me, Mike, how did a Berkeley grad with a master's in English become a probation officer in Serra?"

"That's a great question, Harold!" Iggy bellowed from the front seat. "Want me to answer it, Mike?"

Mike chuckled and shook his head. *Old guy doesn't miss a beat. Don't recall providing the detective with my educational background, but I'll play along.*

"My dad was an Oakland cop. Shot on the job on my foost boothday."

"Oh, God, I'm sorry," said Harold.

Cheryl had put down her reader and looked back at Mike with a mixture of affection and sadness. She had heard all about Mike's youth from Iggy. Mike himself would never share anything so personal, at least not before his stroke. Cheryl decided she liked the new, more open Michael O'Shea.

"I wealy only went to gwad school so I could keep playin' rugby at Cal," said Mike.

"Rugby!" said Harold. "Now there's a sport!"

"My plan was to become an Oakland cop like my dad, stay in the Bay Awea, and mooch off Iggy," said Mike.

"I would have loved it!" yelled Iggy from the front seat.

"So what happened with OPD?" asked Harold.

"Couldn't pass the eye exam," said Mike, pointing to his thick glasses. "And the physical down heah was okay with my eye."

"Ah, the boxing injury," said Harold.

"Mike was an excellent young fighter, Harold. One of the best I ever coached," said Iggy.

Mike maintained his neutral smile. *How'd you know I hurt my eye boxing, Detective? Don't shit yourself. This guy's done his homework.* "So I got lucky. Got a job with pwobation in Serra, close enough to Oakland to visit Iggy on weekends but far enough away to feel like a gwown-up. It was a pwetty good gig," said Mike.

Cheryl smiled. "Harold, when I got hired as the chief, Michael was the first officer I asked to meet. I knew I needed him on my side right off the bat."

"We kind of stayed outta each othoos way," said Mike.

The trip to the Staples Center in downtown Los Angeles took a little over three hours door-to-door from Mike's apartment. Jason had been able to negotiate midcourt seats from a ticket broker. The group of five arranged themselves into their seats. Jason took the end next to Iggy. Mike sat between Iggy and Cheryl with Harold on the other end. By the end of the first quarter, it was clear to the four men that the lone female had forgotten more about basketball than they would ever know. Obviously, Cheryl's interest in the game hadn't ended with her collegiate career at Howard University.

After two beers and a hot dog, Iggy was asleep by the beginning of the fourth quarter. Mike felt his head lightly resting on his shoulder. He rolled up his sweatshirt and gently slid it under Iggy's head.

The Lakers defeated the Sacramento Kings handily. Iggy awoke with a start when the final buzzer signaled the end of the game.

"Atta baby! Go get 'em!" he yelled.

Mike looked at the priest with amusement. *Now you become the party boy.* After the obligatory trip to their respective bathrooms and comments about the effects of aging on the male bladder by Jason and Harold, the group made their way back to the van. Mike noticed that Jason looked tired and offered to drive. Jason happily accepted. Mike felt mischievous when he realized that technically, he wasn't *completely* authorized by the California Department of Motor Vehicles to drive.

Much to his dismay, according to the State of California, Michael Ignatius O'Shea was no longer physically fit to operate a moving vehicle. As Mike's physician, Jason Shapiro had received an inquiry from the DMV. Not wanting to violate his professional ethical standards but also not wanting Mike to become dependent on others—or worse, a shut-in—Jason conveniently misplaced the questionnaire, thus stalling the inevitable. In the absence of a physician's response, Mike's license was suspended.

"I'll ride up front with you, Mike," said Harold almost gleefully. "You don't mind giving up the copilot's seat, do you, Father?"

"Not at all, my amigo. I'll be asleep by Encino," said Iggy, still feeling the effects of his $15 beers.

Swell. Just me and the detective who investigated a double murder I was intimately involved with for the next three hours. Super. Mike maneuvered the van through the postgame traffic north onto Highway 405 and then Highway 101 up the coast toward Serra. By the town of Ventura, he was absolutely amazed at Harold Davis's ability to seamlessly transition from one topic to another. Sports of course—local, state, national—world politics, and pop culture all flowed from Harold in an endless supply of stories, comments, and observations.

This guy must never stop reading. Mike had to constantly remind himself to remain on guard so as not give away some seemingly trivial but incriminating piece of information about his stay in Pacific Dunes. *Rapport. He's establishing a rapport with me. Nice try, Detective.*

CHAPTER 30

Two months following the Lakers game, Mike had comfortably eased into his retirement. He had taken a part-time instructor's position teaching criminal justice classes at Serra Community College, or "Harvard by the Highway," as locals called the school on the coast north of Serra. Most of Mike's students were terrified of him, but his credibility as a former law enforcement officer kept them in rapt attention.

Each morning, except for Sundays, Mike rose early and walked up to the Cal Coastal campus, where he engaged in a forty-year habit—a slow jog up one aisle of the football stadium, ten push-ups, and down the other. After a brief pause, he repeated the routine until he was at the opposite end of the stadium. Physically, Mike was a shell of his former self, but still formidable. The push-ups looked like someone had placed a twenty-pound weight on his left shoulder, somehow weighing him down, but he got the job done. Several times a week, Sylvia Almeida joined Mike for the stadium workout. Mike suspected she was holding back and could have easily completed the workout in half the time, but he enjoyed the Brazilian's company and kept his suspicion to himself.

Cheryl Jackson and now retired Harold Davis were married on a cliff overlooking the Pacific on a warm Sunday afternoon. It was a small affair, the invitees consisting of Jason, Tommy and Alma Sagapalu, Harold's sisters, and Mike and Iggy. Although he was slightly concerned about the canon legalities of marrying two non-Catholics, Iggy had agreed to officiate. Much to Harold's chagrin, Michael O'Shea would walk his future wife down the aisle.

Why not complete this little circus and have a cold-blooded murderer give my bride away? Harold had mused while changing into his "weddin' clothes," as he referred to a dark suit Cheryl had chosen for him to wear.

Cheryl had quickly settled into married life. She and Harold arose early each morning for a walk on the beach. While she showered, he prepared Cheryl her mandatory morning smoothie, a combination of iced green tea, a half cup of chopped kale, seasonal fruit, and a generous helping of protein power. Once Cheryl left for work, Harold had the rest of the day to himself. Not necessarily a good thing, he soon discovered. Thus, he took over the household shopping and cooking responsibilities. Harold's application to bring Pop's Gourmet Snow Cones to the town of Clam Shell Bay was making a slow but steady journey through the County Planning Department, prompting Harold to begin pursuing online sites for a stand which could be transported to and from the beach. However, as Harold soon discovered, Pop's Gourmet Snow Cones was about to take a slight detour.

Two months after Mike's release from Pacific Dunes and four months following the murders of Troops and Simpson, Harold received a phone call from the Mussel Shores Police Chief.

"Harold, it's Sam Gutierrez calling. How's retirement?"

Harold paused for a moment, not sure why his former boss was calling. "Great, Chief. Just swell," said Harold reluctantly.

After obligatory chitchat, Chief Gutierrez got to the point. "Listen, Harold, we kind of need you." Harold's heart leaped. *Thank God someone does. Retirement is overrated.*

"Yes, Chief, I'm listening."

"I don't know if you've read about this, but we got a big deal federal grant to take a second look at cold cases."

Oh, do you really need this? Harold thought.

"Well, Harold, here's the deal. We have some bucks to hire a part-time investigator to take another look at unsolved cases within the city, and, well…I thought the Pacific Dunes case might be a good place to start, and you might be the guy."

Harold met with the Mussel Shores Police Chief in his office the following morning.

"Here it is," said the chief, handing Harold the Pacific Dunes case file. "You ran this investigation, so you're the best guy to take another look. I have enough money budgeted to give you twenty hours a week. But if you need more, I may be able to swing it."

Harold took the hefty file and flipped through the contents, including pages of his handwritten notes. *What are you getting yourself into?*

Chief Gutierrez motioned to an outer office and said, "Take your old cubicle and see HR about getting a temporary badge. You'll have to be sworn back in, but that's no big deal. You pretty much know the drill around here."

One week later, Harold stared out of the kitchen window, racking his brain and trying to figure out why he had agreed to reinvestigate the Pacific Dunes murders. He had thoroughly eliminated any of the victims' associates, family, friends, and coworkers from his list of suspects. As with the initial investigation, there really was only one suspect. Harold hadn't wanted to admit that to himself, but deep down, his suspicion that the sole suspect and guilty party were one and the same had grown, especially after taking a second look at the case file. *Maybe deep down, I was hoping something would pop up to eliminate him. Not going to happen.*

When he was with the Los Angeles Police Department, Harold had injured his knee chasing a burglary suspect through a vacant lot and was temporarily assigned to teach ethics at the LAPD Training Academy. He enjoyed the few classes he taught, not real police work but a tolerable way to spend his rehabilitation.

A former ethics instructor in a police academy is now faced with the biggest ethical decision of his life. You are in a real mess. He glanced at his watch. It was 11:30 a.m. *Almost lunchtime. Wonder what Shapiro's up to.*

Harold was relatively well-known to the Pacific Dunes staff. He greeted several clerks as he entered the hospital lobby and walked toward the desk of Officer Hugo Sanchez. Sanchez leaped to his feet and gave Harold a snappy salute.

"You look well, Detective. How is Mrs. Davis?" asked Sanchez.

"Top-notch, Sanchez," said Harold. "How is your family?"

"They are safe and in good health, my friend," replied Sanchez with a slight bow.

"Is Dr. Shapiro in?"

Sanchez checked a clipboard with the comings and goings of the Pacific Dunes staff. "He is, Detective. I shall escort you." Sanchez looked toward another security officer standing in the corner of the atrium and snapped his fingers. The young officer immediately replaced him at the front desk.

"Come on in!" Jason Shapiro's voice bellowed from behind the door of his office.

"Dr. Shapiro, may I present Detective Davis," said Sanchez with all the pomp and circumstance of a Buckingham Palace butler.

"Harold, you magnificent son of a bitch. I was just thinking of you!"

Harold brushed by Sanchez into Jason's cluttered office. The two shook hands warmly.

"That will be all, Officer Sanchez," Jason said with a salute.

Sanchez bowed and backed out of the office, closing the door gently behind him.

"Sanchez is a little tightly wound, I'll tell ya, but no trouble around here since we brought him on," said Shapiro happily. "Well, other than, well, you know."

Of course not, Doc. Also, no more crazed probation officer with a vigilante complex staying in your little clinic.

"I found a great photo of you and Cheryl at the Lakers game on my phone. I'll send it to you," said Jason, motioning Harold to a chair. He allowed silence to permeate the room. Jason could tell his police detective friend had something on his mind but wasn't altogether convinced he was ready to talk.

"You look like a man with something on his mind," Jason said quietly after the silence grew uncomfortable. "Harold, you okay?"

"Huh?" asked Harold with a shake of his head, almost as though he was being awakened from a nap.

"Harold, what the hell is wrong with you? What's up?" asked Jason.

Harold focused and realized he had drifted off in thought. "No, nothing at all. Just thought you might want to grab a bite."

Jason smiled. *Bullshit. You got something on your mind, my friend. But we'll start with a sub sandwich.*

Harold wiped juice from his massive sandwich from his chin. The sea below the picnic table where he and Jason customarily ate their lunches was thick with white caps. Harold had told Jason about the grant for cold cases. Jason feigned slight interest but internally felt his midsection tighten.

"Any new leads?" asked Jason, taking a bite of the first of three Kosher pickles he ordered along with his sandwich.

Harold shrugged. "Nothing new since we closed the case. Jason, I know I asked you this during the investigation, so forgive my memory lapse, but do you have any recollection of any, how should we say, unsavory characters coming around the hospital to see Troop or Simpson?"

Almost on cue, Shapiro dropped his pickle, looked out across the water, and said, "Ya know, now that you ask, there was a guy who used to come around and see those bums. He would hang around the parking lot, and they would go out and talk during their breaks. Yeah, rough-looking character, that one."

Harold grabbed a yellow legal pad from his file folder and a pen from his shirt pocket. "Description?" he asked hopefully.

"Well, he was a big guy."

"How big?" asked Harold.

Jason looked back toward the water. "Pretty frickin' big, I'll tell ya. Hey, how about this coleslaw? Feel like I'm back in Brooklyn!"

"Six feet? Six two? Six four?" asked Harold. *C'mon, Doc, play along with me.*

"Well, I'll tell ya, he was a big fella. Mean-looking too."

That narrows it down. Nice work, Doctor. "White, Black, Latino, Asian…something else?"

Jason scratched his head as if he was attempting to interpret the original Code of Hammurabi's position on deceptiveness. He snapped his fingers and grinned.

"Wasn't Asian, I'll tell ya that. Could have been Black, White, or Latino."

Harold set his pen down. "Could have been?"

Jason tapped an index finger to his forehead. "Hey, pal, this is California. Did you know that if current demographic projections hold steady, the majority ethnic group in the Golden State will be what?"

Harold looked perplexed. "Ya got me."

Jason gave Harold an expression projecting intellectual superiority. "Mixed race! We won't know what the hell we are. We'll be the perfect melting pot! A salad bowl, really. What do ya think about that?"

Harold grabbed his pen. "So you're saying this mysterious visitor was of mixed race?"

Jason snapped his fingers and folded his arms in victory. "You got it, baby!"

"Where were you when you saw this subject?" asked Harold.

Jason paused for a moment. "Well, my office looks over the parking lot, and I work long hours, so I have a pretty fair idea of the activities germane to the Pacific Dunes parking lot," said Jason officiously.

Sounds like he's been prepped by a very experienced defense attorney. "Let's get back to height and weight."

"Hmm. I would go for between 180 and 220, five ten to six two."

Harold frowned. "That's quite a variance, Doc."

Jason looked up gleefully. "You're right! I'm just not much help, am I?"

Harold took the last bite of his sandwich. *No, idiot. You're no help at all. But then you know that, don't you?*

"Hair color?" asked Harold.

Before he could finish his sentence, Jason blurted out, "Bald! The guy was bald as a cue ball!"

Harold jotted down something on his legal pad. "So I guess hair texture is out?"

Jason smiled, quite pleased with himself. "You bet your ass it's out!"

Ease up, Doctor, and try to contain your enthusiasm. "Clothing?" asked Harold, making a valiant effort to at least give the appearance this was a legitimate police investigation.

"Oh, that's easy. He was dressed like a real badass," said Harold confidently.

"Such as?" asked Harold.

"Well, he wore a white tank top, really baggy pants, and a kerchief on his head," said Jason with as much sincerity as he could generate.

"If he wore a rag on his head, how do you know he was bald?" asked Harold.

Jason once again tapped his forehead. "He didn't wear it *all* the time!"

Harold was beginning to find Jason's smugness irritating. "How often did this subject visit?"

"Oh, at least weekly," replied Jason with absolute confidence.

"So when you were observing this interaction between this mysterious subject and the decedents, did you see anything unusual? Anything stand out?"

Obviously not satisfied with his own lunch order, Jason grabbed a plastic fork and began picking at Harold's partially consumed macaroni salad.

"Hmm. Yeah, now that I think about it, it seems to me that they used to exchange something. Something small, like a little plastic baggie. Yep, little plastic baggie."

Harold took more notes. *Good lord, Shapiro. Can't you do better than that?*

"Wait a minute," said Shapiro, slamming his palm on the picnic table. "You don't think those punks were dealing *dope* here in the hospital parking lot, do you?"

Harold gave him a look that fell somewhere between that of approval and disgust. "You never know, Doc. You just never know."

CHAPTER 31

Iggy fished a ring of keys from his chinos and opened the heavy wooden door. The only source of light was a small pane of stained glass brought up from Mexico by one of the early padres. The white-washed walls were bare except for two small paintings. The first was Father Junipero Serra, who founded the chain of twenty-one California missions and the city's namesake. The second was of the Virgin Mother holding the Christ child up to a bright beam of light from the heavens. In the corner of the room was a small wooden altar with a padded kneeling bench. A carved crucifix hung in front of the altar. Other than those objects, the room was bare and predictably cool, insulated from the outside heat by thick adobe and plaster walls.

Iggy crossed himself, knelt at the altar, clasped his hands together, and gave a reverential nod to the crucifix. With a tired sigh, he brought his head down and rested it on his hands. *God, I feel old. Lord, I pray for the soul of Michael O'Shea. If he had anything to do with this, I pray for your forgiveness and mercy. He's a good man, Lord. I must believe that if he killed those men, he had to have just cause in his heart.* Iggy looked up at the altar for a moment and felt more alone than he had in a very long time.

*****

Harold was taking his investigation in circles. He knew there were only two options. First, find sufficient evidence to charge Mike with one or both murders. If he couldn't make a case, simply declare the matter closed and move on. Of course, there was no guarantee that five or ten years from now, *another* retired detective with too much time on his or her hands and an interest in cold cases wouldn't come to the same place, but that would be their business. *Tie up one more loose end and then let's end it.*

The following afternoon, Harold had a two o'clock meeting with Missy Delonte from the district attorney's office. Harold had worked with her on other cases. Missy Delonte's career would have most certainly progressed more quickly had she possessed a semblance of personality or had any interest in the banter and jokes that were usually exchanged in meetings between law enforcement and the prosecution.

Missy sat in a chair in front of her desk and motioned for Harold to shut the door to her office.

"What's up, Detective?"

Harold pulled a thin manila file from the same worn leather briefcase with the LAPD emblem stamped on the front he had been carrying for as long as he had been a detective. Cheryl had wanted to buy him a much nicer replacement, but Harold would hear nothing of it. Although he wouldn't admit it to his wife, Harold got a kick out of seeing the eyes of young police officers and attorneys light up when they saw confirmation that Harold hailed from the famous and, at times, infamous Los Angeles Police Department.

Harold tapped the insignia on the side of the briefcase. "See that, young lady? That's the badge of the *LAPD*. Got this old briefcase the day I got my gold detective's shield."

Harold had dramatically emphasized "LAPD."

Missy stared at Harold expressionless. "What do you have for me, Detective?" she asked coolly.

Harold summarized the murders and his investigation and the dead ends he had encountered.

"Cellies in the joint?" asked Missy.

Harold nodded. "Checked. All cellmates of both victims either dead or still in."

"Known enemies?" asked Missy.

Harold nodded again. "None that stand out, although both slung a lot of dope, so who knows? But none that are willing to talk."

"Gang ties?" asked Missy hopefully.

"Both flirted with White separatists. But that appears to have been mostly for protection in the joint."

Missy eyed Troop's coroner photo and saw a blue stain of ink about the size of an apple on the left side of his neck. "What the hell's that?" she asked.

"Good question," said Harold. "Started out as a swastika in prison to get in good with the Peckerwoods. But once he got out, he got pumped up on ecstasy and meth and tried to bleach it out. Ended up just making a mess."

"Mr. Troop was none too bright, I take it?"

Harold smiled and nodded. "Safe bet."

Missy pushed the photos and documents across the table toward Harold. "So what do you want to do? Close them out?"

"Not just yet," said Harold.

"What are you thinking?"

"Pacific Dunes is a rehabilitation hospital filled with lots of patients who are in pretty bad medical shape. Everything from head injuries to strokes and lots of debilitating conditions in between."

"Go on," said Missy wearily.

"Think of each one of those patients as possible connections to the murders," said Harold.

"Are you thinking medical records?" Missy asked.

"Yep," said Harold.

"HIPAA [Health Insurance Portability and Accountability Act]. That will be the biggest roadblock between you and a warrant," said Missy as she stood and walked over to a stack of law books on a credenza behind her desk.

Harold looked over her shoulder and saw that book was filled with handwritten notations, assorted pieces of note paper, and small colored labels.

"There is one old case from the seventies we might be able to cite," Missy said under her breath. "Serial rapist infected some of his victims with a nasty strain of gonorrhea. Also gave it to his wife. Local DA got the court to release the wife's medical records, and they had a match. Guy got consecutive life sentences. I think we got something, Harold."

*****

Two days after his meeting with Missy Delonte, Harold strolled into Jason Shapiro's office with a warrant from the State of California, Superior Court of the County of Serra, ordering him to release *all* medical files of Pacific Dunes patients for a two-week period prior and following the murders.

"C'mon in," Jason said through his office door. "Harold, my friend!"

"You may not be so pleased to see me, my friend, when you discover the purpose of my visit." Harold handed Jason the warrant.

Jason read the warrant and looked up with a confused stare. "No shit? Heard of one of these, but they're rare. No skin off my ass, but you have to keep the files here. Can't leave the premises."

Harold held his palms up as if surrendering. "Understood completely."

"I'll give you a private room with a desk where you can go over them. Now let's get lunch," said Jason, rubbing his hands together.

After corned beef sandwiches, Harold followed Jason into an empty office with a single chair, desk, and reading light. He took a key and unlocked a cabinet in the corner. After briefly thumbing through the files, Jason turned to Harold.

"Okay, they should all be here. Taking off early this afternoon, so if I miss you, give your bride my love," said Jason with a smile.

"Will do. And, Doc," said Harold.

Jason was halfway out the office door and turned back. "Yeah?"

"I appreciate your help."

"What, a warrant's a warrant. Think I want to get sideways with the judge? I know you're all in cahoots!" Jason chuckled and closed the door.

Not that he didn't trust his friend, but Harold pulled a list of patients' names already provided by the State Department of Health and Human Services, as ordered in a similar warrant. He would start off by cross-referencing the names on the list against the names on the files in the cabinets. Harold would do this at the beginning of each search on the off chance that someone tried to remove or maybe even add a file. After confirming the files were in order, he was ready to begin.

Fortunately, the files were easier to read than Harold thought, and after the first few, he had a reasonable sense of how the information was arranged. Reports on the right, physicians and physical therapists' notes on the left. The only challenge was in interpreting the handwriting of some of the doctors, but most made audio tapes of their notes and then had them transcribed, which simplified the process.

When Harold was an undergrad at UCLA, he studied the arguments of Supreme Court Justice Potter Stewart. When Justice Stewart was asked to define pornography, he gave a classic response: "I don't know what it looks like, but I'll know it when I see it."

Going through the files, Harold had a similar sense. His intuition told him to simply look for any major medical changes with the patients during the window before and after the murders. While he would never admit this to anyone but himself, Harold fully intended to dissect Mike's file more closely than the others. *I don't care if he's your new BFF. You're still a cop.* Although he was making good progress, Harold noticed that his eyes were starting to become tired, which increased the chance he would miss something. *Best to break this down into short spurts.*

On the third day of his reinvestigation of the Pacific Dunes murders, Harold found something. A patient by the name of Joan Petracelli. Prior to her death, Mrs. Petracelli was a critical care patient. She had just suffered a stroke and was in a late stage of Alzheimer's disease. She had a case of rheumatoid arthritis that kept her heavily medicated around the clock. Other than those maladies, Joan Petracelli was medically stable when she was admitted to Pacific Dunes.

Several months after her arrival, a nurse's aide was getting Mrs. Petracelli ready for her evening bath and noticed a rancid-smelling discharge in her diaper. The on-duty doctor was summoned, who ordered a battery of tests. The results came back positive for gonorrhea. The doctor placed Mrs. Petracelli on antibiotics and completed an Elder or Dependent Adult Suspected Abuse Report, which is similar to a Child Abuse Report and mandated by law in similar cases. By the time investigators from Adult Protective Services received the abuse report, Mrs. Petracelli had passed, rotating the case to the end of a very long line of victims.

Harold reread the report as he took notes on his ever-present legal pad. *How does a senile old lady who can barely move pick up a case of the clap in a rehab hospital?* Unless the hospital missed the gonorrhea when she was admitted, she contracted the disease *after* her arrival. Which meant Joan Petracelli had been raped while she was a patient at Pacific Dunes Hospital.

*****

Harold rubbed his eyes. Both orbs felt like someone had poured fine grains of sand into them. He pushed himself away from the desk and wandered around the townhouse, straightening pictures, rearranging books, anything to occupy his mind. He ended up in the kitchen and opened the pantry doors. *Cookies, peanuts, and some pretzels. Hmmm. Getting fat won't do you much good.* He looked at the bottom shelf where Cheryl had carefully arranged their bar supplies and eyed a bottle of twelve-year-old scotch. *Now we're talkin'.*

He rejected the idea of having a cocktail and quietly closed the pantry. Getting out of bed in the middle of the night for a light snack of scotch and cookies could quickly become a habit he didn't need. Harold turned toward the large granite counter and eyed the instant coffee maker given to him and Cheryl as a wedding gift by Mike and Iggy. The thing looked like a spaceship, and Harold stayed clear for several reasons, not the least of which was his assumption that it was ridiculously complex to operate. After focusing on a mysterious series of international symbols, he found a small plastic tub of what he assumed was filled with tea leaves and slid it into a compartment at the top of the device. With a flick of a switch, a glowing blue light came on, and Harold heard water filling a holding tank.

Harold was roused out of his trancelike state by the sound of hot water spilling out of the coffee maker. He pulled some paper towels from a roll attached to the bottom of a large cabinet and did his best to clean up the small pool of now cooling tea. Harold grabbed the cup and stared at the half serving with disappointment. *Put the damn cup under the spout before you turn the thing on, dummy.*

He returned to his desk and opened the Pacific Dunes file. Harold was all but certain Mike either knew who had murdered Richard Troop and David Lee Simpson or, more than likely, killed them himself. How and why he pulled that off while recovering from a major stroke that left him physically debilitated was, at this phase of his investigation, the real mystery.

"Harold, what are you doing in here, baby?" Cheryl's soft voice belayed an underlining agitation that something was going on in her home without her knowledge.

"Couldn't sleep. Came in here to do a little work. Guess I nodded off." Harold sat up from the small couch in the den where he must have laid down sometime early in the morning.

Cheryl picked the Pacific Dunes report up and glared at Harold accusingly.

"How in the world do you expect to get any rest at all, sir, if you allow a murder investigation to cloud your mind?"

"Oh, it's not that," Harold said in a half-hearted attempt to sound reassuring. "It's my damn knee. Must have torqued it at the beach. Didn't want my tossing and turning to wake you, sweet pea."

"That is a lie, and you know it. Now I don't want to see that file in my home again. Are we clear, sir?" Cheryl was in full domineering Southern wife mode.

"It's clear that when you refer to me as sir and I see fire in your hazel eyes, little Harold stands up and wants to salute." Harold was up and off the couch now and grabbed Cheryl around the waist. Cheryl made a half-hearted attempt to break free and giggled. *Dodged the bullet once again.*

After more tossing and turning, Harold crept from bed for the second time in one night. He made his way to a small bathroom adjacent to the living room to relieve a bladder partially filled by the tea he had made earlier. As Harold stood before the toilet, he maneuvered his penis to urinate in a figure eight pattern. He smiled when he realized that a little-known secret of most men is that they rarely outgrow their "peeing is fun" stage.

Harold recalled a conversation he had had with his former partner, Rebecca Santiago, who was bemoaning having to house train a new puppy. *I miss that young lady. Have to meet for breakfast soon. When was the last time I saw her? Coroner's office. Autopsy. Which autopsy?*

Harold was now staring at his own image in an antique mirror Cheryl had hung on the wall above the toilet. He saw his eyes bulge and mouth drop.

Oh my God. Simpson's autopsy! He had a nasty case of gonorrhea when he was murdered! O'Shea knew he raped the old lady, and he killed him for it. Damn, how could I have missed that?

CHAPTER 32

Six months later

Mike looked out at the thirty-seven fresh faces taking their final exam in his Introduction to Criminal Justice course at the Serra Community College. He enjoyed teaching but wasn't sure just how much of an impact he was having. Some of his students were in the very early stages of preparing for careers in law enforcement. Some wanted to satiate a curiosity wetted by Hollywood and dramatic news headlines. Some heard that Mike's classes were interesting, and some just wanted what they perceived as an easy way to earn three college credits. Mike's classes had become so popular that some of the more serious criminal justice students were bumped to a waiting list, creating a dilemma for the college administration.

The college had recruited Mike to join the faculty within a few weeks of his release from Pacific Dunes, but he was not quite ready to stand in front of a group of postadolescents. Although his speech issues had improved dramatically thanks to hours of therapy, if Mike was going to become a college instructor, he wanted to be in top form. By the time the college made a second attempt to add Mike to their teaching cadre, Iggy convinced him that his speech was virtually flawless. While flawless was a stretch of the truth, he considered this little white lie to be in Mike's best interest, thus morally acceptable.

In the end, students noticed irregularities in his speech patterns but attributed it to an exotic accent of some form.

His instructional evaluations were as high as an instructor could hope for. There were some malcontents, mostly bitter students whose hopes and dreams for a career in law enforcement were dashed when Mike told them their criminal histories would hinder them in a background investigation. But for the most part, Mike's students rated him as an outstanding teacher. His administrative evaluations were more critical but still placed him in the upper echelon of college instructors. During his first faculty evaluation, the department chair brought the textbook Mike was *supposed* to be using. Midway through his lesson, it was obvious that Mike had no intention of following the text but seemed to know what he was talking about, and he certainly kept the attention of the students with his dry humor and real-life experiences. One evaluator compared Mike to a "well-informed stand-up comedian." Another referred to him as an "edutainer." Mike took these evaluations about as seriously as he took his annual performance evaluations as a probation officer, with a mixture of amusement and a complete lack of regard.

"All right, ya got ten minutes, and then you're rid of me either forever or at least until you take another of my classes, so make it count," Mike barked to his class. It was 7:45 p.m. on a Thursday, and if he hustled, he could collect the final exams, close down the classroom, and be home for the second half of the Lakers game.

Mike made a point of memorizing the last name of each of his students. He decided early on that unlike other college instructors, he would not be on a first-name basis with his students, nor he with them. They could call him Mr. O'Shea or simply O'Shea, and he would refer to them by their last name, preceded by Mr. or Ms.

"I hope you have a nice Christmas break, Mr. O'Shea. Really enjoyed your class," said one student.

"Likewise, Ms. Broadhurst," Mike replied.

"I'm trying to get into your gang class for next semester, but it's hard. Any suggestions?"

"If you can't get in, show up the first night. There's usually a few no-shows."

Mike bid farewell to the rest of the students as they turned in their exams. He tried to offer some words of kindness, encouragement, or at the very least, a simple, "Thanks for takin' my class," as the students ushered out. He glanced at the end of the line and let out a quiet sigh. A potential blockade to his evening plans was quickly approaching. Jimmy McGinnes, twenty-six years old, newly paroled from the California Department of Corrections and Rehabilitation and official college student, had strategically completed his exam last to have a private conversation with Mike.

Got to clear the air with the man, Jimmy thought.

"Mr. McGinnes, I couldn't help but notice that the sun set almost three hours ago, but you still have your sunglasses on," said Mike pleasantly as he took Jimmy's test.

"Fuck the shades, man. We need to have a 'cussian."

Mike looked perplexed. He slid his hand down his left leg as if to scratch his ankle, made sure the Glock was securely in place, and smiled at Jimmy.

"First, do you mean a *discussion?*"

Jimmy nodded in the affirmative.

"Okay. Second, watch your mouth. This is an institution of higher learning, and we don't tolerate any toilet tongues…got it?" Mike tried to sound firm.

"Here's the thing, O'Shea. You messed up my self-esteem." Jimmy took off his baseball cap, which had been strategically placed backward on top of his greased back mop of red hair.

Mike rolled his eyes. "Jimmy, trust me. Self-esteem is overrated. Where'd you hear that term anyway?"

"My counselors in the joint, man," said Jimmy, clearly disappointed in Mike's response.

Mike leaned back in his chair and tried to remember if he had ever supervised Jimmy on probation. "Hey, did I supervise you before you went to prison?"

Jimmy smiled broadly. "Nope. You had my old man, Frank." There was some pride in his voice.

Mike felt very old. "Your father was *Frank McGinnis?* What the hell happened to him?"

Jimmy's demeanor saddened. "Dead. Got hooked on the shit in the joint and died of the AIDS."

Mike recalled Frank McGinnes. Actually, he was a heroin addict who used dirty needles with no compunction *prior* to becoming a guest of the state, but why spoil his son's little fantasy?

"So how'd I mess with your self-esteem?" asked Mike, now curious.

"You said the first night of class, 'If you got a felony or criminal history, you ain't gonna pass no background check.'"

"Hmm." Mike made the same statement on the first night of each class in hopes of weeding out the ex-felons and make room for students who might really become law enforcement officers.

"You want to be a *cop*?" asked Mike, trying to disguise his shock.

"A probation officer, man, like you were," said Jimmy in earnest.

Ah, shit. "I'm sorry, Jimmy. I really am. But with your jacket, it just not gonna happen." Mike made a show of organizing his exams and placing them in the canvas messenger's bag Iggy had given him as a birthday gift. *End it. Can't let this turn into a counseling session.*

"Listen, Jimmy, you're a smart kid. I've seen your tests and essays."

"Be straight with me, O'Shea. I can take it!" said Jimmy, dramatically pounding his chest with a fist.

Mike pulled a business card from his messenger bag, jotted down a name and number, and handed it to Jimmy. "Okay, here's the plan. This is the name of the head of the welding program here at the college. Call him first thing tomorrow. Tell him I gave you his name."

"A welder?" asked Jimmy guardedly.

"Yeah, a welder," said Mike. "Trust me, you'll make a ton more dough than I ever made as a PO, and you'll be able to build and fix stuff. Good skills. I almost killed myself last week tryin' to get my old toaster to work."

Jimmy stared at the card and slipped it into his shirt pocket. "A welder, huh? I had an uncle who was welder."

"It's a good living, Jimmy. Call him," said Mike quietly.

Jimmy got up and walked toward the classroom door and turned. "Hey, O'Shea, you got it wrong, man. Not just welders fix shit. You fix shit too."

"Oh really? Just what do I fix, Mr. McGinnes?" asked Mike as he tossed the messenger bag over a shoulder.

"You fix people, man!"

Mike offered a tired smile. "Make that call, damnit!"

*****

All hopes for the Lakers game now lost, Mike tried to plot out what was left of his evening. He had done little to broaden his social contacts since his release from Pacific Dunes. Usually, he liked it that way, but tonight, he wouldn't have objected to company. Contacting Sylvia Almeida was at the top of his list, but she was on an extended road trip with the Cal Coastal women's volleyball team.

It was a moonless night, and had it not been for the lights of the parking lot and the exterior lights of the buildings, the campus would have been completely dark. He walked out into the cool evening, the fog from the Pacific starting to creep south down Highway 1 from Granite Bay. The parking spaces reserved for faculty members were empty except for a few cars, probably custodians and night mainte-nance people. Mike drew the keys to his ancient Jeep Wrangler from the pocket of his jeans and searched for his vehicle.

Where's my Jeep? He turned and walked back toward the entrance of the faculty parking lot. No Jeep. *Check the next lot over. Getting old is rough business*, Mike thought, still in good humor. He walked up and down the parking lot. No Jeep.

This is stupid. Find your damn Jeep and let's go home. Maybe Wong can rustle up some dim sum and you can catch the game highlights on Sports Center. Mike repeated the previous search pattern with the same results. *Either some shit bird stole my decrepit Jeep or something's happening to me.* While Mike's memory had deteriorated over the years, it seemed to have stabilized due in part to medication prescribed by Jason Shapiro and a reduction of his stress since retiring. For the first time in a long time, Michael O'Shea was afraid.

*****

Mike was in his early twenties and an undergrad at Cal when Iggy convinced him to help chaperone a group of Catholic Youth Organization boxers on a trip to Lake Tahoe. Mike had helped coach some of the boys, and a few days in the Sierras sounded appealing, so he accepted, knowing that Iggy would guilt him into it regardless. The group had stayed in tent cabins on the shore of Echo Lake, one thousand feet above Lake Tahoe. Mike had been tasked with minding a cabin of ten tough-as-nails young boxers from East Oakland. The first night went smoothly with Mike making it clear that he would tolerate no foolishness from the boys. Iggy stood outside the cabin listening to Mike's admonishments and loosely veiled threats and smiled. The following morning, after a breakfast of oatmeal and pancakes in the camp kitchen, Mike's group set off on a hike around Echo Lake and her sister Lake, Upper Echo.

Mike had a natural affinity with youngsters, especially tough Oakland kids, and turned the hike into a competition.

"First, hiking is for sissies," Mike advised his charges. This would be a "training run." Second, Mike would lead the way. Anyone able to pass him would get an ice cream cone at the Echo Lake Lodge at the end of the outing.

Iggy had given Mike explicit instructions. "Nobody gets lost, hurt, or dehydrated." As soon as the last boy caught up, Mike rewarded each with a bottle of water and energy bar he had carried in his backpack.

"This ain't shit, O'Shea. Let's keep goin'!" shouted one of the boys. The rest of the group agreed even though most would have been content to return to their cabin and comic books.

"I like your attitude, boys. Follow me!" said Mike with all the bravado of Davy Crockett leading his Tennesseans into the Alamo.

Mike found a trail above the lake which wound its way north toward the Desolation Wilderness. It had been a heavy winter, and much of the trail was still covered in hardpack snow. Mike began to feel uneasy. The trail blended in with the hard snow and left no footprints. Mike stopped, took a head count, and told the boys to sit down. He jogged a hundred yards or so beyond the trail to a ledge overlooking a deep valley.

Shit, we're lost. For all his talents, Michael Ignatius O'Shea had not been blessed with a stellar sense of direction. He found himself completely turned around with no clarity regarding the correct trail back to the lodge. *Damnit, Iggy. I don't know what the hell I'm doin'. Why'd I let you talk me into this?*

"Hey, O'Shea, you lost?" asked Alfonse Montrose, a diminutive but scrappy young fighter from Oakland's Diamond District.

"Whose askin', Alfonse?" said Mike suspiciously.

"I is. Shoot, follow me," said Alfonse.

Mike followed the boy down what appeared to be a very vague trail to a stack of felled trees ringing a clearing of snow. Twigs in the form of an arrow lay in the snow.

"What's that, Alfonse?" asked Mike.

"It's my secret signal. I stopped to pee along the way and had a feelin' you didn't know where the fuck you was goin', so I broke off some branches and made a arrow pointin' back to the lodge. We gotta to go that way," said Alfonse.

Mike looked back up the trail he and Alfonse had just walked down. *I'll be damned. Little reprobate is right.* That had been the last time Mike had experienced the jolt of fear that accompanief realizing that one was truly lost.

Either my Jeep's stolen or I'm having some medical problem. Kind of hope it's stolen. Last time I visited a medical facility, things got a little dodgy.

Mike circled the entire campus once and was working on a second pass. The longer his search, the stronger his belief that the Jeep was indeed in the hands of a thief. The stronger his sense he was the victim of a vehicle theft, the more relieved he felt. As he walked across a perimeter campus road toward another parking lot, the lights of a light-colored sedan flicked on. Mike walked past the car and saw the words "Serra Community College Public Safety" stenciled to the doors. He walked over to the car. A window lowered, and a young officer poked her head out.

"Hey there, Mr. O'Shea. It's Yolanda." Yolanda Gomez was a part-time public safety officer at the college and one of Mike's former students.

"Hi, Yolanda. How are ya?" Mike didn't know whether to be relieved to see a friendly face or mortified that his secret that he might be having some type of medical episode was about to revealed.

"Having a little trouble finding my Jeep. Either it's been jacked or I just lost it," said Mike.

"Old red Wrangler?" asked Yolanda.

"That's it," said Mike, trying to hide his relief.

"It's parked in the loading area of building A. You parked in the dean's *special parking spot*, and he demanded we have it towed to an impound lot in town. He's kind of a prick, if you excuse my language. I recognized it as yours and had it towed, all right...around the back of the building!" said Yolanda. "Hop in. I'll run you over to it."

Mike breathed a sigh of relief. *At least my memory's okay...for now.*

CHAPTER 33

Four months later

Summer had come to Clam Shell Bay, and Harold Davis was now and forever "Detective Harold Davis, Retired." Numerous sleepless nights and endless walks on the beach had led him to the same conclusion. Any police officer who would intentionally deem a case "closed" while knowing the identity of the guilty party should do the honorable thing and move on. It was time. Harold had certainly earned his second retirement, and Cheryl had applied pressure, both subtle and overt, for him to leave the Mussel Shores Police Department.

Harold quickly found not being responsible for responding to the malfeasance of others in an official capacity was invigorating.

"Pop's Snow Cones" was now a reality. A family of six were Harold's first customers. He marveled at their immense girth. *Good grief. The parents combined alone must be over five hundred pounds, and the kids aren't far behind. Maybe I should offer sugar-free syrup?*

"Good morning. What can I get you folks?" asked Harold.

Harold took orders from the family but came to an impasse with their last child, a boy of around twelve years, valiantly attempting to cover up his Buddha-like waist with an oversized Chicago Bulls jersey.

"Give me a chocolate cone," the lad demanded.

"Well, sonny, you have me stumped," said Harold. "I have just about every flavor but chocolate. How 'bout pineapple?"

The boy looked up from his cellular phone. "What do ya mean you got no chocolate?" he asked.

"Look, son, these are the only flavors I offer," said Harold, pointing to a sign attached to the front of his stand.

"Fuckin' poser," said the boy as he stomped away.

Harold wasn't sure what a poser was but sensed it amounted to an insult of some form. *I have absolutely no urge to throttle the boy. Why didn't I retire sooner?*

Harold finished his third snow cone of the day toward the end of the afternoon. *This needs to end or I'll be as big as a house, and the wife will put me on one of her wacky diets.* Harold enjoyed thinking of Cheryl as "the wife." It gave him a sense of domesticity he had missed as a bachelor. Beachgoers were packing up to leave, and the evening crowd was starting to congregate in the patios of the town's three beachside bars.

Harold began his closing chores, cleaning surfaces and preparing the cart to be hitched to the rear of his truck for the short drive home. He looked up toward Front Street as the rider of a vintage Triumph motorcycle backed the bike into a parking space reserved for two-wheeled vehicles. The rider, a stocky man in jeans, work boots, and white T-shirt, eased himself off the bike. Sunglasses and a half helmet shielded his face, but Harold thought the man's gait, an odd swagger really, looked familiar. *I'll be damned. O'Shea bought a new toy.*

"Heard it was opening day," said Mike as he reached out and shook Harold's hand. "Thought I'd take a ride to the beach and bum a snow cone from the proprietor. We're old friends, you know."

"I know how it is," said Harold, turning on a small machine that shaved blocks of ice into tiny chips. "You law enforcement guys are always trying to get over on independent business owners like myself. What flavor would you like?"

Mike reached for his wallet just to clarify that he didn't actually expect any gratuities. "Peach, please."

Harold poured an orange-colored syrup over the ice and handed it to Mike. "Tell me about the new acquisition," said Harold, motioning his head toward the Triumph.

"Well, I find myself with a little more time on my hands," said Mike sheepishly. "Rode one in college and thought it'd be a good way to play tourist and cruise up the coast now and then."

"Don't get me wrong, O'Shea. I love married life, and you know how I feel about Mrs. Davis." Harold looked around to confirm there were no eavesdroppers in the vicinity. "But I do admire your freedom. Gosh, I'd love one of those babies, but can you imagine Cheryl's wrath if I even brought it up?"

"I wouldn't mind a little domesticity in my life," said Mike.

"Hey, speaking of which, how is the volleyball coach of yours?" asked Harold. He and Cheryl had socialized with Mike and Sylvia Almeida on several occasions, and both hoped that Mike's eternal bachelorhood might be coming to an end.

"She is pretty darn good. Travels a lot for her work, but that seems to be okay with both of us," said Mike. "In fact, thinkin' of poppin' the old question to her one of these days…but keep that 10-36 from the wife, would ya?"

"Great news!" said Harold. "What's keeping you from just doing it now?"

"Afraid Iggy would keel over dead of happiness," said Mike with a wink.

"I've been on my feet all day. Let's sit down for a minute," said Harold, motioning to a bench near stairs leading down to the beach.

"I could go for a beer," said Mike. "You?"

"I would *love* one," said Harold.

"Be right back," said Mike.

Harold watched Mike half jog to a small grocery store a block away. *Guy is truly amazing. Stroke almost two years ago and now barely any signs.*

Mike returned and pulled two large cans of ice-cold Australian beer out of a large brown paper bag. Both cans were in their own smaller bags, lest the two men appear to be doing what they were— consuming alcohol in a public place.

"I know most of the Harbor Patrol guys, but I'm a little old for an open container cite," Mike said as he and Harold clicked the cans together in a casual toast.

Harold opened his can and took a sip. *Isn't this cozy? Wonder what we're going to discuss.* Mike stared out into the surf and remained silent. He held the can to his forehead, as if trying to soothe a fever.

This isn't a random visit just to show me his new toy. He's here for a reason. Let's shake things up a little. "How did you find out the old lady was being raped?"

Mike felt a sense of relief pour over him. While he was sure beyond a reasonable doubt what was going on the night he found David Lee Simpson zipping up his pants as he emerged from the room of a comatose patient, Mike had been unable to dismiss doubts that visited him from time to time. *What if you're wrong? You killed a man for no reason. How you gonna explain that away, big guy?* Harold's question confirmed Mike's suspicions about not just David Lee's intent but also, more importantly, his actions.

"Shapiro gave me a pass to roam around at night. I was getting a little stir-crazy."

"On one of your trips around the hospital, you saw something," Harold said in more of a statement than question.

Mike stared at the horizon as the sun started to set over the Pacific. He thought about a lecture he had given to his Introduction to Criminal Law class the week before.

"Two kinds of admissions," Mike often told his students as he held up two fingers.

"Implied and expressed. Expressed admission…I did it," he would say forcefully. "Implied admission…I simply shrug when you ask me if I did it."

Mike took a sip of his beer. *I think I just gave Officer Snowcone an implied admission. Let's see what he does with it.*

"Boy, that Richard Troop was a real piece of work," said Harold with a lighthearted chuckle that belied the severity of the conversation. *Now we know the motive to take out Simpson. Stop him from raping a coma patient. What about Troop?* thought Harold. "You two had quite a history together. Hey, I read the report about the brawl in his gentleman's club he built in his garage. What a shitshow that must have been!"

Mike smiled at the memory of the Cal Coastal football player trying to spin around Troop's hastily constructed stripper's pole.

"After the beating you and your fellow officers gave Troop, I'll bet finding you incapacitated must have been like a kid finding the key to the candy shop.

"I got a warrant to gain access to your medical files from Pacific Dunes," said Harold. Gosh, *this conversation is becoming quite cathartic. Rare a detective—well, former detective—gets a chance like this.* "My guess is you were never in as bad a shape as you let on."

Mike continued to stare at the water with no expression.

"Your file said you were making great progress and then suddenly and with no explanation, really tanked." Harold allowed the statement to hang in the air. Again, no response from Mike.

"The file even said you had become incontinent and had to be put into diapers. Gosh, must have been tough for a guy like you."

Mike gave Harold a look as if to say, "It was kind of liberating in a very deviant way."

"One more question, O'Shea. The murder weapons. A garrote made of dental floss and what appeared to be an ice pick."

Mike twirled his sunglasses around, making it abundantly clear to Harold that he had no interest in responding to his line of questioning.

Harold was making a valiant attempt to contain his exuberance. "If it were me, I would have taken one big dookie in my diaper, hidden the weapon in the poopy, wrapped it up, and dropped it in one of those red biohazard cans."

Dookie and poopie? C'mon, Harold, what are you, nine? "I'm guessing you were a fine detective, Harold," said Mike, raising his beer can in a salute. "I predict you're going to enjoy your retirement and kick ass down here selling snow cones to fat tourists."

Mike stood, tossed his beer can in a trash can, and began the walk back to his motorcycle. After a few steps, he turned back to Harold.

"Hey, Detective. Thank you."

Mike felt better than he had in a long time.

EPILOGUE

The Cal Coastal Lady Wranglers were hosting the Bruins from the University of California, Los Angeles, in a volleyball contest "of epic proportions," according to the headline in the sports section of the *Serra Tribune*.

Mike had scuttled his jeans and work boots and was now dressed in his "semiretirement togs," as he called them: khaki cargo shorts, beach sandals, and a plaid camp shirt. The shorts were comfortable, especially in the mild Central California climate, but Mike had trouble concealing the Glock pistol he still carried in a pocket holster. As a retired probation officer, he took full advantage of the arming privileges afforded to retirees who left their agencies in good standing and wasn't interested in attending large events like a collegiate volleyball game unarmed. Unconsciously, he pulled a small piece of paper from his shirt pocket and glanced at it. It was a receipt from a jeweler in downtown Serra. Earlier in the day, he had dropped his mother's wedding ring off to be sized to fit Sylvia's finger.

He sat in a row of seats directly behind the Cal Coastal Woman's Volleyball Team, nibbling on a bag of popcorn and sipping from a bottle of water, both purchased from a concession stand in the lobby of the cavernous gym.

"Oooh, Coach, that *man* is here again," said a Cal Coastal setter. "Are you two an item? He looks badass! But what's up with his ears?"

Sylvia jerked her head in the direction of the player. "You get your head in the game, young lady, or you're going to become intimately familiar with the seat on the end of the bench."

Mike observed the interaction between coach and player and grimaced. *Kind of like to steer clear of her bad side.* Sylvia hadn't changed during Mike's time at Pacific Dunes. If anything, time had been good to her. The striking silver streak down the middle of her massive brown mane had become more pronounced, making her even more attractive to Mike. After admonishing her athlete, Sylvia glanced in Mike's direction and gave him a subtle wink and slight nod. *I think I'm in real trouble with this woman.*

After dinner at a local Mexican restaurant near campus to celebrate Sylvia's victory, the couple returned to their respective addresses. Mike slept uninterrupted for the first time in years. He arose with the sun, threw on a pair of shorts and a T-shirt, and strolled the three blocks to the Our Lady Church. Although it was warm enough to skip a sweatshirt, Mike shivered as he opened the massive oak door leading into the old church.

Mike quietly walked to a pew adjacent to a small door at the side of the church. Several parishioners waited patiently in line. He took his position next to a young tattooed woman with her hair dyed a deep magenta. *Bet she's gonna really unload on the old guy.*

The line moved surprisingly quickly. When it was Mike's turn, he opened the door and stepped inside. The room was warm and gave off a familiar musty smell. There was a thin wooden divider separating the tiny room into two distinct sections. A thin dark material covered a small opening that connected the two sections.

"Forgive me, Father, for I have sinned," Mike said quietly. "It's been…well, it's been a pretty damn long time since I last confessed."

"Good morning, Michael," said Father Ignatius De la Rosa. "I was hoping you'd stop by."

ABOUT THE AUTHOR

Gary L. Joralemon has a bachelor's degree in criminal justice from California Polytechnic State University, San Luis Obispo, and a master's degree in leadership from St. Mary's College of California. After thirty-three years in law enforcement, he retired from the San Luis Obispo County Probation Department, having risen to the rank of chief deputy probation officer. Gary has served on the faculties of the Alan Hancock College Law Enforcement Academy, Cuesta College, and California State University, San Luis Obispo. He specializes in issues pertaining to law enforcement use of force and ethics.

Photo courtesy of
Tamara Lalanne

He is a former Police and Fire Olympic wrestler and participated in the 2005 Outrigger Canoe World Championships in Molokai, Hawaii. As with his character Michael O'Shea, Gary spent untold hours running the steps of Edwards Field on the University of California campus.